THE

RESURRECTION OF THE DEAD;

CONSIDERED IN THE LIGHT OF

HISTORY, PHILOSOPHY,

AND

DIVINE REVELATION.

BY

REV. HIRAM MATTISON, D. D.

WITH AN INTRODUCTION

BY REV. MATTHEW SIMPSON, D.D.,

ONE OF THE BISHOPS OF THE M. E. CHURCH.

He will swallow up death in victory.—ISAIAH.

THIRD EDITION.

PHILADELPHIA:

PERKINPINE & HIGGINS,

No. 56 NORTH FOURTH STREET.

WESTCOTT & THOMSON, STEREOTYPERS.

Jas B. Rodgers, Pr.
52 & 54 N. 6th St.

CONTENTS.

CHAPTER I. PAGE

Preliminary Observations and Definitions......... 11

CHAPTER II.

Belief of the Ancient Jews touching the Resurrection.................. 17

CHAPTER III.

Belief of the Early Christians, Martyrs, and Confessors.............. 28

CHAPTER IV.

Views of Various Sects and Denominations to the present time. 45

CHAPTER V.

Teachings of the Old Testament as to the Resurrection of the Dead. 68

CHAPTER VI.

Teachings of Christ.. 96

CHAPTER VII.

The Resurrection of Christ.. 100

CHAPTER VIII.

The Resurrection of Christ and the "New Church" Theory....... 131

CHAPTER IX.

Teachings of the Apostles... 145

CHAPTER X.

Various Theories Considered—Does the Resurrection take place at Conversion?.. 167

CHAPTER XI.

Theories Considered—Does the Resurrection take place at the Death of the Body?.. 173

CHAPTER XII.

Theories Considered—"Germ Theory" of Mr. Drew and others... 189

CHAPTER XIII. PAGE

Theories Considered—A new body of Common Elements............ 199

CHAPTER XIV.

True Theory of the Resurrection.. 210

CHAPTER XV.

Objections to a Corporeal Resurrection Considered.................. 224

CHAPTER XVI.

Nature and Characteristics of the Resurrection Body................ 247

CHAPTER XVII.

Speculative Questions Considered, Physical Defects, Infants, Nationalities, etc.. 269

CHAPTER XVIII.

Uses of the Resurrection-body in another Life......................... 282

CHAPTER XIX.

Time and Extent of the Resurrection.. 296

CHAPTER XX.

The First Resurrection.. 304

CHAPTER XXI.

The Millennium.. 311

CHAPTER XXII.

Order and Accompaniments of the Resurrection......................... 327

CHAPTER XXIII.

Natural Emblems of the Resurrection.. 345

CHAPTER XXIV.

Practical Observations and Reflections..................................... 363

Index of Authors Cited.. 393

Index of Poetic Quotations.. 395

Index of Scripture Quotations.. 397

General Index.. 401

PREFACE.

If the writer has succeeded in what he has undertaken, the following are the characteristics of the present volume.

1. It fairly and specifically *defines* the true doctrine of the Resurrection.

2. It discusses the general subject, and all collateral issues, *from an orthodox stand-point;* and is emphatically evangelical in its expositions and reasonings.

3. As the result of a wide range of reading and of much thought and study for years, it embodies a large amount of matter upon the subject not otherwise accessible to the public.

4. It is a complete *history* of the doctrine of the Resurrection, as held by the Jews and the early Christians, and by the various modern denominations.

5. As an investigation of the teachings of Moses and the Prophets, and of Christ and his Apostles, it is exhaustive of the subject.

6. The proofs of the Resurrection of Christ are more fully stated, and more logically arranged, than in any other work of which we have knowledge.

7. The various *objections* to the orthodox view are fully and fairly stated, and thoroughly answered.

8. In discussing the *nature* and *characteristics* of the Resurrection Body, and its *uses* in the life to come, we have furnished what no other writer has supplied; and yet what, in our view, is indispensable to a full and fair view of the subject, and a complete vindication of the orthodox faith.

9. By discussing the nature of the *first resurrection*, and of the *millennium*, and the *order and accompaniments* of the resurrection, we have furnished what was also indispensable and yet what we have not elsewhere met with.

These, we are aware, are high claims; and such as should not be put forth, especially by the author, unless abundantly sustained by the facts.

But believing that after much study and labor we have at length produced such a volume, neither too intricate or scholastic on the one hand, nor too superficial on the other; but logical, clear, orthodox, non-controversial, comprehensive, philosophical, evangelical and complete in all its details, we frankly state our convictions; only asking that the work be read with candor by all classes, and judged upon its intrinsic merits.

That others, with the same expenditure of time and labor, could have written a much better book, we are free to admit; and that others *have* written admirably upon the subject, is also conceded. But some have confined themselves to a small portion of the general subject, while others have been too controversial, or too prolix and heavy, or even too learned, for the mass of readers. If we have succeeded in our purpose, we have avoided all these errors; have so written that all can understand us, and have given to the whole an evangelical cast and application.

And now may the blessing of HIM who died for us and rose again, accompany this volume wherever it may go, and by whomsoever it may be read, to the edification of his saints in the earth, and the glory of his name forever.

H. MATTISON.

JERSEY CITY, *March 6th,* 1866.

INTRODUCTION.

THE theme discussed in this volume is one of deep and intense interest to every rational mind. Life is short. The grave opens before us. Every avenue and every pathway, whatever its apparent direction, or by whomsoever trod, leads thither its journeying millions. As we approach nearer, and cast a glance towards its gathering shadows, how frequently and how forcibly the question arises, "If a man die, shall he live again?" Never do we follow loved ones to the tomb without asking, "Shall we see them again?—Shall there be a resurrection of the dead?"

Were the question merely speculative, wholly destitute of moral bearings, no other could surpass it in interest. We rejoice in the education and development of humanity on earth—but how fleetly we pass away. What shall we be in eternity? Shall we have conscious existence? If not, why this intense longing to pierce the vail of the future? why this feeling that we can not wholly die? Revelation comes to our aid, and proclaims that man is immortal. Reason approves the tidings.

But, if so, how shall man live? Is he to be a spirit dissevered from the body, and having no intimate connection with organized matter? In his power to come in contact with matter and to govern it, as well as in his moral nature, he was made in the image of God. He was formed to reign on earth. Cursed and crushed by his sin, the earth too has been accursed, and death, seizing the sceptre from humanity, has reigned in his stead. But the earth is to be renewed. A new heaven and a new earth are to be fashioned, resplendent with glory. Who shall govern that new earth, wherein is to dwell righteousness? The angels can not; for "unto the angels hath he not put in subjection the world to come." Shall not man, redeemed from sin, be restored to dominion? Shall he not again be body, as well as spirit?

Then other inquiries press upon us. Is his memory to retain the images, and sayings, and deeds of his fellow-men? Shall he know his friends, and shall he have communion with them? Will the past of earth be related to, and potential upon the future of eternity?

Revelation again comes to our aid, and assures us that the body shall rise. Its infirmities and defects, its weakness and corruption shall all pass away, and it shall be clothed with power and glory. Precisely when this shall occur—what change shall take place,—how the dead shall rise, and how much of each body shall come forth we are not definitely informed. The finite mind cannot comprehend the full plans and designs of the Infinite.

To these speculations is added a moral grandeur. The bliss of the future body is to be affected by the deeds performed on earth. The resurrection is to be through Christ. He is our life. Our Saviour on earth, he is to be our judge in eternity. We are to appear before him in these bodies to give account for all our doings, and to stand justified by our faith in his atonement, or to be condemned for our rejection of proffered mercy. In religious teaching, this doctrine should have great prominence. The apostles gave witness to the resurrection of Christ with "great power." They loved the theme, and under its proclamation, thousands were won to the cross.

In later days because there are philosophical objections, efforts have been made to explain away the resurrection by visionary theories. So far as these theories obtain, the power of the gospel over the hearts of men is invariably weakened. The gospel is the "*power of God.*" There is in it, and there must be in it the supernatural. Nor are these objections new. They were made by the schoolmen and sophists of Corinth as forcibly as at present. They furnished the occasion for the beautiful and forcible remarks of St. Paul, wherein light is thrown beyond the grave, and glimpses are given us of the glorified body. We know not what we shall be, but raised by Christ's power we shall be transformed into his glorious image. Thus is it, that by the wisdom and power of God, the assaults of enemies ever occasion the truth to appear in greater beauty and majesty.

The author of this volume has performed a good work for the church. Its plan is simple, clear and full. He has collected and condensed the views of the principal writers on this subject in all ages, and has faithfully presented and classified their theories. He has shown the faith of the Jews both from the Holy Scriptures and rabbinical sayings—the belief of the early Christians, and the creeds and confessions of the leading churches in Christendom, thus presenting the uniform consent of the vast majority of the believers in revelation in reference to this article of Christian faith. He has also noticed the various theories devised to explain apparent difficulties, and to deny the resurrection of the body laid in the grave, and has clearly shown that these theories are without Scriptural warrant.

I commend this volume to the Christian public for the research, ability and fidelity displayed by the author. I believe it to be the best work now published in small compass, for the information of the general reader. May all its readers attain to the resurrection of the just.

MATTHEW SIMPSON.

THE RESURRECTION OF THE DEAD.

CHAPTER I.

PRELIMINARY OBSERVATIONS AND DEFINITIONS.

I. THAT the Holy Scriptures teach the doctrine of a resurrection of the dead, is admitted by all who read them, whether they believe in their divine inspiration or not. But all are not thus agreed as to the *nature* of the resurrection. Upon this point there is some diversity of opinion, even among those who receive the Bible as an infallible revelation, and bow in implicit reverence to all its teachings.

One theory is that the resurrection taught in the Scriptures is simply the quickening of the soul, or of the moral powers, by the Holy Spirit in regeneration; and that therefore every regenerate person is already in the resurrection state.[1] Another is that the resurrection is the emerging of the soul from the body at the hour of death.[2] A third is that it is the construction of a new body out of common elements, having no reference to the material of which the former body

[1] The *Gnostics* of the first century. See Col. ii. 8. Also, Mosheim's Eccl. Hist. Vol. I. pp. 89–91, and Macknight's preface to 1 Cor. Sec. 4, with notes on 2 Tim. ii. 18.

[2] The "New Church," or Swedenborgian theory. See "*Anastasis, &c.*," by Prof. Geo. Bush, and the writings of Emanuel Swedenborg.

was composed.[1] A fourth theory is that the new body will be evolved in some way from a small portion of the old one—a germ or nucleus around which shall be gathered the remaining elements necessary for a new body;[2] while others hold to the literal resurrection of the identical body laid in the grave.[3]

These five theories, we believe, embrace the principal views held upon the subject; so that their distinct consideration will cover the whole ground of discussion, and will draw in every question and argument that properly belongs to the general subject.

II. *What, then, is the true doctrine of the resurrection, as taught in the Scriptures?* For it is admitted on all hands that this doctrine is one of pure revelation; and that "Reason and Nature," even as interpreted by their self-styled special votaries, promise no future life for the body of man beyond its sad decay in the tomb. And as we are dependent upon the Inspired Volume for all we know as to the *fact* of a future resurrection; so are we dependent upon the same blessed book for all we know or hope to know in this life as to the *nature* of that promised event. And just here is the only issue, so far as professed Christians are concerned. That there is, or is to be a "resurrection," we all agree; but *in what that resurrection consists,* and *when* and *how* it shall be accomplished, we are not agreed. How shall we arrive at the truth? How,

[1] An idea first promulgated by Origen, and held by Archbishop Whately, Dr. Hitchcock and others.

[2] See Drew on the Resurrection, Chap. v., and Hitchcock's Religion of Geology, pp. 401, 402.

[3] The popular or prevailing idea at the present time.

"Set the false witnesses aside,
But hold the truth forever fast?"

III. There are usually two methods of reasoning, the *direct* and the *indirect*. Both these methods are applicable, we think, in the present instance. If it be admitted on all hands that the Scriptures clearly teach *a* resurrection from the dead, and, in the second place, that some one of the preceding theories must be the true one; then, if it could be shown from the Bible that four of the five theories named are false, it would follow of necessity that the remaining one was true: its truth being thus established by the indirect process.

Again: so essentially different are these theories from each other, that it is impossible in the very nature of things that more than one of them should be true. If, then, it can be proved directly from the Scriptures that any one of them is true, it follows inevitably that all the rest are false. This would be to establish the truth by the direct process, and refute all opposing errors by the indirect. And if it be possible to arrive at the same conclusion by *both* these processes,—the direct and the indirect,—independently of each other, the moral demonstration will be complete.

IV. Believing most implicitly in what we have called the popular theory of the resurrection, and that despite all cavils and new interpretations of the Scriptures it is susceptible of proof by both the processes above indicated, we shall adopt this two-fold process in the present investigation; showing first that the popular doctrine of the resurrection as held by the great mass of Christian believers at the present time,

2

is the true doctrine of the Bible; and secondly, that the various theories proposed to obviate the supposed philosophical and rational difficulties in the way of accepting the popular belief, are not only in obvious conflict with the inspired writings, but are themselves beset with difficulties even more formidable than those they were designed to obviate.

V. We have spoken thus far of the "popular theory," without explaining definitely what we mean by the phrase. The prevailing idea, as we understand it, when expressed in general terms, is, that the same body which is laid in the grave at death, shall hereafter arise out of it, and live again forever; or, to be still more explicit, that *all that constitutes and properly belongs to the body at the hour of death, and is essential to its corporeal identity and integrity, will be raised again to life; and will go to constitute the resurrection body.*

Such we understand to be the popular theology upon the subject, as well as the doctrine of the Holy Scriptures; and such is the doctrine we propose to vindicate and illustrate in the succeeding chapters.[1]

VI. In carrying out this design, we shall show first that the Jews before Christ, and at the time of his advent, held to the doctrine of a physical resurrection; that such was the belief of the early Christians; and

[1] "It is not a little remarkable," says Whately, "that the prevailing opinion should be (as I believe it is,) that the very same particles of bodily substance which are laid in the grave, or otherwise disposed of, are to be reassembled and reunited at the resurrection; so as to form, as is supposed, the *same* body in which the soul resided before death; and that Scripture teaches us to believe this."—*Lectures on a Future State, Phila. Ed.* p. 95.

that such has been the belief of the general Church of Christ, in its various denominations, from the days of the apostles to the present time. Turning then to the Sacred Writings, we shall show that the Old Testament fully warrants the belief of the Jews, and the faith of the early saints, as touching the nature of the resurrection—that our Lord Jesus Christ taught a physical resurrection, and demonstrated it by his own resurrection from the tomb of Joseph; and that the apostles, following the teachings of Moses and the prophets, and of Jesus Christ; and with the fact of his resurrection from death ever before them, taught and everywhere insisted upon the literal resurrection of the body from the dust of the earth, to glory and immortality.

From this *direct* argument we shall pass to the *indirect*, by showing first that the various objections urged against the popular belief are either unscriptural or unphilosophical, or both, or otherwise unfounded; and secondly, that the various rival theories, designed to avoid the supposed difficulties of the popular belief, are both unscriptural and unphilosophical, and liable to many objections far more formidable than those they were designed to obviate.

The true doctrine being thus evolved and vindicated, both by the direct and the indirect processes, we shall conclude with a discussion of the characteristics and utility of the resurrection body, the order and circumstances of the resurrection, and such other topics and reflections as may give to the whole a practical and devotional bearing.

VII. To avoid circumlocution, and save space in our pages, and at the same time to allow of some variety of expression, we shall use the terms *literal*, *physical*, *material* and *corporeal* interchangably, as qualifying the term resurrection, and as purporting in all cases the raising up again of the body laid in the grave at death. Whenever, therefore, we speak of a literal or corporeal, a physical or a material resurrection, we wish to be understood as referring to the popular theory of the raising again to life of the identical body from which the soul goes forth at the hour of death.

With these preliminaries and definitions we may now pass to the consideration of the general subject.

CHAPTER II.

BELIEF OF THE ANCIENT JEWS TOUCHING THE RESURRECTION.

As stated in the previous chapter, the prevailing idea at the present time, and in all ages of the Church, is that of the literal resurrection of *the same body laid in the grave;* or, in other words, that whatever properly belongs to and constitutes the body at the hour of death, and is essential to its corporeal identity and integrity, will be raised again to life, and will go to constitute the resurrection body.

The Jews had their sacred writings in possession from four to fifteen centuries before the advent of Christ. From these writings of Moses and the prophets they derived the doctrine of the resurrection of the dead. Moreover, they read these writings in their own tongue wherein they were born, and would be more likely on that account to understand their true spirit and meaning than any modern Hebraist. How then did *they* understand Moses and the prophets? Did they look for a *literal* resurrection of the body, or merely for a spiritual regeneration, a transmigration, or a new creation?

Without at this time affirming or denying as to

either of these views, we propose in the present chapter to show that, whether right or wrong, philosophical or unphilosophical, the Jews, before and at the time of our Lord's ministry, *believed in a corporeal resurrection*, and had no idea of any other.

I. *Rabbi Akiba*, one of the Jewish fathers, as cited from *Wetstein* by Dr. Clarke, says: "How shall the holy blessed God raise the dead? We are taught that God has a *trumpet* a thousand ells long, according to the ell of God. This trumpet he shall *blow*, so that the sound of it shall extend from one extremity of the earth to the other. At the *first* blast the *earth* shall be shaken; at the *second* the *dust* shall be separated; at the *third* the *bones* shall be gathered together; at the *fourth* the *members* shall *wax warm;* at the *fifth* the *heads* shall be *covered with skin;* at the *sixth* the *souls* shall be rejoined to their *bodies;* at the *seventh* all shall revive and stand clothed."[1]

Fanciful as all this may be as to the exact *process* of the resurrection, it is every way pertinent, as showing, beyond question, the belief of the writer in a physical resurrection; and for that purpose alone we quote the passage.

II. The books of the *Apocrypha* are supposed to have been written from two to six centuries before Christ; and, though uninspired, contain many allusions to the theology of the Jews at the time they were written. In the second book of Maccabees, chapter vii., we have the following concerning the martyrdom of certain Jews for refusing to eat swine's flesh:

[1] Notes on 1 Cor. xv. 52.

"And when he was at the last gasp, he said, Thou like a fury takest us out of this present life, but the King of the world shall raise us up, who have died for his laws, unto everlasting life."

* * * * * * * *

"Now when this man was dead also, they tormented and mangled the fourth in like manner.

"So when he was ready to die, he said thus, It is good, being put to death by men, to look for hope from God to be raised up again by him: as for thee, thou shalt have no resurrection to life."

And so again in chapter xii.:

"And when he had made a gathering throughout the company to the sum of two thousand drachms of silver, he sent it to Jerusalem to offer a sin-offering, doing therein very well and honestly, in that he was mindful of the resurrection:

"For if he had not hoped that they that were slain should have risen again, it had been superfluous and vain to pray for the dead."

In 2 Esdras, chapter ii., we have the following:

"And those that be dead I will raise up again from their places, and bring them out of the graves: for I have known my name in Israel."

* * * * * * * *

"Wheresoever thou findest the dead, take them and bury them, and I will give thee the first place in my resurrection."

These passages show that in the time of Esdras and the Maccabees, the doctrine of the resurrection of the dead was well understood among the Jewish people, and that it was understood in the sense of a physical resurrection.

III. The *Chaldee Paraphrase* of Solomon's Song has the following: "The prophet Solomon said, When the dead shall revive, it shall come to pass that the Mount of Olives shall be cleft, and all the dead of Israel shall come out from thence. And the just, too, that died in captivity, shall come through the way of the caverns under the earth, and shall come forth out of the Mount of Olives." [1]

Taking this gloss literally, the Jews believed that those who died and were buried elsewhere would have to pass through the earth to Jerusalem in order to rise there. "This," say they, "was the reason why Jacob and Joseph, who died in Egypt, were carried into Canaan to be buried there, that they might not be obnoxious to the trouble of the caverns;" that is, that they might not be obliged to pass a long way through the earth, in order to rise from the Mount of Olives.

An English traveler of the last century found this idea still extant among the Jews of Palestine. "In what part soever they die and are buried, their bodies must all rise to judgment in the Holy Land, out of the Valley of Jehoshaphat, and that therefore the greater and richer sort of them [the Jews] have their bones conveyed to some part thereof by their kindred or friends; by which means they are freed of a labor to scrape thither through the ground, which with their nails they hold they must who are not there buried, or conveyed thither by others." [2]

"Whole barks full of Jews' bones are wont to arrive at Joppa, to be interred at Jerusalem, because they imagine that the soul is delighted by it, and at the general judgment they shall have a quicker dispatch." [3]

"This desire of the Jews to be buried near Jerusa-

[1] Chapter VIII. 5.

[2] Voyages to the Holy Land, by John Sanderson.

[3] Sandys' Travels, old edition, p. 148.

lem is mentioned by Morrison, and the same reason assigned for it."[1]

In the sixteenth century Thevenot thus speaks of the same desire: "The Jews who now live in Jerusalem give a chequin a day for permission to bury their dead in the Valley of Jehoshaphat, that they may be the sooner dispatched at the day of judgment, because, as they believe, it will be held at that place."[2]

"They think that those who are there buried will be sooner dispatched, because they are the first that will make their appearance, it requiring some time for those who are buried elsewhere to come thither."[3]

IV. In the ancient prayer book of the Jews entitled "*The Mahzar of the Holy Roman Synagogue*," they are directed whenever they look upon the grave of one of their nation to offer this prayer: "Blessed be the Lord our God, the King of the world, who formed you with judgment, nourished you, preserved you alive, delivered you up unto death; who knows the number of you all, who will raise you up again, who will restore you again with judgment. Blessed art thou, O Lord, who givest life to the dead. May thy dead live, with thy dead body may they arise. Awake and rejoice ye that lie in the dust, because the dew of the light is your dew, and the earth shall cast out the dead."[4]

The same prayer is pronounced at the grave by the *Hazan*, or minister of the Synagogue, at the burial of a Jew; and in the hymn chanted at the grave we find

Travels, old edition, p. 223. [2] Travels, p. 184.

[3] Hody on the Resurrection. London, 1694, p. 72.

[4] This last sentence is a version of Isa. xxvi. 19, 20.

the following: "God is perfect in all his works. Who will say unto him, What doest thou? He who governs in things beneath and in things above, who delivers up to death, who gives life, who brings down to the grave, and brings back again." To which is added, "See now that I, even I, am he, and there is no God with me. I kill and I make alive. I wound and I heal. Neither is there any that can deliver out of my hands." [1]

When the corpse is laid in the grave, the mourners signify their hope of the resurrection by throwing grass over their heads, and saying, "Your bones shall bud as the grass;" [2] and as they return from the grave and enter the porch of the Synagogue, they say, "God shall destroy death forever, and wipe away all tears from their eyes, and will take away their reproach from all the earth, for the Lord hath spoken it."

V. *Flavius Josephus*, the celebrated Jewish historian, wrote about A. D. 80. In his *Discourse to the Greeks concerning Hades*, we find the following:

"This is the discourse concerning Hades, wherein the souls of all men are confined until a proper season which God hath determined, when he will make a resurrection of all men from the dead; not procuring a transmigration of souls from one body to another, but raising again those very bodies, which you Greeks, seeing to be dissolved, do not believe [their resurrection.] But learn not to disbelieve: for while you believe that the soul is created, and yet is made immortal

[1] A Jewish version of Deut. xxxii. 39.

[2] Isa. xliv. 4. "And they shall spring up as among the grass, as willows by the water courses."

by God, according to the doctrine of Plato, and this in time, be not incredulous, but believe that God is able, when he hath raised to life that body which was made as a compound of the same elements, to make it immortal; for it must never be said of God, that he is able to do some things and unable to do others. We have therefore believed that the body will be raised again, for although it be dissolved, it is not perished; for the earth receives its remains and preserves them. . . . . So that we have not rashly believed the resurrection of the body; for although it be dissolved for a time on account of the original transgression, it exists still, and is cast into the earth, as into a potter's furnace, in order to be formed again, not in order to rise again such as it was before, but in a state of purity, and so as never to be destroyed any more. And to every body shall its own soul be restored." [1]

VI. The gospel history affords numerous proofs that both the Pharisees, who believed in, and the Sadducees, who denied the resurrection of the dead, understood that doctrine in its literal and corporeal sense, as held by Christians generally at the present day. Of these proofs a few specimens will suffice.

"The same day came to him the Sadducees, which say that there is no resurrection, and asked him,

"Saying, Master, Moses said, If a man die, having no children, his brother shall marry his wife, and raise up seed unto his brother.

"Now there were with us seven brethren: and the first, when he had married a wife, deceased; and having no issue, left his wife unto his brother.

"Likewise the second also, and the third, unto the seventh.

"And last of all the woman died also.

[1] Works, in one vol., pp. 608, 609.

"Therefore, in the resurrection, whose wife shall she be of the seven, for they all had her?"—Matt. xxii. 23–28.

How obvious from this passage that the Sadducees understood the doctrine in its most literal sense, and regarded our divine Redeemer as at least a defender of the doctrine of such a resurrection.

The response of Martha to the declaration of our Lord (John xi. 23), shows conclusively that in her view the resurrection was the literal raising up again of the body. "Thy brother shall rise again," said the Saviour, to which she mournfully replied, "I know that he shall rise again in the resurrection in the last day." Here she speaks of "the resurrection in the last day" as a thing well understood, and concerning which there was no dispute or doubt, except on the part of the small sect of the Sadducees.

Again: The remark of Herod concerning John the Baptist (Matt. xiv. 2,) shows that even that guilty ruler believed in the resurrection of the dead. When he heard of the miracles of Christ, under the influence of remorse and fear, he concluded that John, whom he had wantonly beheaded, had risen to life. "This is John the Baptist;" said he. "He is risen from the dead; and therefore mighty works do shew forth themselves in him."

VII. Various passages in the discourses of St. Paul, as reported in the Acts of the Apostles, refer to the doctrine of the resurrection as a doctrine generally believed by the Jews at that time. In the twenty-fourth of Acts we have this passage:

"But this I confess unto thee, that after the way which they call heresy, so worship I the God of my fathers, believing all things which are written in the law and in the prophets:

"And have hope towards God, which they themselves also allow, that there shall be a resurrection of the dead, both of the just and unjust."

Here it is more than implied that his belief in the resurrection of the dead was based upon what he found written in the law and the prophets; and that the Jews, his accusers, professedly "allowed," (that is, believed,) the same doctrine, and cherished the same "hope toward God."

Another similar passage may be found in the twenty-sixth chapter of Acts, where, standing before Agrippa, the Apostle said:

"And now I stand and am judged for the hope of the promise made of God unto our fathers:

"Unto which promise our twelve tribes, instantly serving God day and night, hope to come. For which hope's sake, king Agrippa, I am accused of the Jews.

"Why should it be thought a thing incredible with you, that God should raise the dead?"

Here he affirms that he is accused of the Jews on account of the "hope of the promise" which he cherished. And yet he elsewhere defines the accusation by saying, "Of the hope and resurrection of the dead I am called in question." And the closing sentence, "Why should it be thought a thing incredible with you, that God should raise the dead," shows conclusively that by the "hope of the promise" St. Paul meant the hope of the resurrection of the dead. And yet he affirms that the "twelve tribes" "hoped to come" to this same "promise;" or, in other words, hoped for the resurrection of the dead.

VIII. In the modern ritual of the Jewish synagogues

3

entitled "Prayers of Israel," there is a "Service for the Dead" in which the following passages occur:

"Blessed art thou, our God! King of the universe; he hath created you in justice, and fed and maintained you in justice, and knoweth the numbers of all you in justice. Blessed art thou, O Lord, who *revivest the dead*. . . . He ruleth below and above, he slayeth and *reviveth*, and bringeth to the grave and *bringeth up again*. . . . Thou art righteous to slay and *revive*. Blessed be the righteous Judge, who slayeth and *reviveth*. . . . May his great name be exalted and sanctified throughout the world, for he will in future renew the same and *revive the dead*, and bring them up to everlasting life."[1]

"The whole nation," says Lightfoot, "did so generally assert and hold the resurrection of the dead, (the Sadducees only excepted,) that they made the deniers of this point one of the three parties that should never have part in the world to come: as they speak in the Talmud: . . . 'These are they that have no portion in the world to come; he that saith, the resurrection of the dead is not taught from the law, etc.'"[2]

"In the latter times indeed of the Jewish church," says Archbishop Secker, "not a few denied this doctrine; but much the greater part held to it, *allowing*, as St. Paul acquainted Felix, that 'there shall be a resurrection both of the just and the unjust.'"[3]

From these various testimonies, therefore, we think it indubitably certain, not only that the Jews long before and at the time of our Lord's ministry believed in

[1] Pages 225–229. [2] Landis on the Resurrection, p. 173.
[3] Works, London, 1825, Vol. VI. pp. 170, 171.

the resurrection of the dead, but that *they held that doctrine in the popular sense*, as implying *the raising up again of the same body laid in the grave.* Whether right or wrong, philosophical or unphilosophical, possible or impossible, such was the fact. So *they* understood Moses and the prophets, and so their venerable rabbis believed and hoped. The Apocryphal writers and Chaldee paraphrasts had no other idea. The desire of the Jews to be buried at Jerusalem is based upon the hope of such a resurrection, and the doctrine is unequivocally taught in their ancient and modern burial services. Josephus explicitly defends it, and the gospel history and the discourses of St. Paul, show beyond all question, that such was the belief most prevalent in Judea during our Lord's ministry.

Whoever, therefore, would rightly understand the teachings of Christ and his apostles must interpret them in the light of this fact; and whoever propounds any other view of the resurrection, must admit at the outset that his hope is altogether different from that of God's ancient people for fifteen centuries before Christ, and of the modern Israelites from the advent to the present time.

Having thus ascertained the belief of the ancient Jews, let us next inquire respecting the faith of the early Christians.

CHAPTER III.

BELIEF OF THE EARLY CHRISTIANS AS TO THE NATURE OF THE RESURRECTION.

HAVING shown that, with the exception of the Sadducees, who denied all future existence, all the Jews, before and at the time of Christ, believed in a literal resurrection of the body, let us now ascertain, if possible, what was the belief of the early Christians upon this particular point. And in this immediate inquiry we shall depend wholly upon outside testimony, leaving the evidence of the Scriptures for subsequent examination.

I. The *Catacombs of Rome* are the burial-place of the early Christian martyrs and others during the first three centuries of the Christian church.

Speaking of his visit to this subterranean charnel-house, Bishop Kip says: "We were wandering among the dead in Christ, who more than sixteen centuries ago were borne to their rest. Around us were the remains of some who, perhaps, had listened to the voices of apostles, and who lived while men were still upon the earth, who had seen Jesus of Nazareth as he went on his pilgrimage through the length and breadth of the land. [1]

[1] The *Catacombs of Rome:* as illustrating the Church of the first three centuries, by Rt. Rev. Wm. Ingraham Kip, D.D., p. 22.

In this subterranean city of the dead, excavated in the soft rock, and extending for miles under the modern city, are deposited the ashes of hundreds of thousands who died in the faith of Christ, as then taught and believed, and whose remains were deposited here by their friends and brethren of like precious faith. Along the sides of the narrow streets their graves are cut in the rock, one above another, the bodies deposited, and the front closed by mason work, or by slabs nicely fitted and hermetically cemented. Upon these slabs or upon the adjoining rock are to be seen numerous inscriptions and symbols, indicative as well of the faith of those who were buried as of those who buried them.

Some of these inscriptions date back as early as the time of Vespasian; that is, not forty years after the crucifixion; and most of them are of a very early date.

Now these inscriptions and symbols furnish conclusive evidence, not only that the Christians of that period believed in *a* resurrection, but that they looked for the revival of the *identical bodies* laid in the tombs. Hence the Phœnix (fabled as rising to life from its own ashes, and therefore a striking emblem of the resurrection) is one of the common symbols upon their tombs. [1] The *cock*, suggesting the *morning* of the resurrection; and a fish, or a *sea monster*, ejecting a man from his stomach, are often to be met with; the latter chosen in reference to our Lord's words, Luke xi. 29:

[1] The ancients seemed really to have believed this fable. Hence Clement, in A. D. 95, in his first Epistle, presents an argument for a literal resurrection, drawn from the supposed phenomenon of the Phœnix.

"There shall no sign be given it but the sign of the prophet Jonas," etc. Another symbol consists of sculptured representations of the resurrection of Lazarus—a scene employed for the same purpose at the entrance of Greenwood Cemetery, near New York. [1]

"They sought not the sculptured marble to enclose their remains, but were content with the rude emblems which were carved above, merely to show that for the body resting there they expected a share in the glory of the resurrection." [2]

Though many of the inscriptions speak of the "rest" or "sleep" of the dead, they also speak of their future resurrection. "You will arise; a temporary rest is granted you." And the number of symbols representing the resurrection of Christ, shows that in his glorious triumph over death they recognized the proof and pledge of their own resurrection and future glory.

"This is the theme, Christ's resurrection, and that of the Church in his person, on which, in their peculiar language, the artists of the catacombs seem never weary of expatiating; death swallowed up in victory, and the victor, crowned with the amaranth wreath of immortality, is the vision ever before their eyes, with a vividness of anticipation which we, who have been born in this belief, can but feebly realize." [3]

This all-pervading and inspiring hope of the resurrection of the body, invested the remains of the dead in Christ with a peculiar sacredness in the eyes of the early confessors and martyrs.

"The only case," says Bishop Kip, "in which any-

[1] Bishop Kip's Treatise. [2] Ibid., p. 21.

[3] Bishop Kip, p. 126.

thing like denunciation is found, is where it is directed against those who should violate the sanctity of the grave. To the early Christians even this frail tabernacle had acquired a higher value and dignity when they learned the lesson of the resurrection, and that it was THIS MORTAL which hereafter was to 'put on immortality.' Precious in their eyes, therefore, became the remains of the saints. They could not burn them upon the funeral pile, nor would they gather them into an unmeaning urn, for they felt that these lifeless relics had been consecrated to the Lord, and were now to be placed in charge of the Angel of the Resurrection until the end of all things. Therefore it was, that somewhat in the spirit of the Hebrew Psalms, in inscriptions like the following, they record their curse against any who should disturb the rest of that body which was one day to be united again to its spiritual partner:—

> "If any one shall violate this sepulchre,
> Let him perish miserably and remain unburied;
> Let him lie down, and not rise again;
> Let his portion be with Judas." [1]

"And yet, in this very imprecation it is implied that to 'rise again' is at least the allotment and hope of the righteous dead. So full was the hope of the martyrs of the first three centuries of the Christian Church with the idea of immortality for the body as well as the soul, that despite the gloom which darkness and silence and death would otherwise have thrown over this home of slumbering millions, the countless inscriptions and symbolical monograms to be

[1] Bishop Kip, pp. 81, 82.

seen on every hand, all pointing away to the "better country," and to victory over death and the grave, have filled all these subterranean corridors and arches and crypts with the light of an eternal day.

"It is not alone a place of gloom and desolation. It reminds us not even primarily of death. Its dominant sentiment is that of *immortality*. From the distant past—from their rock-hewn tombs—we hear the voices of the buried martyrs calling on us to rejoice and hope, because the darkness has rolled away from the sepulchre, and Christ has become to us, as he was to them, THE RESURRECTION AND THE LIFE.[1]

II. We have seen that this doctrine was assailed by the Greeks in the time of Josephus, on the very ground that it is now assailed by some, namely, that *such* a resurrection is a physical impossibility. And so during the first ages of the Christian Church assaults were made upon Christianity in general upon the same ground, calling forth replies from several of the Christian Fathers. Now it is a well-known fact that the only notion of the resurrection indicated by Clement, Justin, Irenæus, Tertullian, Cyprian and others, as well as by Josephus,) is that of a *physical resurrection.* As one has well said, "Most of the Fathers believed in the resuscitation of the body, and of the very same body which man possessed while on earth.[2]

Of the proofs of this fact we shall here cite a few specimens.

III. *Clement*, Bishop of Rome, was a companion of St. Paul, who mentions him, Phil. iv. 3, as a "fellow-

[1] Bishop Kip, p. 83.

[2] Hagenbach's History of Doctrines, Vol. I., p. 217.

laborer, whose name is in the book of life." This Clement, though claiming for them no inspiration, wrote several letters to different churches, and among them two to the church at Corinth—the very church to whom St. Paul addressed his overwhelming argument on the resurrection of the dead. (1 Cor. xv.) He also writes upon the same *subject* upon which the apostle had written.

Now in the first Epistle of Clement to the Corinthians, he labors to prove a resurrection possible by referring to the fable of the Phœnix, in which the new and living bird was produced out of the ashes of the dead one. Believing this to be a literal fact in nature, he says: "Why do we esteem it a great matter, and wonderful, that the Creator of all things should raise up all those that have served him holily, since by a bird he manifests to us the magnificence of his promise?" In his second Epistle he says, "Let no one of you say, that THIS FLESH shall not be judged, nor rise. Do you know in what you were saved, in what you were converted, unless it were in the flesh? . . . . As ye were called in the flesh, *so shall ye come in the flesh.* The Lord Jesus Christ, who has saved us, being first a spirit, was made flesh, and so called us. So we likewise, *in this flesh, shall receive a reward.*"

Now if Clement held to any other view than that of a literal resurrection, his reference to the Phœnix is altogether inappropriate, and his language misleading.

IV. *Polycarp* was a disciple of St. John, and suffered as a martyr under Antonius, A. D. 166. Eusebius tells us that he was "a man who had been instructed by the apostles, and had familiar intercourse with many who had seen Christ;" and that "he always taught what he had learned from the apostles, what the Church had handed down, and what is the only true doctrine."[1] Now when bound to the stake, this venerable martyr of eighty-six years offered a last prayer to God, in which he says, "I bless thee that thou hast thought me worthy of the present day and hour, to have a share in the number of the martyrs and in the cup of Christ, unto the *resurrection* of eternal life, both of the soul and *body*, in the incorruptible felicity of the Holy Spirit."[2]

V. The *Sybilline Oracles*, says Hody, were "published by Christians about thirty years after the death of St. John. In one of the verses it is said, that 'God, after he has destroyed the world and all mankind by fire, will restore their *ashes* and *bones*, and form them again as they were before.'"[3]

VI. *Justin Martyr* flourished about A. D. 140. In his dialogue with Trypho the Jew, he says: "If you meet with any who have the Christian name but deny the resurrection of the dead, do not esteem them as Christians. For I, and all those Christians who in all respects hold the true opinion, do know that there will be a *resurrection of the* FLESH." And the title of a book which he wrote expressly upon the subject of the resurrection, is, "*Concerning the Resurrection of the* FLESH." "In those days," says Hody, "they did not call it 'the resurrection of the *body*,' because some of

[1] Eccl. Hist., Book IV., chap. xiv.

[2] Ibid., Book IV., chap. xv.

[3] Hody on the Resurrection, p. 140.

the heretics who denied the resurrection of the flesh, pretended nevertheless to believe in the resurrection of the *body*. But that all might know that they intended the very same *human body*, they called it in downright terms, 'the resurrection of the FLESH.'" [1]

VII. *Titianus Syrus* was a disciple of Justin Martyr. In his oration against the Gentiles he says: "We shall be restored to what we are, and be judged by God the Creator. This we believe, though you look upon us as filthy triflers, and babblers for it. For as once I had no being, and then was begotten, so, being born and again reduced by death to what I was, I shall be restored to my being again. Though all my flesh shall be consumed by fire, yet the world contains the evaporated matter. Though I shall be drowned and dissolved in a river or the sea, or be devoured by wild beasts, yet I am laid up in the repositories of God. The ignorant indeed, and the Atheist, know not where my substance is deposited; but God who reigns, and who alone sees it, will restore it in his due time to its former state." [2]

VIII. *Irenæus*, who was born before the death of John, and was a pupil of Polycarp, declares that the doctrine that "Christ should come and raise up all flesh" was received from the apostles, and believed by the Church throughout the world." [3] He also devotes a large portion of his fifth book to proving that "we shall rise perfect men with the same body of flesh."

IX. *Athenagoras* was a Christian philosopher of the time of Irenæus, who was teacher in a divinity

[1] Res. of the Body, pp. 141, 142. [2] Book I., chap. ii.
[3] Hody, p. 142.

school at Alexandria, and wrote a treatise "concerning the Resurrection of the Dead." In that treatise he represents all who had written upon the subject before him as holding to a *physical resurrection;* and his whole effort is to establish this doctrine against the objections and cavils of the heathen. [1]

X. In the year of our Lord 177, the Churches of Vienne and Lyons wrote an epistle to the Churches in Asia and Phrygia, recounting their terrible persecutions. This epistle, entitled "*The Number and Sufferings of those that Suffered for the Faith in Gaul,*" is preserved in Eusebius, and contains the following pertinent passage:

"The bodies of the martyrs, after being abused in every possible manner, and thus exposed to the open air for six days, were at length burned and reduced to ashes by the wretches, and finally cast into the Rhone, that flowed near at hand, that there might be no vestige of them remaining on the land. These things they did as if they were able to overcome God, and destroy the resurrection (παλιγγενεσιαν,) as they themselves gave out, 'that they might not have any hope of rising again, in the belief of which they have introduced a new and strange religion, and contemn the most dreadful punishments, and are prepared to meet death even with joy. Now we shall see whether they will rise again; and whether their God is able to help them, and rescue them out of our hands.'" [2]

Two things are evident from this quotation, namely: first, that the Gentiles who put the saints to death un-

[1] Hody, p. 143.

[2] Book V., chap. ii., American translation, p. 180.

derstood the latter to believe in and teach the literal resurrection of their bodies; and secondly, that the Christians made no effort to prevent the persecution or to recover the bodies of their friends for burial, by correcting this materialistic idea of their persecutors. "Among our brethren," says the epistle, "matters were in great affliction, for want of liberty to commit the bodies to the earth. For neither did the night avail us for this purpose, nor had money any effect to persuade, nor could any prayers nor entreaties move them. But they guarded them in every possible manner, as if it were a great gain to prevent them from burial." Now as all this "great affliction" grew out of a desire of the persecutors to prevent the resurrection of the same bodies, how easily could the Christians have obtained relief, and probably averted the persecution altogether, by adding to their "prayers and entreaties" for the bodies of their friends the simple statement, that by "the resurrection of the flesh" they did not mean the raising again of the same body, but a new body made of other elements; or, still better for their purpose, the theory of Prof. Bush and the Swedenborgians, that the resurrection of the dead is the emerging of the soul from the body at the moment of death.

But they availed themselves of no such explanations, for the simple reason that they held to the very resurrection which their enemies proposed to prevent, and the explanations or theories alluded to were not then known among believers.

"It is to be observed," says Osterwald, "that all, both Jews and Christians, when treating of the resur-

4

rection, always understood the resurrection of the body. The objections of the Sadducees suppose the same, (Matt. xx. 24,) and the judgment of the heathen concerning this doctrine, (Acts xvii. 32.) We learn from Tertullian, Minucius Felix, and other ancient writers, that this was the principal objection of the adversaries of Christianity. How could it be possible that our bodies should be restored? In order to remove which objection, it may be observed, that if there were no resurrection of the body, Christ and his followers would have plainly said, that the Sadducees and heathens did not understand their doctrine, and that the bodies were not to be raised. But they said no such thing, but took their answers from Scripture, and the omnipotence of God, which supposes the resurrection of the bodies." [1]

X. *Tertullus*, who flourished about A.D. 180, wrote a book upon the subject of the resurrection, with the title, "*De Resurrectione Carnis*,"—*the resurrection of the flesh*. This writer affirms that "Christ shall come to judge the quick and the dead," and that the "resurrection of the *flesh*" was an article of faith which was "received by the whole Church with one accord," and was "*immovable and unalterable*." [2]

XI. The compend of Christian doctrines known as *The Apostles' Creed* is certainly of very great antiquity. Ruffinus affirms that it was composed by the Apostles themselves during their stay at Jerusalem soon after our Lord's ascension. But of this there is no sufficient proof. It was in existence, however, in the time

[1] Osterwald's Theology, (Amer. ed., 1788,) pp. 379, 380.

[2] Hody, pp. 145, 146.

of Ruffinus, in the fourth century, and is quoted in full by him, as it stands in the English Liturgy. It is also cited by Ambrose, in the third century, and was doubtless in existence much earlier. Mosheim says, "It appears to have been the general creed of the Christian Church from at least the close of the second century down to the Reformation.[1] It may therefore be regarded as embodying the faith of the early saints at a period not later than a century after the death of John the beloved disciple.

Now among the doctrines embodied in this most ancient symbol or confession of faith is that of "*the Resurrection of the Body.*" And observe, it is not "the resurrection of the *dead*" in general terms, but of the "*body,*"—thus definitely restricting the meaning to a corporeal resurrection. Nor is this all. "The Greeks," says Bishop Pearson, "always use *σαρκὸς ἀνάστασιν*; the Latin, *carnis resurrectionem,* both of which mean 'the resurrection of the flesh.'" And this was to be observed, because being we read of spiritual bodies, some would acknowledge the resurrection of the body who would deny the resurrection of the flesh." [2]

And even this was not sufficiently explicit to satisfy all, as expressive of their belief. Hence we are told that "they of the church at Aquileia, by the addition of a pronoun propounded it to every single believer in a more particular way of expression,—"*the resurrection of this flesh.*" [3]

[1] Mosheim's Eccl. Hist., Vol. I., p. 79. Vol. 2.

[2] Pearson on the Creed, American Ed., p. 553, note.

[3] Pearson on the Creed, p. 553.

XII. The *Apostolic Constitutions*, compiled near the end of the second century, has a long chapter in defence of a literal resurrection. "God Almighty will raise us up . . . in the same form which now we have, without any mutilation or corruption. For whether we die in the sea, or have our particles dispersed in the earth, or devoured by beasts or birds, he will raise us up by his power by which he holds the whole world in his hand. Not a hair of your heads shall perish. . . . Through this certain persuasion we endure stripes, persecutions and deaths." [1]

XIII. *Lucian*, an atheistic writer of the same period, in condemning the Christian faith, thus defines it: "These wretches persuade themselves that they shall be, *the whole man*, both body and soul, immortal, and shall live forever. And on this account they contemn death, and many of them offer themselves voluntarily to be put to death." [2]

XIV. *Minucius Felix*, who flourished near the beginning of the third century, thus writes:—"Who is so foolish and brutish as to deny, that God who first made man, can form him again, as he was before? 'Tis harder to make that which before had no being, than to restore that which once had a being. All bodies, when dissolved, whether crumbled to dust or dissolved into moisture, are reduced to ashes or rarefied into vapor, are lost to us, but to God, the keeper of the elements, they are still preserved."

XV. *Hippolytus*, who lived and wrote in the third century, "ranked very high both among the writers

[1] Book V., Chap. vii. [2] Hody, p. 149.

and the martyrs" of his time.[1] He also wrote a book "*Concerning the Resurrection of the Flesh*," and is supposed to have been the author of a work "*Concerning the Cause of the Universe, against the Heathen*." In this last work he tells the heathen, that "God will raise us all up, not by shifting the soul out of one body into another, but raising up the same bodies. You, O ye heathens, because you see that these bodies were dissolved, do not believe that they will rise again. But learn you to believe. For since ye believe, according to Plato, that the immortal soul was made by God, you ought not to disbelieve but that God is able to raise up to life this body, which is compounded of the elements, and to make it immortal."[2]

XVI. The celebrated *Origen*, who flourished in the third century, was the first Christian writer of whom we have knowledge, who attempted in any wise to modify the commonly received idea of the resurrection. "Being fascinated with the Platonic philosophy, he ventured to apply its laws to every part of religion, and persuaded himself that the philosophy which he admired could assign the cause and ground of every doctrine, and determine its precise form and nature;"[3] and though the resurrection, as generally understood, is a *miracle*, and consequently *above* reason and nature, he attempted to modify the idea of the resurrection, in order that it might be susceptible of rational explanation upon the principles of his philosophy. Yet it is

[1] Mosheim's Ecclesiastical History, Harper's Ed., Vol. I., p. 168, at top.

[2] How much like the quotation from Josephus, page 22!

[3] Mosheim, Vol. I., p. 177.

difficult to ascertain precisely what he taught or believed upon the subject. In his book against Celsus, who had attacked the Christian faith violently, and especially the doctrine of the resurrection, Origen admits that 'the resurrection of the flesh was the doctrine preached in the churches.' He also speaks of the 'resurrection of the body,' 'our own bodies,' 'that which fell,' etc., as if he held to the common belief, and yet he is accused by cotemporaneous writers of teaching, that though in the resurrection 'we shall have the same species of body, the same form or appearance, yet it will not be the same matter, as our bodies in old age retain the same species, yet have not any of the same particles which we had in our youth."

"The followers of Origen," says *Epiphanius*, "acknowledge the resurrection of the dead, and of our flesh, and of the body of our Lord, the same that was conceived of the Virgin Mary; and yet they did not own that the same flesh shall rise, but that another will be substituted by God in its place." This was probably the substance of the departure of Origen from the common faith,—a defection of so much moment in the estimation of the early Christians, as to induce the Council of Trollo to declare that "he spoke wickedly and contumeliously of the resurrection of the dead," that he "foolishly said that these very bodies we now have are not to rise, etc." Several books were written against him, and his views were condemned and anathematized by three different synods, from A.D. 399 to 553.

"I could easily fill you a volume," says Hody, "with the testimonies and authorities of the Doctors of the fourth and the following ages; and could show you with how great zeal the doctrine of *the same human body* has been always maintained by the Church."[1]

XVII. Early in the fourth century, Ruffinus wrote to Pope Anastasis as follows: "Moreover also we acknowledge that the resurrection of our flesh shall be complete and perfect; of this our very flesh in which we now live, no member of it being amputated, nor any part of it cut away, and to which nothing of its whole nature will be wanting, excepting only corruption."[2]

XVIII. From the time of Origen his opinions were repeatedly condemned, both by councils and individual writers, and the true faith asserted. In A. D. 400, the Council of Toledo said, "We believe there will be a resurrection of the flesh of mankind." Another council, at the same place, in 633, said, "We are to be raised up by Christ in the same flesh in which we now live, and in the same form in which he himself rose." At still another council held at Toledo in 675, they said, "According to the example of our Head, we confess that there will be a true resurrection of the flesh of all the dead. Neither do we believe that we shall rise in an aerial or any other kind of flesh, (as some have deliriously fancied,) but in that in which we live, have our being, and move."

In a Confession of Faith written by *Boethius*, a noted Christian philosopher and writer of the sixth century,

[1] A very full account of the sayings of Origen, upon the subject, is furnished by Dr. Hody (pp. 151–168,) but our limits forbid further quotations.

[2] Macknight on 1 Cor. xv. 43.

he says: "This is principally required in our religion, that we believe, not only that our souls do not perish, but also that our bodies themselves, which are dissolved by death, are restored in the life to come to their former state."

Such is the testimony of the early Christian martyrs and confessors, not only to the *fact* of a resurrection from the dead, but especially as to the *nature* of a resurrection for which they hoped, and for the hope of which many of them died. From the tombs in which their ashes slumber; from the accusations of their enemies; from the records of their religious synods and councils; and the written vindications of the faith which they have left behind them, but one voice arises; and that is, that whether right or wrong, philosophical or unphilosophical, visionary or Scriptural, *they believed in a literal resurrection of the* FLESH, BONE FOR BONE, AND MUSCLE FOR MUSCLE!

The bearing of this indisputable fact upon the general inquiry is obvious. If such was the faith of the early saints, despite the persecutions it brought upon them, the presumption is very strong, to say the least, that *such was the doctrine taught by the apostles;* and that in the opinion of the primitive martyrs, to abjure the doctrine of a physical resurrection, was to abjure the faith of Christ.

CHAPTER IV.

VIEWS OF VARIOUS SECTS AND DENOMINATIONS TO THE PRESENT TIME.

HAVING shown in the last chapter that the confessors and martyrs of the first six centuries of the Christian era held to the literal resurrection of the body, we shall now proceed to show, in the present chapter, that with few exceptions this has been the faith of the Christian world from that time to the present. In so doing we shall consult confessions of faith, catechisms, and systems of theology, the sermons of eminent ministers of different denominations, and the hymns of the various churches and Christian poets.

I. From time immemorial the ROMISH CHURCH have expressed their views upon this subject in the language of the apostles' creed. In all ages and countries they have been wont to say, "I believe in * * * CARNIS *resurrectionem—the resurrection of the* FLESH." And whatever may be thought of their doctaines generally, it will not be denied that they are a very ancient body of professed Christians, whose belief upon this subject is not without its significance.

II. The GREEK CHURCH separated from the Romish about the beginning of the fifth century, and in many respects very much resembles the parent stock.

It comprehends a considerable part of Greece, the Grecian isles, Wallachia, Moldavia, Egypt, Abyssinia, Nubia, Lybia, Arabia, Mesopotamia, Syria, Cilicia, and Palestine; Alexandria, Antioch, and Jerusalem; the whole of the Russian Empire in Europe; great part of Siberia in Asia, Astrachan, Casan, and Georgia.[1]

It is the National Church of the Russian Empire, and numbers its votaries by millions.

Upon the subject of the resurrection the Greek Church also holds to the doctrine of the apostles' creed—to *σαρκός ἀναστασιν*—*the resurrection of the* FLESH.[2]

III. The LUTHERAN CHURCH hold to the Augsburg Confession, drawn up by Melancthon, in 1530. In the XVIIth article we are told in general terms that "at the end of the world Christ will appear for judgment, and will raise all the dead."

Messrs. *Storr* and *Flatt*, Theological Professors in the University of Tübingen, Germany, thus speak upon the point in hand, in their *Elementary Course of Christian Theology*, as translated by Dr. Schmucker.

"But those effects, also, which death has on the body, shall be removed. For the same body which was exposed to corruption, and which experienced a dissolution of its particles, while the soul was in a state of happy existence, shall be raised by the power of God, and be brought to a state of renovated life."[3]

[1] Watson's Theological Dictionary, article, *Greek Church*.

[2] See Greek versions of the apostles' creed, in the Appendix to Pearson, American edition.

[3] Elementary Course of Christian Theology, as translated by Dr. Schmucker, p. 369.

Again: in his "*Elements of Popular Theology*," Dr. Schmucker says: "The Scriptures also teach the *identity* of the risen body with that which was laid in the grave. . . . The future body will still embrace the *essential elements* of the present. . . . We are told that our bodies will *rise again*, and not that new ones will be created." [1]

Still again: *Q.* "*Will the body that is raised be the same which was laid in the grave?*

A. "All that is essential to the identity or sameness of the body, will be raised; while its unessential particles will remain mingled with the mass of earth." [2]

IV. The *German Reformed Churches* usually refer to the *Heidelberg Catechism* as their standard of doctrine. In that catechism their faith is laid down as follows:

"*Question* 57. *What comfort doth the resurrection of the body afford thee?*

"*Answer*. That not only my soul, after this life, shall be immediately taken up to Christ, its Head, but also that this my body, being raised by the power of Christ, shall be reunited with my soul, and made like unto the glorious body of Christ!"

Ursinus, a celebrated German divine and author of the sixteenth century, in commenting on the 57th question of the Heidelberg Catechism already cited, writes thus: "In this article the resurrection of the body means the restitution of the substance of our bodies after death out of the very same matter of which they now consist . . .—in the restitution of the

[1] Pages 375, 376.

[2] Evangelical Lutheran Catechism, by Dr. Schmucker, p. 121.

same body, or the bringing together the mass of matter which now constitute, our bodies, but which after death is scattered and dissolved in the different elements." He then proceeds to vindicate the doctrine of the resurrection, as popularly understood.

Again: "The bodies with which we shall rise in the resurrection, will not only be human bodies, but also the very same which we now have, and not other and different bodies created by Christ, as the Anabaptists affirm." [1]

George Christian Knapp was Professor of Theology in the University of Halle, Germany. In answering the question: "*What is understood by the resurrection of the dead?*" he says:—

"By this is meant the revivification of the human body after it has been forsaken by the soul, or the reunion of the soul hereafter with the body which it had occupied in the present world." P. 527. "Notwithstanding the difference between the body which we now have and that which we shall possess hereafter, it is still taught in the schools of theology that our future body will be, in substance, the same with the present." [2]

V. The CHURCH OF ENGLAND have ever held to the doctrine of the Apostles' Creed; that is, to "the resurrection of the flesh."

Bishop Pearson, in his learned and exhaustive Exposition of the Creed, (which the Church of England everywhere endorses,) explicitly advocates and expounds it as teaching a physical resurrection. He

[1] Willard's translation, 1852, pp. 312, 315.

[2] Lectures on Christian Theology, American Edition, 1859, p. 536.

says, "We must therefore undertake to show that the bodies of men, however corrupted, wheresoever in their parts dispersed, how long soever dead, shall hereafter be re-collected in themselves, and united to their own souls."

Again: "The identity of the body raised from death is so necessary, that the very name of the resurrection doth include or suppose it; so that when I say there shall be a resurrection of the dead, I must intend thus much, that the bodies of men which live and are dead shall revive and rise again. For at the death of man nothing falleth but his body, 'the spirit goeth upward,' (Eccles. iii. 21,) and no other body falleth but his own; and therefore the body, and no other but the body, must rise again to make a resurrection."

Such a resurrection, he proceeds to prove, is not only not possible, but upon general considerations highly probable, and "upon Christian principles infallibly certain." [1]

Bishop Beveridge died in 1707. Commenting upon the Apostles' Creed, he says: "By the 'resurrection of the body' I understand and believe, that every body that was ever informed or endued with a reasonable soul, and is afterwards parted from it by death, although it be then reduced to the earth again, or eaten up of worms, or beasts, or fishes, or any other way consumed, and the parts of it scattered abroad and dispersed over the earth, yet, at the last day, all the parts and particles of it shall come together again,

[1] Exposition of the Creed, Appleton's Ed., pp. 555, 568, 569.

every one into its proper place where it was before, so as to make up the same individual body, etc."[1]

Archbishop Secker says: "They shall be so far the same bodies, that every one shall have properly his own, and be truly the same person he was before."[2]

Robert South, who died in 1716, thus wrote: "For who would imagine, or could conceive, that when a body, by continued friction and dissipation is crumbled into millions of little atoms, some portions of it rarified into air, others sublimated into fire, and the rest changed into earth and water, the elements should, after all this, surrender back their spoils, and the several parts, after such a dispersion, should travel from all the four quarters of the world to meet together, and come to a mutual interview of one another, in one and the same individual body again? That God should summon a part out of this fish, that fowl, that beast, that tree, and remand it to its former place, to unite into a new combination for the rebuilding of a fallen edifice, and restoring an old, broken, demolished carcass to itself once more?

"I cannot, I say, find anything in all this either hard or puzzling, and much less contrary to natural reason, if we do but acknowledge an omniscience in the agent who is to do this great thing, joined with omnipotence in the same manner.

"The sum of all, therefore, is this, that every human body, upon its dissolution, sinks by degrees into the elementary mass of matter; whereof a great part passes by several animations into other bodies, and a

[1] Works, London Ed. 1824, p. 49.

[2] Works, London, 1835, Vol. VI., p. 172.

great part likewise remains in the same elementary mass, without undergoing any further changes. To which reserved portion, at the last day, the soul, as the prime, individuating principle, and the same reserved portion of matter, as an essential and radical part of the individuation, together with a sufficient supply of more (if requisite) from the general mass, shall, by the almighty power of God joining all these together, make up and restore the same person."[1]

In 1725, *Dr. Henry Felton*, of England, published a sermon, entitled, *The Resurrection of the Same Numerical Body, and its Re-union to the Same Soul*, against Mr. Locke's notion of personality and identity. It was so well thought of at the time as to pass through three editions.[2]

The learned *Isaac Barrow* thus reasons:

"That which never had fallen could not be said to be raised again; that which did never die could not be restored from death; nor could men be said to rise again, but in respect to that part which had fallen, or that state which had ceased to be." And after citing various Scriptures, he says: "which expressions and the like occurring, do clearly and fully prove the separation of our bodies, and their re-union to our souls, and our persons becoming in substance completely the same that we were."[3]

Thomas Scott (Rector of Ashton, etc.,) says:

"As the body is a part of our nature, and the instrument of the soul in doing good or evil; so it is

[1] Sermons, London, 1850, p. 359.

[2] Doddridge's Lectures, Vol. II., p. 363, note.

[3] Works, 1845, Vol. II., p. 565.

meet that it should be raised from the dead, to share the happiness or misery which shall be awarded to every one according to his works." . . . "Our bodies will be raised so far the same, that we shall know ourselves to be the same persons who did such and such things on earth: but 'as we must all be changed,' our bodies will not be *in all respects the same, etc.*" [1]

Bishop Hopkins (of England) says:

"It shall be raised *an entire and perfect body.* Not a dust, not an atom, that is necessary to the integrity of it, shall be lost: and though they be scattered up and down the world, and confusedly mixed with other beings; yet, by the omnipotence of God and the ministry of angels, every dust shall be picked up again, and set in its due place and order." [2]

VI. The Reformed Dutch Church in America thus express their adherence to the common faith:

"For all the dead shall be raised out of the earth, and their souls joined and united with their proper bodies, in which they formerly lived." [3]

Dr. Samuel Helffenstein thus expresses the same general views:

"A question is asked, whether the dead will be raised with the same bodies which were laid in the grave, or with different bodies. That the same body which was laid in the grave shall be raised, is necessarily implied in the very nature of a resurrection. If it were a different body, composed of different par-

[1] Theological Works, first Amer. ed., Vol. V., pp. 492, 493.

[2] Works, London, 1809, Vol. IV. p. 90.

[3] Constitution of the Reformed Dutch Church of North America, article xxxvii.

ticles of matter, it would be a creation, and not a resurrection."[1]

John Frederic Osterwald was a celebrated divine of Switzerland, who died in 1741. In his *Compendium of Christian Theology* he says:

"But it may be inquired whether the same bodies shall be raised, or if men shall be clothed with new bodies? The former ought by all means to be maintained, otherwise there would be no resurrection, but only a new creation; neither would the Scriptures have taught us, that those who sleep shall come out of the dust, and that the dust of the earth shall deliver up its dead. Again, since man consists of soul and body, it seems entirely requisite, in order that the same man should rise that he should have the same body."[2]

VII. The PROTESTANT EPISCOPAL CHURCH in this country follow the Church of England in the use of the apostles' creed as an embodiment of their belief. Hence they also believe with the mother church, and with Pearson, and Beveridge, and South, and Secker, in "the *resurrection of the* FLESH."

VIII. The METHODIST EPISCOPAL CHURCH hold to the same creed, and, of course, to the same doctrine. But this may be made more clear, perhaps, by a few quotations from prominent Methodist writers.

John Wesley thus writes: "The plain notion of a resurrection requires that the self-same body that died should rise again. Nothing can be said to rise again but that very body that died. If God gives to our souls at the last day a new body, this cannot be called

[1] Doctrines of Divine Revelation, p. 375. [2] Page 379.

a resurrection of our body; because that word plainly implies a fresh production of what was before. There are many places in Scripture that plainly declare it," etc.

He then proceeds to cite and interpret the Scriptures referred to, as teaching a physical resurrection; and to show at length that *such* a resurrection has nothing unphilosophical or incredible in it.[1]

So, also, in his Notes on 1 Corinthians, xv., he interprets it throughout as teaching a physical resurrection.

Charles Wesley is equally explicit. In that inimitable hymn commencing, "I call the world's Redeemer mine," we find the following:

"Then the last judgment-day shall come;
And though the worms this skin devour,
The Judge shall call me from the tomb,
Shall bid the greedy grave restore,
And raise this individual me,
God in the flesh, my God, to see.

"In this identic body, I,
With eyes of flesh refined, restored,
Shall see that self-same Saviour nigh,
See for myself my smiling Lord;
See with ineffable delight,
Nor faint to bear the glorious sight."

So in the hymn commencing, "Our great Creator, God."

"Who breathed into our earth
The breath of life divine,
Can, by a new celestial birth,
God and the sinner join:

[1] Works, Vol. II., p. 507.

Thus we the pledge receive
Of immortality,
Sure that our bodies too shall live
Forever one with thee."

John Wesley endorsed and published all these hymns.

Richard Watson inculcated the same view. "It cannot, however, fail," says he, "to strike every impartial reader of the New Testament, that the doctrine of the resurrection is there taught without any nice distinctions. It is always exhibited as a miraculous work, and represents the same body which is laid in the grave as the subject of this change from death to life by the power of Christ." . . . . "That the same body which was laid in the grave shall arise out of it, is the obvious doctrine of the Scriptures."[1]

The above views of Mr. Watson are quoted without dissent in the *Encyclopædia of Religious Knowledge;* showing that they were regarded as the correct views, by the author and editors of that elaborate work.

Joseph Benson was equally orthodox. He says: "The Scripture speaks consistently when, in describing the state of the righteous after the resurrection, it represents them as having their mortal bodies refashioned," etc.[2]

Though *Dr. Adam Clarke* nowhere states distinctly that he believed in a corporeal resurrection, yet he explains 1 Cor. xv. throughout as teaching that doctrine.

Bishop Kingsley thus speaks in his admirable little work upon the subject: "It is the body that *dies* that

[1] Theological Institutes, Part II., chap. xxxix.

[2] Notes on 1 Cor. xv. 44.

is raised again, whether that body sleeps in the grave, or in the dust of the earth, or in the sea." . . .

"Cannot *he* who is present to every particle of matter, who knows every particle by *name*, and whose power has brought every particle into *being*, collect together again the scattered fragments of the human frame, although mingled with the elements, and driven to the four winds of heaven? May we not reply to those who make this objection, ['that it is not possible that the same identical body can ever be raised'] 'Ye do err, not knowing the Scriptures, nor the *power* of God?' " . . .

"The doctrine of a literal resurrection of the body is as positively taught in the Scriptures as any proposition can be expressed in *language*."

"The bodies of mankind after the resurrection, although composed of the same matter as was laid in the grave, will be very different," etc.[1]

IX. All other Methodist bodies throughout the world—the Wesleyans in England, Canada, Australia, and the West Indies; the Methodist Free Churches, the Primitive Methodists, and the "Bible Christians" in England; the M. E. Church in Canada; the Methodist Protestant, Wesleyan, and Independent Methodist Churches in this country, as well as the M. E. Church, South, all hold to the same doctrine—"*the resurrection of the flesh, and the life everlasting.*"

"If the new body should not be a material organization," says Dr. Stockton, "human nature, instead of being restored to its original perfection, would be

[1] Treatise, pp. 32–34, and 153, 154.

exchanged for another mode of being. Its very identity would be lost." [1]

Rev. Thomas N. Ralston, of the M. E. Church, South, thus speaks of the term *resurrection:* 'It implies not an original creation of new bodies, but a *resuscitation* of the same bodies that are laid in the grave."[2]

X. The BAPTIST CHURCHES also hold to a physical resurrection.

Dr. John Gill was a learned Baptist divine of England, who wrote very extensively, and died in 1771. Upon the nature of the resurrection he says:—

"The resurrection to be treated of is—the resurrection of the body in its literal sense; the quickening of mortal bodies. It may be proved, that the same body that now is, will be raised from the dead.

"It is no contradiction, that dust formed out of nothing, and of it a body made, and this reduced to dust again, that this dust should again form the body it once constituted. . . . If God could, out of the dust of the earth, form the body of man at the first, and infuse into it a living and reasonable soul; then much more must he be able to raise a dead body, the matter and substance of which now is, though in different forms and shapes. . . . It is not impossible nor improbable that the dead should be raised; since he knows all the particles of matter bodies are composed of; and when dissolved and transmitted into ten thousand forms, knows where all are lodged, whether in the earth, air or sea; and his all-discerning eye can distinguish those which belong to one body, from

[1] Sermons for the People. [2] Elements of Divinity, p. 438.

those of another, and his almighty hand can gather and unite them, what are necessary, and range them in their due place and order." [1]

"We believe the Scriptures teach, that at the last day Christ will descend from heaven, and raise the dead from the grave for final judgment." [2]

XI. The FREE-WILL BAPTIST Churches also hold to a literal resurrection of the body. In a "*Treatise on the Faith* of the Free-Will Baptists," written under the direction of their General Conference, the writer says:

"As the transgression of Adam secured temporal death to all his posterity, so the obedience and resurrection of Jesus Christ render it certain that the bodies of all men will be raised from the dead." [3]

In a work entitled "*Natural and Revealed Theology*," by *John J. Butler, D.D.*, Professor of Christian Theology in the Theological School at New Hampton, N. H., in alluding to the views of Prof. Bush and Mr. Drew, the author says:

"But all such theories are not only foreign from the Scriptural representation, but subversive of the Scriptural doctrine. They deny that there is to be any literal resurrection of our mortal bodies. Whereas the Scriptures explicitly teach that the body of Christ was literally raised, etc." [4]

On p. 333 in answer to the objection that the body may be scattered or absorbed into another body, he says:

[1] *Body of Divinity*, London, 1769, pp. 956, 962, 963.

[2] *Baptist Church Directory*, by Edward T. Hiscock, D.D., p. 174.

[3] Chapter XV., p. 126.

[4] Page 331.

"Cannot Omnipotence, then, so guard our dust as to secure our physical identity in the resurrection? It is enough that Divine revelation has assured us of the fact." [1]

XII. The PRESBYTERIAN CHURCH in Scotland, and both the Old and New School Presbyterian Churches in this country, hold to a corporeal resurrection.

John Calvin, whose theology they generally follow, thus speaks upon the point under consideration:

"Equally monstrous is the error of those who imagine that souls will not resume the bodies which at present belong to them, but will be furnished with others altogether different. It was the very futile reasoning of the Manichæans, that it is absurd to expect the flesh which is so impure will ever rise again. . . . Nor is there any point more clearly established in Scripture than the resurrection of our present bodies."

Again: "That those bodies which God has dedicated as temples for himself, should sink into corruption without any hope of resurrection, would be absurd in the extreme. What is to be concluded from our being members of Christ? from God's enjoining every part of them to be sanctified to himself, requiring their tongues to celebrate his name, their hands to be lifted up with purity to him, and their bodies altogether to be presented to him as a 'living sacrifice;' this part of our nature, therefore, being dignified with such illustrious honor by the heavenly Judge, what madness is betrayed by a mortal man in asserting it to be reduced to ashes without any hope of restoration." [2]

[1] Lecture XXXI. [2] Institutes, Book III., Chap. xxv., Sec. vii.

The same doctrine is taught in the *Confession of Faith* as follows: "At the last day, all the dead shall be raised up with the self-same bodies, and none other, although with different qualities, which shall be united again to their souls forever."[1]

The *Catechism* is equally explicit. "*What are we to believe concerning the resurrection?*

"We are to believe that the self-same bodies of the dead which were laid in the grave shall be raised up by the power of Christ."[2]

Dr. Edwards says: "The resurrection of the wicked is seldom spoken of in the New Testament, and rarely included in the meaning of the word; it being esteemed not worthy to be called a rising to life, being only for a great increase of the misery and darkness of eternal death."[3]

Dr. Dwight thus reasons upon the subject: "That the body will be the same in such a sense as to be known, appears sufficiently evident from the Scriptures; mankind will know each other in the future world, and their bodies will so far be the same as to become the instruments of such knowledge."[4]

Dr. Griffin, in his sermon on *The Better Resurrection*, thus describes the rising of the dead: "The universal convulsion has opened all the graves. The dead bodies begin to move. The scattered dust is collecting from all quarters, and is flying in all directions to seek its kindred dust."[5]

[1] Article xxxii. [2] Larger Catechism, question 89.

[3] Works, Vol. II. p. 445.

[4] System of Theology, Glasgow, pp. 868, 869.

[5] Sermons, Vol. II., p. 302.

Dr. John Dick, of Glasgow, says: "The very word, resurrection, and the corresponding term ἀναστάσις, both signify the rising or standing up of something which had fallen or laid down; and if it is a different body from their present with which men will hereafter be clothed, a word has been chosen by the inspired writers which conveys a fallacious idea. This single argument, I think, is conclusive."[1]

Rev. Charles Buck, author of the Theological Dictionary, says: "As to the nature of the resurrection, it will be of the *same body*. It is true, indeed, that the body has not always the same particles, which are continually changing, but it has always the same constituent parts, which proves its identity. It is the same body that is born that dies, and the same that dies that shall rise again."[2]

Rev. A. Alexander Hodge, of Fredericksburg, Va., says, "ἀναστάσις signifies, etymologically, 'a raising or rising up.' It is used in the Scriptures to designate the future general raising, by the power of God, of the bodies of all men from the sleep of death." [3]

XIII. The REFORMED PRESBYTERIANS (or Covenanters,) hold to the Westminster Confession and Catechism, which are the same as those of the Old and New School Presbyterian Churches. They must therefore be orthodox on the subject of the resurrection.

XIV. The INDEPENDENTS of England, and the CONGREGATIONALISTS of this country, also hold to a physical resurrection.

David Bogue, D. D., a distinguished Independent

[1] Lectures on Theology, Cincinnati, 1858, p. 439.

[2] Dictionary, article, Resurrection. [3] Outlines of Theology, p. 440.

minister of England, was one of the founders of the London Missionary Society, and for many years at the head of its Seminary at Gosport. In his Theological Lectures, speaking of "the properties of the bodies which shall be raised," he declares explicitly that "it is the same body which was laid in the grave." [1]

Philip Doddridge, another eminent Independent minister and writer, says:—

"The Scripture speaks not merely (as Mr. Locke maintains) of the resurrection of *the dead*, but also of the resurrection of *the body*, in such terms as at least to strongly intimate that it may properly be called the same body that was laid in the grave, on some material account, though the organization of it shall no doubt be greatly changed." [2]

XIV. The *Moravians*, (or United Brethren,) like the Lutherans, hold to the Augsburg Confession, and like them hold to a physical resurrection. And so of all minor sects having the least title to the appellation of Christian, unless it should be the orthodox Friends or Quakers. Precisely what they believe upon the subject we have not been able to ascertain from any of their writings.[3] That Deists, Universalists, Spiritualists, and a great majority of the Unitarians, especially of the Theodore Parker School, deny the resurrection of the body, we are well aware; but with these exceptions we aver that the doctrine of the literal resurrection of the body, in all its essential elements,

[1] Lectures, Vol. I., p. 264.

[2] Lectures, London, 1822, Vol. II., p. 363.

[3] A little testimony from outside sources as to their views may be found in Chapter IX.

part for part, and atom for atom, has been the faith of the Church of God in all ages and lands, from the days of Moses to the present time. This even Prof. Bush substantially admits when he says that in opposing this doctrine he is arraigning THE CURRENT CREED OF THE CHURCH FOR THE SPACE OF EIGHTEEN CENTURIES ! [1]

XVI. A few poetic quotations touching the nature of the resurrection may appropriately close this chapter.

It seems as all were over now—
The heavy limbs, the soulless brow;
Yet through these rigid limbs once more
A nobler life ere long shall pour;
These dead, dry bones again shall feel
New warmth and vigor through them steal;
Re-knit and living they shall soar
On high, where Christ lives evermore.[2]

I know the time shall come
When, through the channel dumb,
A voice shall ring upon the slumb'ring ear;
These bones shall startle then,
And feel strange life again,
And these decaying fibres leap to hear.
I know these hands shall wrestle with the turf
That time shall heap upon them all in vain;
Or struggling upward from the stormy surf,
So I be buried in the mighty main.
Yes, 'tis not long ere I shall shake the clay
That years have matted on my mould'ring brow,
And tear the cerements of the grave away
With these same muscles that are lusty now.[3]

Thou shalt rise, my dust! thou shalt arise,
Not always closed thine eyes;

[1] Preface to *Anastasis*, p. 5.

[2] Hermann. [3] A. C. Coxe.

Thy life's first Giver
Will give thee life forever.
Ah! praise his name.[1]

The trumpet! the trumpet! the dead have all heard;
Lo! the depths of the stone-covered chancel are stirred;
From the sea, from the land, from the south and the north,
The vast generations of man are come forth.[2]

Yet these, now rising from the tomb,
With lustre brighter far shall shine,
Revive with ever-during bloom,
Safe from diseases and decline.[3]

Then let the worms demand their prey,
The greedy grave my reins consume;
With joy I drop my mould'ring clay,
And rest till my Redeemer come;
On Christ my life, in death rely,
Secure that I can never die.[4]

The trump shall sound—the dead shall wake;
From the cold tomb the slumb'ring spring.[5]

These ashes too, this little dust,
Our Father's care shall keep
Till the last angel rise and break
The long and dreary sleep.[6]

Forgotten generations live again,
Assume the bodily shape they owned of old,
Beyond the flood.[6]

What though my body run to dust?
Faith cleaves unto it, counting every grain,
With an exact and most particular trust,
Reserving all for flesh again.[7]

[1] Klopstock. [2] Milmann. [3] Samuel Wesley, Jr. [4] Charles Wesley.
[5] Dwight. [6] Henry Kirk White. [7] Herbert.

The blessed in the new covenant,
Shall rise up quickened, each one from his grave,
Wearing again the garments of the flesh,
Ministers and messengers of life eternal.[1]

The time draws on
When not a single spot of burial earth,
Whether on land, or in the spacious sea,
But must give back its long committed dust
Inviolate; and faithfully shall these
Make up the full amount; not the least atom,
Embezzled or mislaid of the whole tale.[2]

Grave, the guardian of our dust,
Grave, the treasury of the skies,
Every atom of thy trust
Rests in hope again to rise:
Hark! the judgment trumpet calls—
Soul, rebuild thy house of clay;
Immortality thy walls,
And eternity thy day.[3]

Bury the dead; and weep
In stillness o'er the loss;
Bury the dead, in Christ they sleep,
Who love on earth his cross;
And from the grave their dust shall rise,
In his own image to the skies.[3]

Corruption, earth and worms,
Shall but refine this flesh,
Till my triumphant spirit comes,
To put it on afresh.[4]

God my Redeemer lives,
And ever from the skies,
Looks down, and watches all my dust,
Till he shall bid it rise.[4]

Restore thy trust—a glorious form—
Called to ascend and meet the Lord.[5]

[1] Dante. [2] Blair. [3] Montgomery. [4] Watts. [5] Ibid.

6 *

Corruption, closely noted, is but a
Dissolution of the parts,
The parts remain, and nothing lost,
To build a better whole.[1]

So uniform and explicit has been the faith of the general Church of Christ in all ages, that Archbishop Whately[2] and Professor Bush,[3] both of whom deny a corporeal resurrection, admit that this is now and has been the faith of the Church of God, from the day of Pentecost to the present hour.

Whatever, then, may prove to be the truth in the end, it cannot be successfully denied that a corporeal resurrection, or a resurrection of the material body laid in the grave, has been the faith of the Church of Christ in all ages of the world. Founding their belief upon the Holy Scriptures, they have understood them to teach this doctrine; and unless the people of God in all ages, have sadly misunderstood the sacred writings, the Bible certainly inculcates the doctrine of the resurrection of the body.

But we have not adduced these evidences of the belief of former ages, as proving anything directly upon the subject; but simply as furnishing a *presumptive* argument in favor of a literal resurrection. For the probability that a physical resurrection is the true re-

[1] Tupper.

[2] It is not a little remarkable that the prevailing opinion should be (as I believe it is,) that the very same particles of bodily substance which are laid in the grave, or otherwise disposed of, are to be reassembled and re-united at the resurrection; so as to form, as is supposed, the *same* body in which the soul resided before death, etc."—*Future State, American edition*, p. 95.

[3] "The current creed of the Church for the space of eighteen centuries."—*Anastasis*, p. 5 (preface.)

surrection of the Bible, is precisely equal to the probability that the Jews of a former dispensation, and the Church of Christ from the day of Pentecost to the present time, have rightly understood the Word of God.

This brings us to the question, What do the Scriptures teach upon the subject? Have both Jews and Christians misunderstood their respective Scriptures, or do they actually teach a physical resurrection?

CHAPTER V.

TEACHINGS OF THE OLD TESTAMENT AS TO THE RESURRECTION OF THE DEAD.

HAVING shown in the preceding chapters that, with few exceptions, the idea of a literal resurrection of the body has been, beyond all question, the faith of the people of God in all ages, let us now examine the Sacred Writings, from which these views have been professedly derived, to ascertain, if possible, what they actually teach upon the subject of the future life of the body.

And here, as we enter upon the investigation of the Scriptures, it may be proper to remind the reader of what we shall have occasion again to suggest, that throughout the Sacred Volume, whenever the subject of the resurrection is spoken of, it is almost exclusively *in reference to the righteous.* Though they clearly teach that the unjust shall rise as well as the just, and *how* they shall rise,[1] the veil is lifted no further; and we are left, with these few and brief disclosures, to the revelations of the last day. If, therefore, we would not be wise above what is written, we should adopt the same course in our investigations, having in view and speaking of the righteous dead only, except where

[1] See our Lord's declaration, John v. 29.

the language plainly shows that we include all, or are speaking particularly of the unforgiven and the lost.

Another preliminary observation should be repeated, and that is, that, so far as we know, there is no dispute as to whether or not the Scriptures of both Testaments teach *a* resurrection. *That* is conceded on all hands. But the question is, *do they teach a* PHYSICAL *resurrection*, that is, the resurrection of the *body* as defined in our first chapter, and as held by Jews and Christians in all ages of the Church? For the present our attention will still be directed mainly to this point (the main issue, as we conceive,) leaving all other theories for consideration in subsequent chapters.

And now what does the Old Testament teach as to the *nature* of the resurrection?

I. The fact that, with few exceptions, both Jews and Christians of all ages have *understood* the Bible to teach a corporeal resurrection, is a strong presumptive evidence that such is its true intent and meaning.

1. The Jews had the books of Moses and of Job some fifteen hundred years before Christ, and the other portions of the Old Testament from four to fourteen centuries. These books were read in the temple, and in their Synagogues every Sabbath day,[1] and that, too, in their own tongue in which every Jewish hearer was born. With the same degree of attention, therefore, they had a better opportunity to understand the true meaning of their Scriptures than any modern reader can have; whether he read those Scriptures as translated, or in the original Hebrew. For it is impossible for the most profound student to understand an ancient

[1] Acts xv. 21.

language as perfectly as those who lived when and where it was written, and spoke it as their native tongue.

2. As to the early Christians, some of them heard Christ and the apostles preach, while others heard their immediate successors. The gospels and epistles were read in private and in their religious assemblies; and as the triumph of Christ over death by a resurrection from the dead, was the great fact to which the apostles and early Christians constantly pointed, in proof of the divinity of their religion, and through which they preached the resurrection of the dead,[1] everything was calculated frequently to call up the subject, and to lead to clear statements and specific defenses of the true doctrine; thus enabling all who heard them to understand distinctly what kind of a resurrection they designed to set forth.

3. During the last few centuries the general Church has been divided into a great variety of sects or minor churches; and numerous controversies have arisen leading to great research in the study of the Scriptures. Indeed, no field of inquiry has had more numerous or learned explorers, or can exhibit more enduring and lofty monuments of patient toil. Now, taking all these circumstances into the account, it does seem to us that the fact that nearly all of this host of students —the Jews before Christ, the primitive saints and martyrs, and modern Christians—have understood the Bible to teach a physical resurrection, furnishes a strong presumptive proof that such *is* its true intent and meaning.

[1] See Acts iv. 2; xvii. 18; and 1 Cor. xv. 13.

It is not far more probable that theirs is the correct understanding, than it is that with the Bible open before us the true theory of the resurrection has remained undiscovered for three thousand years; and that a vast majority of the people of God have lived and died in error upon so vital a question, from the days of Solomon and Isaiah to the present time.

II. *The Paradisiacal promise of restoration by Christ* involves the idea of the literal restoration of the body to life and immortality.

1. It will scarcely be denied that the normal condition of man is that of soul and body united. His creation was not complete at the first, when the body was formed out of the dust of the earth, till the living spirit was breathed into it. *Then* he became *man*, and not before. Till then he did not *live*, but now the heart throbbed, the eyes saw, the ears heard, and the muscles moved. Then sin came, and natural death followed in its train. "By one man sin entered into the world, and death by sin; and so death passed upon all men, for that all have sinned."[1] Hence "the dust returns to the earth as it was, and the spirit returns to God who gave it."[2]

Now who does not see, that man's normal or natural condition, is that in which his two component natures —soul and body—are united? and that consequently when these two natures are separated, he is in an abnormal state? And just so long as his body remains in the grave, so long he is under the dominion of death, wears a badge of subjugation, and his redemption is practically incomplete.

[1] Romans v. 12. [2] Ecclesiastes xii. 7.

But we are redeemed by the blood of Christ, and are to be restored through faith in him from *all* the effects of sin. Now if sin has thus reigned unto death, by sending the body to corruption, shall not grace reign through righteousness unto eternal life by raising it again and restoring it to its former immortal condition?

2. St. Paul teaches us most explicitly that "the promise," or covenant of God made first to Adam in Eden, and subsequently renewed to Abraham, included, among other blessings, the resurrection of the body.

The substance of this promise was, "in thy seed" [*i. e.*, in Christ] "shall all the nations of the earth be blessed."[1] On a certain occasion when Paul was defending himself before the Jewish council at Jerusalem, perceiving that part of his persecutors were Pharisees and part Sadducees, and therefore directly opposed to each other upon the subject of the resurrection, he adroitly divided his opponents, and arranged the stronger party on his side by crying out in the council, "Men and brethren, I am a Pharisee, the son of a Pharisee: of the hope and resurrection of the dead I am called in question;"[2] and in the twenty-sixth chapter he declares this hope of the resurrection to be "the hope of the promise made of God unto our fathers." But read the whole statement:

> "And now I stand and am judged for the hope of the promise made of God unto our fathers:
>
> "Unto which promise our twelve tribes, instantly serving God day and night, hope to come. For which hope's sake, king Agrippa, I am accused of the Jews.
>
> Why should it be thought a thing incredible with you, that God should raise the dead?" Acts xxvi. 6–8.

[1] Genesis xxii. 18. [2] Acts xxiii. 6.

How obvious, therefore, not only that St. Paul understood the doctrine of the resurrection as the Pharisees understood it, (as explained by Josephus,[1]) but that he also understood the resurrection of the body as among the blessings included in the covenant of redemption by the promised Messiah.

3. If Adam and Eve had never sinned, they would never have died. The analogy of our removal from this world at death, and of the removal of our bodies also after they are raised from the dead, as well as the translations of Enoch and Elijah and the ascension of Christ, justify the belief that if Adam and Eve had never sinned, they too would have been translated bodily to heaven. It is absurd to suppose they would have remained on earth forever, or that in leaving this world they would have left their bodies behind them.

4. If, then, the original state of man was that of a soul in a material but immortal body; if sin dislodged the soul from its tabernacle of flesh, and consigned it to the tomb; and if Christ, as the second Adam, is to undo this work of death, and restore man (especially those who believe in him) to their former state, what less *can* the resurrection be than the restoration of the same body laid in the grave to glory and immortality?[2] Any thing short of this, it seems to us, would come short of an actual and complete restoration; and would disparage the Redeemer of our bodies.

[1] See pages 22 and 23 of this work.

[2] As part of that curse consists in the death of the body, it cannot be completely taken away but by the resurrection of the body. "That this will be done was probably implied in the general promise made to our first parents, that *the seed of the woman*, our blessed Lord, should bruise the serpent's head."

If death is to hold our bodies under his power forever, and, so to speak, compel Christ to reconstruct them of other elements, or resort to some other similar expedient, where is his victory over death? Where the deliverance of his saints from the captivity of the tomb?

We argue, therefore, that the idea of redemption by Christ involves the doctrine of a literal resurrection of the body. And as the resurrection from the dead is one of the unconditional results of the atonement, *all* will be thus raised, whether they accept or reject the proffered salvation of the gospel.

III. The *translation of Enoch and Elijah to heaven in their material bodies,* strongly supports the idea of a corporeal resurrection.

That they were thus taken, without seeing death, is plain from the accounts of their translation. Of the first it is said,

> "And Enoch walked with God, and he was not: for God took him."[1]

This brief narrative is somewhat amplified by St. Paul:

> "By faith Enoch was translated, that he should not see death; and was not found, because God had translated him."[2]

How plain it is from this language, first, that the expression "he was not," in the first passage, means, "was not found;" and second, that the reason why he was not found was not that his body had been miraculously concealed or dissolved into its original elements, but because "God had translated him," soul and body in union, to the regions of eternal life.

[1] Genesis v. 24. [2] Heb. xii. 5.

And so of Elijah; the thing proposed was, to "take up Elijah into heaven;" not his *soul* merely, but "*Elijah*"—the whole *man*. So the sons of the prophets understood it, and hence they "went and stood to view afar off," to see him ascend. And as they went on, Elijah talking to Elisha about being "taken from" him, "there appeared a chariot of fire, and horses of fire, and parted them both asunder; and Elijah went up by a whirlwind into heaven."[1] No body or parts or elements of the body are left behind, from which a spiritual body has been evolved. Though the mantle which clothed it "fell from it," the *body* has gone up to heaven. In vain do fifty men search for it for three days: as Elisha had told them it would be, their search was vain.

How puerile in the light of this history is the gratuitous assumption of Prof. Bush that his body did not ascend, but was dissolved to dust![2] To what strange imaginings will a false theory sometimes drive an apparently candid and otherwise reliable writer.

But the fact stands unimpeached and indisputable that in two instances, at least, where holy men have been taken to heaven, they have been taken up *bodily*, that is, *in their normal state* as complete men, soul and body united. As flesh and blood in its mortal and corruptible state, cannot inherit incorruption, it follows that their bodies were "changed" in the transition, as the vile bodies of all the saints shall be; and in that same body, no doubt, made thus glorious and immortal, Elijah appeared on Mount Tabor nine centuries afterward.[3]

[1] 2 Kings ii. 1–18. [2] Anastasis, p. 166. [3] Matt. xvii. 1–3.

IV. The numerous instances in which *dead bodies were raised to life* recorded in the Scriptures, are important facts in this discussion. The son of the widow of Zarephath was raised by Elijah,[1] and the son of the Shunemite by Elisha.[2] As a dead body touched the bones of Elisha, after he had been long buried, it came to life and "stood up on its feet."[3] Our Lord raised Lazarus after he had been dead four days, and had begun to decompose.[4] He also raised the daughter of Jairus from death,[5] and at his bidding the son of the widow of Nain arose from the bier upon which he was being borne to the grave, "sat up and began to speak."[6]

Now while it is admitted that none of these are legitimate instances of resurrection, inasmuch as they were not raised incorruptible and immortal, and consequently all died again and saw corruption; they nevertheless show that there is and ever has been connected with the true religion of Christ a power superior to death; and that the *body*, laid low in the dust in consequence of sin, is a proper subject upon which that Almighty restoring power may be legitimately exerted. Though Christ was the first to arise from death "to die no more," yet even these resurrections of dead bodies to life were not only precursors of the "better resurrection" to come, but most significant intimations that as they were temporarily wrested from the grasp of the destroyer, though again allowed to fall under his power, they will be the subjects of that

[1] 1 Kings xvii. 17–22. [2] 2 Kings iv. 18–36. [3] Ibid., xiii. 21.
[4] John xi. 17–44. [5] Mark v. 35–42. [6] Luke vii. 11–15.

final resurrection power, which shall swallow up death in victory.

V. In the twentieth chapter of Luke, and elsewhere, our Lord quotes Exodus iii. 3, in proof of the resurrection of the dead:

> "Now that the dead are raised, even Moses shewed at the bush, when he calleth the Lord the God of Abraham, and the God of Isaac and the God of Jacob.
>
> "For he is not a God of the dead, but of the living: for all live unto him."

That the resurrection spoken of in this passage is that of the body, in the usual acceptation of that term, is obvious from the question of the Sadducees which called it forth, namely, that respecting the woman who had seven husbands. "In the resurrection, whose wife of them is she, for seven had her to wife."[1]

But it may be asked, how the continued life of Abraham, Isaac and Jacob, while their bodies were still in the grave, can be regarded as proof of the resurrection of the body?

To one who believed in the immortality of the soul, but denied the resurrection of the body, it would be no proof; but to one who denied both alike, the proof of the continued life of the soul would go to overthrow his theory of no life after death, and would thus go indirectly to establish the doctrine of the resurrection of the body.

Now the Sadducees, with whom our Lord was arguing, *did* deny alike the resurrection of the body, the immortality of the soul, and all angelic or spiritual existence.

[1] Luke xx. 37, 38.

> "For the Sadducees say that there is no resurrection, neither angel, nor spirit; but the Pharisees confess both."[1]

It was therefore quite sufficient with *such* disputants, to cite a clear proof of the immortality of the soul; inasmuch as, *in their estimation*, the two doctrines were substantially identical, and must stand or fall together. But we shall recur to this passage again in a subsequent chapter.[2]

VI. The ancient Jews understood Deut. xxxiii. 39, 40, as teaching a physical resurrection:

> "See now that I, *even* I, *am* he, and *there is* no god with me: I kill, and I make alive; I wound, and I heal: neither *is there any* that can deliver out of my hand.
>
> "For I lift up my hand to heaven, and say, I live for ever."

That this passage was understood by the ancient Jews to teach the resurrection of the dead, is obvious from the fact that it constituted part of their burial service at the graves of their kindred.[3] And what else can we understand by the expressions "I KILL, and I MAKE ALIVE?" To "make alive" is as much in contrast with killing, as healing is to wounding. It plainly means *to restore from death;* which can have its accomplishment only by a resurrection of the body. Well, therefore, might the *Hazan*, or minister of the Synagogue repeat these words of the Omnipotent as

[1] Acts xxiii. 8.

[2] Since the above was written, we find the same view thus concisely stated by Dr. Hody:

"It was not so much the resurrection of the body, as the immortality of the soul, that the Sadducees stuck at. If it could be once proved out of the books of Moses that the soul was immortal and did not die with the body, they were ready and willing to grant that there would be a resurrection of the body." *Resurrection of the Body, p.* 107.

[3] Hody, p. 75.

he consigned the body to the tomb: "I kill, and I make alive; I wound, and I heal: neither is there any that can deliver out of my hands."[1]

VII. The passage 1 Sam. ii. 6, was also understood to teach the same doctrine:

> "The Lord killeth, and maketh alive: he bringeth down to the grave, and bringeth up."

This passage also constituted part of the Jewish burial service, which was sung at the grave by the *Hazan* and the congregation. By "maketh alive," and "bringeth up" from the grave, they understood the resurrection of the body.

VIII. The book of Job is supposed to have preceded the books of Moses as to the date of its composition, and to be in fact the oldest book in the Sacred Volume. In the fourteenth chapter of this book, which is devoted especially to the subject of the decay and future prospects of the body, we have the following remarkable passage:—

> "But man dieth, and wasteth away; yea, man giveth up the ghost, and where is he?
>
> "As the waters fail from the sea, and the flood decayeth and drieth up:
>
> "So man lieth down and riseth not: till the heavens be no more, they shall not awake nor be raised out of their sleep.
>
> "O that thou wouldest hide me in the grave, that thou wouldest keep me secret, till thy wrath be past, that thou wouldest appoint me a set time, and remember me!
>
> "If a man die, shall he live again? all the days of my appointed time will I wait, till my change come.
>
> "Thou shalt call, and I will answer thee: thou wilt have a desire to the work of thy hands."

Here observe, it is first declared that man riseth not

[1] See page 22 of this volume.

"*till the heavens be no more,*" that is, till the time when "the heavens shall pass away with a great noise, and the elements shall melt with fervent heat."[1] In the second place, though Job desired to be hid in the grave on account of his indescribable misery, he nevertheless expected to be "remembered" there at the "set time" of the resurrection. And to make his meaning indubitably clear, he asks and answers the specific question: "If a man die, *shall he live again?*" And mark the answer: "All the days of my appointed time will I wait, *till my change come.*" Not, as some suppose, his "appointed time" to *die*, and the change of *death*, (for he is not speaking of *death*, but of the prospect of living again after death,) but his appointed time to *rise*—the "set time" when God should "remember" him. All these days he would wait *in the grave* till his "change" from corruption to immortality should come,—the change that shall take place with both the living and the dead at the last day.[2] Dr. Adam Clarke renders the passage "*till my renovation come;*" and citing the Hebrew term rendered "*change*" in our version, says: "This word is used to denote the springing of grass, Ps. xc. 5, 6, after it had once withered, which is in itself a very expressive emblem of the resurrection." "*Thou shalt call*"—and "all that are in the grave shall hear thy voice."[3] "I will answer thee," that is, will respond to the summons and "come forth." "Thou wilt have a desire to the work of thy hands,"—the body formed by God out of the

[1] 2 Peter iii. 10.
[2] See 1 Cor. xv. 51, and Phil. iii. 21.
[3] John v. 28, 32.

dust of the earth, now fallen and perished; and though it be dead will cause it to live again.[1]

That this passage teaches the resurrection of the body in its most literal sense, seems to us clear beyond all cavil. Speaking of it as a whole, Dr. Clarke says: "Here is no doubt, but a strong persuasion of the certainty of the general resurrection." And yet, often as it is quoted by the advocates of the popular theory, it is a remarkable circumstance that it is not even alluded to by Prof. Bush in his celebrated work against a physical resurrection.

IX. In the nineteenth chapter of Job we have another equally remarkable passage. He had just before exclaimed, "My face is foul with weeping, and on my eyelids is the shadow of death."[2] "My breath is corrupt, my days are extinct, the graves are ready for me." "I have said to corruption, Thou art my father: to the worm, Thou art my mother and my sister."[3] But his fortitude and his faith seem to rally, and, as if about to utter some sentiment of great moment and worthy of the most enduring record, he exclaims:[4]

> "Oh that my words were now written! oh that they were printed in a book!
>
> "That they were graven with an iron pen and lead in the rock for ever!

And then comes the momentous and triumphant utterance:—

> "For I know that my Redeemer liveth, and that he shall stand at the latter day upon the earth:

[1] The celebrated John Flavel gives a similar exposition of this passage, in his *Treatise of the Soul of Man,* London, 1789, p. 306.

[2] Chapter xvi. 16. [3] Chapter xvii. 1, 14. [4] Chapter xix. 23, 24.

> "And though after my skin worms destroy this body, yet in my flesh shall I see God:
>
> "Whom I shall see for myself, and mine eyes shall behold, and not another; though my reins be consumed within me."

Notwithstanding the efforts of Prof. Bush to fritter away the meaning of this passage, we doubt if human language could more clearly express the hope of a physical resurrection. Look at the several parts of the text. "*I know that my Redeemer liveth*"—the promised seed, who was to bruise the head of the serpent, and destroy his works. "*And that he shall stand,* etc.," that is, shall become incarnated, and stand on the earth, as he did some fifteen centuries afterward. "*And though after my skin*" (which was already clothed with worms, and broken, and become loathsome[1]) "*worms shall destroy this body,*" thus completing the work of dissolution already begun, "*yet,*" despite this dissolution, "*in my* FLESH *shall I see God.*" And lest he might be understood to speak of his posterity, and not of himself personally, he adds, "*whom I shall see* FOR MYSELF, *and mine eyes shall behold* NOT ANOTHER; *though my reins be consumed within me.*"

It is of no avail to say, "In our translation it does teach a physical resurrection, but the Hebrew does not warrant such a translation." The translators of the authorized version understood Hebrew quite as well as Prof. Bush; and they thought otherwise. So of Pearson, and Clarke, and Horn, and Secker, and Beveridge, and scores of eminent scholars, the opinion of any one of whom is more than a counterpoise to that of Prof. Bush. We shall therefore waste no time in consider-

[1] Chapter viii. 5.

ing his various expositions of this passage, nor in answering his puerile criticisms of the English version.[1]

X. The sixteenth psalm indirectly inculcates the doctrine of a physical resurrection:

> "I have set the Lord always before me: because *he is* at my right hand, I shall not be moved.
>
> "Therefore my heart is glad, and my glory rejoiceth: my flesh also shall rest in hope.
>
> "For thou wilt not leave my soul in hell; neither wilt thou suffer thine Holy One to see corruption.
>
> "Thou wilt shew me the path of life," etc.

This passage was quoted by Peter in his celebrated discourse on the day of Pentecost,[2] as having had its fulfilment in the resurrection of Christ:

> "For David speaketh concerning him, I foresaw the Lord always before my face, for he is on my right hand, that I should not be moved:
>
> "Therefore did my heart rejoice and my tongue was glad: moreover also my flesh shall rest in hope:
>
> "Because thou wilt not leave my soul in hell, neither wilt thou suffer thine Holy One to see corrnption.
>
> "Thou hast made known to me the ways of life; thou shalt make me full of joy with thy countenance.
>
> "Men *and* brethren, let me freely speak unto you of the patriarch David, that he is both dead and buried, and his sepulchre is with us unto this day.
>
> "Therefore being a prophet, and knowing that God had sworn with an oath to him, that of the fruit of his loins, according to the flesh, he would raise up Christ to sit on his throne;
>
> "He, seeing this before, spake of the resurrection of Christ, that his soul was not left in hell, neither his flesh did see corruption.
>
> "This Jesus hath God raised up, whereof we all are witnesses."

[1] This passage is quoted and its popular interpretation defended by Pearson, in his Exposition of the Creed, page 562; by George Smith, in his Patriarchal Age, p. 410–413; and by Moldenhauer, Dr. Hales, Dr. Samuel Lee, Dr. John Mason Goode, and others; any one of whose opinions are, to say the least, a sufficient offset against the criticisms of Prof. Bush and other Swedenborgians.

[2] See Acts ii. 25, and onward.

And so also St. Paul, preaching to the Jews in the Synagogue at Antioch:[1]

> "And we declare unto you glad tidings, how that the promise which was made unto the fathers,
>
> "God hath fulfilled the same unto us their children, in that he hath raised up Jesus again; as it is also written in the second psalm, Thou art my Son, this day have I begotten thee.
>
> "And as concerning that he raised him up from the dead, *now* no more to return to corruption, he said on this wise, I will give you the sure mercies of David.
>
> "Wherefore he saith also in another *psalm*, Thou shalt not suffer thine Holy One to see corruption.
>
> "For David, after he had served his own generation by the will of God, fell on sleep, and was laid unto his fathers, and saw corruption:
>
> "But he, whom God raised again, saw no corruption."

Now if it be admitted that the inspired apostles Peter and Paul understood the Jewish Scriptures aright, it is certain that not only in the sixteenth psalm was the resurrection of Christ predicted, but also in the second, as well as in the fifty-fifth chapter of Isaiah. So far then we have the authority of the apostles that the Old Testament promised the resurrection of Christ, and to that extent at least, taught the doctrine of the resurrection of the dead. This is admitted even by Prof. Bush.[2]

But upon this collateral point, (namely, the opinion of the apostles as to what the Old Testament teaches,) we have, if possible, still clearer testimony. In his discourse before Agrippa,[3] after narrating his conversion, St. Paul says:

> "Having therefore obtained help of God, I continue unto this day, witnessing both to small and great, saying none other things than those which the prophets and Moses did say should come:

[1] Acts xiii. 32–37. [2] Anastasis, p. 104. [3] Acts xxvi. 22, 23.

"That Christ should suffer, *and* that he should be the first that should rise from the dead, and should shew light unto the people, and to the Gentiles."

Notice especially the declaration that in witnessing that Christ "should be the first that should rise from the dead;" he had taught "*none other things than those which the prophets and Moses did say should come.*" In his opinion, therefore, both Moses and the prophets taught the resurrection of Christ, and to that extent at least taught the resurrection of the dead.

XI. Another pertinent passage is found in the seventeenth psalm:

"As for me, I will behold thy face in righteousness: I shall be satisfied, when I awake, with thy likeness."

That this passage is explicit as to the *nature* of the resurrection, we do not assert. But that the "awaking" is the revivifying of the dead, who sleep in the dust, is very evident. Then the righteous, with bodies fashioned like unto Christ's glorious body, will behold the King in his beauty, and come before his presence with exceeding joy.

XII. The forty-ninth psalm is still more explicit:

"Like sheep they are laid in the grave; death shall feed on them; and the upright shall have dominion over them in the morning; and their beauty shall consume in the grave from their dwelling.

"But God will redeem my soul from the power of the grave: for he shall receive me. Selah."

"That is," says Dr. Clarke, "by the plainest construction, I shall have a resurrection from the dead, and an entrance into his glory; and death shall have no dominion over me."[1] The term "*soul*" is here

[1] Dr. Adam Clarke's Commentary.

used in the sense of *life*, which, so far as the body is concerned, is extinguished by death. This extinct life "God will redeem from the power of the grave," by a resurrection to immortality.

XIII. The prophet Isaiah was favoured with a bright and cheering vision of the final victory over death:

> "He will swallow up death in victory; and the Lord God will wipe away tears from off all faces; and the rebuke of his people shall he take away from off all the earth: for the Lord hath spoken *it*."—Isa. xxv. 8.

This passage also is included in the ancient Jewish burial service; and that it is a prophecy of the general resurrection is placed beyond all doubt by its citation by St. Paul, 1 Cor. xv. 54:

> "So when this corruptible shall have put on incorruption, and this mortal shall have put on immortality, then shall be brought to pass the saying that is written, Death is swallowed up in victory."

If the general resurrection is the "bringing to pass of this saying," or, in other words, the fulfilment of this prophecy, then the prophecy *must* have related to the resurrection; and to *such* a resurrection as the apostle was setting forth and defending at the time he quoted it. It is therefore an unmistakable prophecy of the literal resurrection of the dead.

XIV. Another very explicit passage is found in Isa. xxvi. 19:

> "Thy dead *men* shall live, *together with* my dead body shall they arise. Awake and sing, ye that dwell in dust: for thy dew *is as* the dew of herbs, and the earth shall cast out the dead."

This is another of the passages embodied in the Jewish burial service; and it would be difficult to announce the doctrine of a physical resurrection in clearer language than that employed in the first sentence. And the apostrophe to the dead is scarcely less explicit. "Awake and sing, ye that dwell in dust." Here again we have "the voice of the Son of God" calling his saints to their glorious reward. And as they awake they are to "*sing*"—sing for joy at their victory over death, and their new birth to immortality. "*For thy dew is as the dew of herbs.*" As the heavy dews revive the plants and flowers which the scorching sun has smitten with blight and decay, so an influence from above shall rest on every grave, that shall revive its mouldering tenant to die no more.

Or, to dwell a little more at length upon this beautiful passage; the figure seems to be that of a flower, on the borders of some sandy desert. In the morning it is seen with its stem erect, its calyx opened, and the soft dew-drops sparkling upon its bosom. But the day rolls on. The hot winds of the desert dry up its moisture, and the meridian sunbeams rob it of all its strength and beauty. At length it yields to the heat and drouth, and bending over toward the earth, pillows its fainting head upon the burning sands. At length the wild sirocco sweeps over the desert, leaving upon its wings clouds of sand, and the little flower, so gay and beautiful a few hours before, is buried from the sight of the passing traveler.

But the night rolls on. The heavy eastern dews fall copiously on forest and plain, and moisten even the bed where the sleeper reposes. Life begins to return again to the withered stalk. Again it seeks to rise, and stirs the sands that overlay it. At length it rises, refusing longer "to dwell in dust." It drinks in the descending dews, takes on all its wonted vigor, and when the sun again arises, there it stands, beautiful and fragrant, sparkling again with dew-drops,—a bright and lovely emblem of the resurrection!

Nor is this all. To represent the joy and gladness of God's people as they rise from the dead, the new-risen flower borrows a song from the songsters of the neighboring grove, and stands forth in all its new life and beauty *a singing flower!*

So shall it be with man. "He cometh forth as a flower," and "as a flower of the field" for a time he flourisheth. But sickness, decay and death soon bear him down to the dust, and the grave covers him. But the night of the passing ages rolls on, and the morning of the resurrection draws near. The dews of immortality distil where his ashes slumber, and anon the fiat is heard, "Awake and sing, ye that dwell in dust;" and behold he lives! His dew is "as the dew of herbs," and he awakes, not like them again to fade and die, but like his glorious forerunner, "to die no more." Oh, blessed and glorious morn, when "the earth shall cast out the dead," and "death shall be swallowed up in victory!"

XV. The scene of resurrection presented before the mind of the prophet Ezekiel, is not without its bearing upon the subject under consideration.

"The hand of the Lord was upon me, and carried me out in the Spirit of the Lord, and set me down in the midst of the valley which was full of bones,

"And caused me to pass by them round about: and, behold, *there were* very many in the open valley; and lo, *they were* very dry.

"And he said unto me, Son of man, can these bones live? And I answered, O Lord God, thou knowest.

"Again he said unto me, Prophesy upon these bones, and say unto them, O ye dry bones, hear the word of the Lord.

"Thus saith the Lord God unto these bones; Behold, I will cause breath to enter into you, and ye shall live:

"And I will lay sinews upon you, and will bring up flesh upon you, and cover you with skin, and put breath in you, and ye shall live; and ye shall know that I am the Lord.

"So I prophesied as I was commanded: and as I prophesied, there was a noise, and behold a shaking, and the bones came together, bone to his bone.

"And when I beheld, lo, the sinews and the flesh came up upon them, and the skin covered them above: but *there was* no breath in them.

"Then said he unto me, Prophesy unto the wind, prophesy, son of man, and say to the wind, Thus saith the Lord God; Come from the four winds, O breath, and breathe upon these slain, that they may live.

"So I prophesied as he commanded me, and the breath came into them, and they lived, and stood up upon their feet, an exceeding great army."—Ezek. xxxviii. 1–10.

That the dry bones in this vision were to represent the people of Israel who were morally dead, and that the whole vision was a figurative representation of a *moral* resurrection, is admitted. But if there never had been and never was to be a *literal* resurrection, the figure was not founded upon what had been or might be, as is usual in the Scriptures, but upon a mere vagary of the prophet's imagination. But as the doctrine of a literal resurrection was held by the Jews, it naturally furnished the basis of this figurative resurrection; and tne *figurative* necessarily implies the *literal*. And the "bones," "sinews," "flesh," and "skin" coming to their places in order, and at length revivified by the divine "breath," is all in perfect keeping with the prevailing belief that the different

8 *

parts of the body should be re-collected and re-united, and then re-inhabited by its immortal spirit. We therefore regard this vision as a legitimate instance in which the doctrine of a literal resurrection is at least implied and recognized, if not directly inculcated.[1]

XVI. The prophet Daniel also saw the coming day when the dead shall live again:

> "And many of them that sleep in the dust of the earth shall awake, some to everlasting life, and some to shame *and* everlasting contempt."—Daniel xii. 2.

It is scarcely possible to pervert this passage to teach anything else than the literal resurrection of the body. The *subjects* of this waking are not the *souls* of men yet in the body, to awake and rise by conversion, or by emerging from the body at death, but "them that *sleep in the dust of the earth*"—a phrase descriptive only of the mouldering body. Neither does the use of the term "*many*" instead of *all* in the least invalidate this exposition, inasmuch as it is no unusual thing for a part to be put for the whole in the Scriptures, as can be seen by consulting Isa. liii. 12, and Rom. v. 15–19.

XVII. The closing verse of the prophecy of Daniel seems also to contain a promise of the resurrection.

> "But go thou thy way till the end be: for thou shalt rest, and stand in thy lot at the end of the days."—Daniel xii. 13.

That the "end" here means the time when they that sleep in the dust of the earth shall awake, and the righteous shall shine as the stars for ever, seems plain.

[1] "This vision of dry bones," says Dr. Clarke, "was designed, *first*, as an emblem of the wretched state of the Jews; *secondly*, of the general resurrection of the body."—See Commentary.

The expression "thou shalt rest" is equivalent to "thou shalt *die;*" and "shalt stand in thy lot at the end of the days" is a figure borrowed from the division of the land of Canaan, and the various tribes standing each in their lot was a cheering promise to Daniel, that though he should "rest" in death, he should live again, and be present at the final consummation, to take and for ever enjoy his portion of the heavenly Canaan.

XVIII. Finally, Jehovah promised "the fathers" victory over death and the grave, by the mouth of Hosea the prophet:

> "I will ransom them from the power of the grave; I will redeem them from death: O death, I will be thy plagues; O grave, I will be thy destruction: repentance shall be hid from mine eyes."—Hosea xiii. 14.

That this passage relates to the resurrection of the dead is certain, from the fact that St. Paul cites it 1 Cor. xv. 54, 55, as to have its fulfilment when this corruptible shall put on incorruption, and this mortal immortality.

> "So when this corruptible shall have put on incorruption, and this mortal shall have put on immortality, then shall be brought to pass the saying that is written, Death is swallowed up in victory.
> "O death, where *is* thy sting? O grave, where *is* thy victory?"

The variation from the original, as the passage is here quoted by the apostle, is no more than we find in other cases, where Christ and his apostles quote the ancient Scriptures. And as there is no other passage "written" in the Old Testament, in which such an apostrophe to death and the grave occurs, it is clear that the apostle refers to this passage in Hosea, and meant to apply it as a prophecy of the general resurrection.

These passages from the Old Testament, with the comments and references to them gathered from the New, are sufficient to show, not only that the ancient Jews had Scriptural warrant for their hope of *a* resurrection, but also for their cherished belief that it would be a literal resurrection of the body laid in the grave. (Even Dr. Priestly admits this much.[1]) It is not strange, therefore, that they chanted these prophecies as they buried their dead, and that imbibing with the hope of the resurrection the rabbinical idea that it would take place near Jerusalem, they sought a resting-place upon Mount Olivet, or ordered their children to convey their bones from distant lands and bury them in the Valley of Jehoshaphat.

Despite, therefore, the efforts of theorizers and unbelievers to obscure the testimony of these Scriptures, even the Old Testament flames with the light of immortality. Every devout Hebrew sought "a better country and heavenly," and "hoped to come" to its endless fruition. Through the resurrection of the body from the grave, they looked for the introduction of the *whole man*, restored and incorruptible, into the presence of God, to go out no more forever.

[1] "That man should really *die*, and after continuing in a state of death, come to life again at a future period, that is, that there should be a proper *resurrection of the dead*, which is the faith of the Jews and Christians, (being, I must now presume, the clear doctrine of both the Old and the New Testament,) I will venture to say, must ever have appeared in the highest degree improbable. Nothing but the express assurances of the Great Being who made men could have satisfied them that he would revive them in those circumstances."—*Priestly's Discourses, Northumberland Edition,* 1805, p. 314.

CHAPTER VI.

TEACHINGS OF CHRIST CONCERNING THE RESURRECTION.

IN order fully to understand the position and teachings of our Divine Lord upon the subject of the resurrection, the following facts should be distinctly borne in mind.

1. The prevailing belief among the Jews at the time of his advent and during his ministry was, that there should be a literal resurrection of the bodies of all men from the grave. This we have abundantly shown in Chapter II., and neither Prof. Bush nor any other respectable writer, so far as we are aware, has ever denied it. Right or wrong, the current theology during our Lord's ministry was that there would be at the end of the world a resurrection of the bodies of all men from their graves.

2. It is equally clear that Christ *never combated* nor *corrected* this theology, as he did many Jewish traditions and errors. Their false ideas as to divorce, retaliation, etc. he corrected; but not their ideas of the resurrection,—thus virtually endorsing their correctness, as he did the doctrine of the being of a God, the immortality of the soul, and future rewards and punishments.

3. While we never find him contending with the Pharisees against their view (which was that of a physical resurrection,) we often find him contending with the Sadducees—a small sect of Jews who denied this doctrine.

These facts alone, aside from all specific teachings from his lips, fully justify the statement, we think, that our Lord *accepted, endorsed* and *defended* the prevailing doctrine of a physical resurrection.

And still further: whatever Christ said upon the subject must be interpreted in the light of these most important considerations. Let us then examine his recorded sayings touching the resurrection of the dead.

I. At the conclusion of his parable of the wedding feast, he said:

> "When thou makest a feast, call the poor, the maimed, the lame, the blind;
>
> "And thou shalt be blessed: for they cannot recompense thee: for thou shalt be recompensed at the resurrection of the just."—Luke xiv. 13.

Here he speaks of the "resurrection of the just," as a well-understood future event; and in such a way that all would understand him as accepting and endorsing that doctrine as popularly understood. To say, therefore, that he did not intend to teach a literal resurrection, is to accuse him of great indefiniteness in his teaching, if not of want of courage and fidelity in refuting what modern opponents of the prevailing theory characterize as gross and dangerous error.

II. As Martha and Jesus were conversing together about the death of Lazarus, he said to her:

> "Thy brother shall rise again.

"Martha saith unto him, I know that he shall rise again in the resurrection at the last day."—John xi. 23.

Here she but gave expression to the faith held by all devout Jews, namely, that the bodies of all their dead should rise "at the last day," or at the end of the world. But instead of saying to her, "Your brother has arisen already at the moment of death," or "His *body* is never to be raised; you mistake the nature of the resurrection," he replied,

"I am the resurrection and the life: he that believeth in me though he were dead, yet shall he live:

"And whosoever believeth in me, shall never die."—Ver. 25, 26.

As the resurrection from the dead is through him and by him, (1 Cor. xv. 21,) he announces the fact; as much as to say, "You need not wait till 'the last day.' In my person is lodged the resurrection power." And as he "cried with a loud voice, Lazarus, *come forth*," the half putrid body teemed with vitality and life, and came forth, a trophy won from death, and a living specimen of physical resurrection!

Is there anything in all this subversive of the faith of Mary and Martha, that there should be a physical resurrection of all the dead "at the last day?" Were not the absence of all correction, either expressed or implied, and this act of resurrection, as well calculated to confirm them in their cherished faith as anything could be?

III. In the fifth chapter of John we find a distinct announcement of a future resurrection of all the dead:

"Marvel not at this: for the hour is coming, in the which all that are in the graves shall hear his voice,

"And shall come forth; they that have done good, unto the resurrection of life; and they that have done evil, unto the resurrection of damnation."—John v. 28, 29.

This passage is all the more explicit from the fact that our Lord had just before spoken of the spiritual resurrection of men by his own life-giving Spirit, rendering it infallibly certain that he here speaks of the literal dead, and of the resurrection of their bodies from the grave. And as any Christian audience, holding to a physical resurrection, would understand such language as distinctly teaching their doctrine, so every Jewish hearer would and did understand him to be teaching their well-known doctrine of a corporeal resurrection.

IV. But the most striking passages to be met with in all his teachings, are those in which he refutes the argument of the Sadducees:

> "Then came to him certain of the Sadducees (which deny that there is any resurrection) and they asked him,
>
> "Saying, Master, Moses wrote unto us, If any man's brother die, having a wife, and he die without children, that his brother should take his wife, and raise up seed unto his brother.
>
> "There were therefore seven brethren: and the first took a wife, and died without children.
>
> "And the second took her to wife, and he died childless.
>
> "And the third took her; and in like manner the seven also; and they left no children, and died.
>
> "Last of all the woman died also.
>
> "Therefore in the resurrection, whose wife of them is she? for seven had her to wife."—Luke xx. 27–33.

Two things are worthy of special attention in this extract. (1.) It is obvious that the Sadducees understood Christ to teach and defend the prevailing doctrine of a literal resurrection of the body. (2.) They supposed the relationships of the present life, as to marriage and being given in marriage, were to be perpetuated in a future state. On these two assumptions they based their objection to the doctrine they opposed.

Now mark the Redeemer's answer: Instead of informing them that there would be no such resurrection as they supposed, (as any Swedenborgian would have done,) thus relieving their difficulties at once, he lets *that* part of their supposition stand, as altogether correct; and by the very tenor of his answer virtually endorses it. But upon the other point he takes distinct issue with them:

> "And Jesus answering, said unto them, The children of this world marry, and are given in marriage:
>
> "But they which shall be accounted worthy to obtain that world, and the resurrection from the dead, neither marry, nor are given in marriage:
>
> "Neither can they die any more: for they are equal unto the angels; and are the children of God, being the children of the resurrection."—Vs. 34–36.

The simple statement that there would be no marriage relation among men in the resurrection state, any more than among the angels, was a complete refutation of their objection, and they were silenced.

But beside this error, they denied the existence of angels, and of the disembodied souls of men. It was needful, therefore, now that they were silenced on one point, to set them right from their own acknowledged oracles—the books of Moses—as to their other cardinal error. Hence our Lord proceeds:

> "Now that the dead are raised, even Moses shewed at the bush, when he calleth the Lord the God of Abraham, and the God of Isaac, and the God of Jacob.
>
> "For he is not a God of the dead, but of the living: for all live unto him."—Vs. 37, 38.[1]

V. In his memorable discourse at Capernaum, John

[1] For exposition of this passage see page 77.

vi.) our Lord repeatedly inculcated the resurrection of the righteous at the end of time:

"And this is the Father's will which hath sent me, that of all which he hath given me, I should lose nothing, but should raise it up again at the last day.

"And this is the will of him that sent me, that every one which seeth the Son, and believeth on him, may have everlasting life: and I will raise him up at the last day.

"No man can come to me, except the Father which hath sent me draw him: and I will raise him up at the last day."—Vs. 39, 40, and 44.

No Jewish hearer could understand this language in any other sense, than as teaching the commonly received doctrine of the resurrection at the end of the world.

VI. On several occasions Christ spoke of his own resurrection, not as a spiritual recovery from a fallen state, or the emerging of his soul from the body at the hour of death, but as the literal raising up of his body from the grave, to die no more. But of these predictions more at length in a subsequent chapter.

So far, therefore, as Christ spoke at all upon the subject, all his recorded sayings show that he recognized and taught the prevailing doctrine of the resurrection of the bodies of all the dead at the end of time.

VII. It in no wise detracts from the weight of our Lord's testimony, that he said but little upon the subject. This is equally true of other important topics. The doctrine of the resurrection of the dead was generally received by the people among whom he preached, and needed no formal announcement. It is enough that he recognized and defended it against its adversaries. This he did, but never by teaching a *different* resurrection from that taught by the Pharisees. He thus emphatically endorsed the doctrine of a physical resurrection, as held by the Jews on the authority of Moses and the prophets.

CHAPTER VII.

THE RESURRECTION OF CHRIST.

In discussing the subject of the resurrection of Christ, the following particulars are worthy of especial notice:

I. *The prophets had* DISTINCTLY PREDICTED *his resurrection.*

1. We have already cited these predictions among the teachings of the Old Testament; but may re-produce some of them here, as pertinent to the present inquiry:

> "Therefore my heart is glad, and my glory rejoiceth: my flesh also shall rest in hope.
>
> "For thou wilt not leave my soul in hell; neither wilt thou suffer thine Holy One to see corruption."—Ps. xvi. 9, 10.

Quoting this passage in his sermon on the day of Pentecost, Peter assured his hearers that David "spake of the resurrection of Christ, that his soul was not left in hell,[1] neither his flesh did see corruption."[2]

2. St. Paul cites the same passage, in connection with two others, in his discourse at Antioch, Acts xiii. 32–37.

> "And we declare unto you glad tidings, how that the promise which was made unto the fathers,
>
> "God hath fulfilled the same unto us their children, in that he

[1] *Hades*, the place of departed spirits. [2] See Acts ii. 25–31.

hath raised up Jesus again; as it is also written in the second psalm, Thou art my Son, this day have I begotten thee.

"And as concerning that he raised him up from the dead, *now* no more to return to corruption, he said on this wise, I will give you the sure mercies of David.

"Wherefore he saith also in another psalm, Thou shalt not suffer thine Holy One to see corruption.

"For David, after he had served his own generation by the will of God, fell on sleep, and was laid unto his fathers, and saw corruption.

"But he, whom God raised again, saw no corruption."

From this passage it appears that the expression Ps. ii. 7, "Thou art my Son, this day have I begotten thee," was a prediction of Christ's resurrection. On this account, probably, and with reference to this very prediction, he is styled "the first-begotten of the dead," Rev. i. 5; and "first-born from the dead," Col. i. 18.

And so of the other quotation, from Isa. lv. 3,—"I will give you the sure mercies of David,"—it was understood and cited as a prediction of the resurrection of Christ.

II. *Our Lord had* REPEATEDLY FORETOLD HIS OWN RESURRECTION.

1. When the Scribes and Pharisees desired a sign from him, he said:

"An evil and adulterous generation seeketh after a sign, and there shall no sign be given it, but the sign of the prophet Jonas.

"For as Jonas was three days and three nights in the whale's belly: so shall the Son of man be three days and three nights in the heart of the earth."—Matt. xii. 39, 40.

This was a plain intimation that the miracle of Jonah's preservation for three days and nights, etc., was a type of Christ's resurrection; and that answering to the type, he would arise from the dead on the third day.[1]

2. During the second year of his ministry, while preaching and healing the sick in the vicinity of Cesarea Philippi, it is said:

> "And he began to teach them, that the Son of man must suffer many things, and be rejected of the elders, and of the chief priests, and scribes, and be killed, and after three days rise again.
>
> "And he spake that saying openly."—Mark viii. 31, 32.

3. Upon another occasion when the Jews desired a sign, our Lord replied:

> "Destroy this temple, and in three days I will raise it up.
>
> "Then said the Jews, Forty and six years was this temple in building, and wilt thou rear it up in three days?
>
> "But he spake of the temple of his body.
>
> "When therefore he was risen from the dead, his disciples remembered that he had said this unto them: and they believed the Scripture, and the word which Jesus had said."—John ii. 19–22.

4. While on his last journey to Jerusalem, he thus addressed the disciples:

> "Behold, we go up to Jerusalem; and the Son of man shall be betrayed unto the chief priests, and unto the scribes, and they shall condemn him to death,
>
> "And shall deliver him to the Gentiles to mock, and to scourge, and to crucify him: and the third day he shall rise again."—Matt. xx. 18, 19.

5. On the night before his crucifixion, we find him again assuring the disciples of his resurrection:

> "Then saith Jesus unto them, All ye shall be offended because

[1] On this account the early Christians often used a *fish* as an emblem of the resurrection, with special reference to these words of Christ. See an account of inscriptions in the Catacombs of Rome, page 29 of this volume.

of me this night: for it is written, I will smite the Shepherd, and the sheep of the flock shall be scattered abroad.

"But after I am risen again, I will go before you into Galilee."
—Matt. xxvi. 31, 32.

6. This prediction was well understood by the Jews at Jerusalem, at the time, as is evident from the remark of the chief priests to Pilate the day after the crucifixion—"We remember that that deceiver said, while he was yet alive, After three days I will rise again."[1]

The evidence is therefore abundant that Christ foretold, and intended publicly to predict, that after his crucifixion he would rise again from the dead.

III. *That the body of Christ was* REALLY DEAD *when it was laid in the tomb, is clear beyond all controversy.*

It has often occurred to us that upon this point modern writers are less specific and tenacious than were the apostles. *They* were wont to insist "that Christ *died*," as well as that he arose from the dead;[2] and the evangelists have left on record as complete a chain of proofs of his death, as of his resurrection.

1. The law under which the three were executed, required that they should hang upon the cross *till they were dead.*

2. The penalty under the Roman law for not carrying out the sentence of death, would have been very severe, probably death itself, to those who allowed the criminal to escape.[3]

3. It will not be denied that it was the *design* of his persecutors to put him to death; and that in carrying

[1] Matt. xxvii. 63. [2] See 1 Cor. xv. 3, and 1 Thess. iv. 14.
[3] See Acts xii. 19.

out this design it was the purpose of those who crucified him to utterly extinguish his mortal life.

4. After hanging upon the cross with nails driven through his hands and feet for three hours, he cried with a loud voice, bowed his head and gave up the ghost.[1]

5. The executioners were fully satisfied that he was dead. As the Jewish Sabbath began at six o'clock, they were anxious to dispose of the bodies before that time; and for this purpose went to Pilate and requested him to hasten their death by having their legs broken:

> "The Jews therefore, because it was the preparation, that the bodies should not remain upon the cross on the Sabbath day, (for that Sabbath day was an high day,) besought Pilate that their legs might be broken, and that they might be taken away.
>
> "Then came the soldiers, and brake the legs of the first, and of the other which was crucified with him.
>
> "But when they came to Jesus, and saw that he was dead already, they brake not his legs:
>
> "But one of the soldiers with a spear pierced his side, and forthwith came thereout blood and water."—John xix. 31–34.

Why his side was pierced we know not, unless it was that the Scripture might be fulfilled—"they shall look upon him whom they have pierced"[2]—and that the world might have this assurance that Christ was at this time actually dead. "It may be naturally supposed," says Dr. Clarke, "that the spear went through the pericardium [popularly called the heart-case,] and pierced the heart; that the water proceeded from the former, and the blood from the latter. . . . . As the law in the case stated that the criminals were to con-

[1] Matt. xxvii. 50, and John xix. 30.

[2] Psalm xxii. 16, 17.

tinue on the cross *till they died*, the side of our Lord was pierced to secure the accomplishment of the law."

6. The body was not given to Joseph until Pilate, as well as the centurion, had been fully satisfied of its death:

> "Joseph of Arimathea, an honorable counsellor, which also waited for the kingdom of God, came, and went in boldly unto Pilate, and craved the body of Jesus.
>
> "And Pilate marvelled if he were already dead: and calling unto him the centurion, he asked him whether he had been any while dead.
>
> "And when he knew it of the centurion, he gave the body to Joseph."—Mark xv. 43–45.

7. The body being thus delivered to Joseph as dead, was taken by him and *embalmed*,[1] like any other dead body, "as the manner of the Jews is to bury:"

> "And there came also Nicodemus (which at the first came to Jesus by night) and brought a mixture of myrrh and aloes, about an hundred pounds weight.
>
> "Then took they the body of Jesus, and wound it in linen clothes with the spices, as the manner of the Jews is to bury."—John xix. 39, 40.

"The Jews embalmed the bodies of their dead by laying around them large quantities of costly spices and aromatic drugs, in order to imbibe and absorb the humors, and by their inherent virtues to preserve them as long as possible from putrefaction and decay. Hence the hundred pounds of myrrh and aloes furnished by Nicodemus. The embalming was usually repeated for several days together, that the drugs and spices thus applied might have all their efficiency in their exsic-

[1] This fact, also, is too often overlooked in contemplating the evidences of our Saviour's death.

cation of the moisture and the future preservation of the body."[1]

The body was swathed in bandages of linen or other cloth, on which the aromatics had been spread. Hence it is said that Joseph "wound the body of Christ" in linen clothes, with the spices, as the manner of the Jews is to bury. Thus Lazarus was bound hand and feet in grave clothes, or bandages; and hence, though raised from the power of death, Christ said, "Loose him and let him go;" that is, unwind the bandages that surround his limbs and his body. There was also placed over the face what was called a "napkin," which was saturated with aromatics, for the purpose of penetrating the eyes and nostrils, and the muscles of the face, to preserve them from decay. Thus we read that the face of Lazarus was bound about with a napkin;[2] and when our Lord was risen, Peter, who went into the sepulchre, saw the linen clothes lie, and the napkin that had been laid over the face, not lying with the linen bandages, but placed by itself.[3] And it was to repeat the application of drugs to the body, and thus to complete the embalming that the women went to the sepulchre early in the morning.

> "And when the sabbath was past, Mary Magdalene, and Mary the mother of James, and Salome, had bought sweet spices, that they might come and anoint him."—Mark xvi. 1.

But the first embalming, as it was called, was as liberal and as perfect as the time and circumstances would allow.[4]

[1] Horne's Introduction. [2] 1 John xi. 44. [3] John xx. 7.

[4] For a full account of the Jewish custom of embalming, see Horne's Introduction, Philadelphia Ed. p. 98.

This embalming of itself, aside from all other causes, would have extinguished life in any human body in far less time than our Lord lay in the tomb. This puts an end to all conjectures that he was merely in a swoon, or state of catalepsy; for even if either of these were possible when he was buried, the embalming would have extinguished life, and made resuscitation impossible.

8. The Jews, with all their efforts to get rid of the fact that Christ had risen, never alleged, so far as we have knowledge, that he was not really dead. The evidence of this fact was so abundant and incontrovertible on every hand that they never dreamed of calling it in question. It was left for the hardihood of modern infidelity to invent this hypothesis.

Such, then, are the proofs that the body of Christ was emphatically *dead* when committed to the tomb of Joseph.

IV. *The circumstances under which our Lord was buried, and slept in the grave till he arose, are such as to render all fraud and imposition impossible.*

1. The tomb was a *new one* which had never before been occupied.[1] There were, therefore, no other bodies there with which that of Christ could in any way be confounded.

2. It was *hewn out of a solid rock,*[2] so that if the entrance was well secured it was impossible for any one to enter it by removing a few bricks or stones in the rear, and thus to get away the body unnoticed by the attendants.

3. It was *near Jerusalem,*[3] so near that it was easy for

[1] Luke xxiii. 53, John xix. 41. [2] Matt. xxvii. 60. [3] John xix. 42.

the Jews to know all the facts; to take such precautions as they saw fit; and to investigate the alleged resurrection after it was reported to have occurred, with the least possible difficulty, and the greatest advantage for securing success.

4. The Jews *knew that Christ had predicted* his own resurrection from the dead, and that if that event should take place, it would demonstrate his prophetic character, give currency to his teachings, and convict them of shedding innocent blood. Hence it is recorded—

> "Now the next day that followed the day of the preparation, the chief priests and Pharisees came together unto Pilate,
>
> "Saying, Sir, we remember that that deceiver said, while he was yet alive, After three days I will rise again.
>
> "Command therefore that the sepulchre be made sure until the third day, lest his disciples come by night, and steal him away, and say unto the people, He is risen from the dead: so the last error shall be worse than the first."—Matt. xxvii. 62–64.

The promised resurrection was therefore well understood, and the consequences of its being even reported to have occurred were fully anticipated. It is also worthy of note that the Pharisees and chief priests seem to have had no idea that he would really arise; but as Joseph, in whose sepulchre the body was laid, had shown himself at least friendly to Christ and his disciples, by begging the body, and laying it in his own new tomb; they either actually feared that the disciples might remove the body, or used this as an argument with Pilate to obtain the desired security against removal or resurrection.

5. In response to the request of the Pharisees and chief priests, *the most effectual means were adopted to*

prevent the removal of the body, in case the terror-stricken disciples had contemplated such a measure:

> "Pilate said unto them, Ye have a watch: go your way, make *it* as sure as ye can.
>
> "So they went and made the sepulchre sure, sealing the stone, and setting a watch."—Matt. xxvii. 65, 66.

"*Ye have a watch.*" "The Jews had a corps of Roman troops to guard the temple," (Acts iv. 1.) "These companies mounted guard by turns." See Luke xxii. 4. "Some of these companies that were not then on duty, Pilate gave them leave to employ to watch the tomb." [1]

This guard is supposed to have consisted of sixty soldiers, though it is not probable that all of them were on duty at the same time.

"*Make it as sure as you can*"—as much as to say, "It would be a calamity indeed if the body should be missing, and the report get abroad that Jesus has risen from the dead; therefore, do all you can, with your ample means, to prevent such an occurrence."

The "great stone" had already been rolled to the door of the sepulchre, to prevent ingress or egress,[2] (for Joseph had no idea of Christ's resurrection,) and now, to make assurance doubly sure, the stone is *sealed*, first, that no one should remove the stone, with this "broad arrow" of the government upon it; and secondly, that if it should be by any means removed, the guard could infallibly detect it, by the broken condition of the seal.[3]

[1] Clarke's Notes. [2] Matt. xxvii. 60: Mark xv. 46.

[3] In the same manner Darius sealed the stone at the mouth of the den of lions, that no man might remove it:—"And a stone was brought

Death has placed his pale and cold seal upon his brow, and the fine linen, and napkin, and myrrh, and aloes, inclose every portion of the body. On all sides save the narrow entrance, the solid adamant incloses the cold remains, and defies approach or escape. The great stone at the entrance is sealed to prevent its disturbance, and in front of it from hour to hour, and with unwearied tread, pace the sturdy Roman soldiers, to and fro, to prevent the fulfilment of the promise of "this deceiver;" or even the removal of the lifeless corpse. *Thus sleeps the Son of God!*

V. *Despite all these precautions,* THE BODY IS GONE! *and the report goes forth that it has risen from the dead!!*

1. The first remarkable and noteworthy fact is that the faithful Roman guards *left the sepulchre,* and went into the city, declaring that the body was gone:

> "Now when they were going, behold, some of the watch came into the city, and shewed unto the chief priests all the things that were done." [1]

> Vain the stone, the watch, the seal—
> Christ has burst the gates of hell:
> Death in vain forbids his rise;
> Christ hath open'd Paradise.

Herod arrested Peter and delivered him to four quaternions of soldiers for safe keeping; but an angel led him forth from the prison.

and laid upon the mouth of the den; and the king sealed it with his own signet, and with the signet of his lords; that the purpose might not be changed concerning Daniel'[2]

[1] Matt. xxviii. 11.

[2] Daniel vi. 17.

"And when Herod had sought for him, and found him not, he examined the keepers, and commanded that *they* should be put to death."[1]

Such was the usual penalty for unfaithfulness on the part of a Roman guard. And yet "some of the watch came into the city, and shewed unto the chief priests all the things that were done." No doubt their report included the particulars of the earthquake, the descent of the angel, the rolling away of the stone, and of the rising of the Son of God.

2. The chief priests were *no doubt satisfied* in their own minds that he had risen from the dead. They do not seem to have questioned the fact. But still, feeling that his resurrection would be a most damaging fact to them and their cause, they fall back upon the old idea of the disciples stealing the body:

"And when they were assembled with the elders, and had taken counsel, they gave large money unto the soldiers,

"Saying, Say ye, His disciples came by night, and stole him away while he slept.

"And if this come to the governor's ears, we will persuade him, and secure you.

"So they took the money. and did as they were taught: and this saying is commonly reported among the Jews until this day."—Matt. xxviii. 12–15.

Had the soldiers told the governor the facts, as they were, it is not likely that he would have even censured them, much less punished them: but to admit that the very thing they were set to prevent, namely the stealing of the body,[2] had actually taken place, was virtually to sign their own death-warrant, unless something was done to avert the penalty of such gross unfaithfulness. Hence it required "large money" to induce

[1] Acts xii. 19. [2] Matt. xvii. 64.

the soldiers to incur the risk of admitting that they were asleep at their posts and deserved death; and hence the promise, "If this come to the governor's ears, we will persuade him, and secure you."[1] And so it seems that they did; for we have no evidence that the guard were ever called upon to account for their self-alleged dereliction.

VI. *The absurdity of the Jewish account of the absence of the body, is of itself a strong indirect proof of its resurrection.*[2]

1. The idea that the disciples would *desire* to abstract the body from the tomb, as a pretext for asserting that it had risen, is absurd upon its face; for we all know that, after all that he had said upon the subject, they had no idea or hope of his resurrection; and, so far as appears, no *desire* even that he should rise again. What motive, then, could they have had for stealing the body?

2. If such an idea had ever occurred to them, their

[1] *We will persuade him* that it is for his own interest and honor to join in the deception; and we will *render you secure*—we will take care that you shall not suffer that punishment for this pretended breach of duty which otherwise you might expect.—*Dr. Adam Clarke.*

[2] The Jewish historian *Josephus* thus speaks of Christ and his resurrection: "Now there was about this time Jesus, a wise man, if it be lawful to call him a man, for he was a doer of wonderful works, a teacher of such men as received the truth with pleasure. He drew over to him both many of the Jews, and many of the Gentiles. He was [the] Christ. And when Pilate, at the suggestion of the principal men amongst us, had condemned him to the cross, those that loved him at the first did not forsake him; for he appeared to them alive again the third day, as the divine prophets had foretold these and ten thousand other wonderful things concerning him. And the tribe of Christians, so named from him, are not extinct at this day.—*Antiquities of the Jews, Book* XVIII., *Ch.* ii., *Sec.* 3.

fear of the Roman guard at the tomb would have banished it in a moment; and if they knew nothing of the guard, they would have gone carelessly about their work, and would have been detected and punished.

"*Stole him away while we slept!*" "Here," says Dr. Clarke, "is a whole heap of absurdities. (1.) Is it likely that so many men would all fall asleep, in the open air, at once? (2.) Is it at all probable that a *Roman guard* should be found off their watch, much less asleep, when it was instant *death*, according to the Roman military law, to be found in this state? (3.) Could they be so sound asleep as not to awake with all the noise which must be necessarily made by removing the great stone, and taking away the body? (4.) Is it at all likely that these disciples could have had time to do all this, and to come and return without being perceived by any person? (5.) If they were asleep, how could they possibly know that it was the *disciples* that stole him, or indeed that any person or persons stole him?—for, being *asleep*, they could see no person. From their own testimony, therefore, the *resurrection* may be as *fully proved* as the *theft*." [1]

3. It is a very remarkable circumstance that, so far as we know, *no effort was ever made to find the body of Jesus*, or to arrest and punish either the guard or the disciples. St. Paul tells us that Enoch, who was translated to heaven, "was not found, because God had translated him;" [2] and so of the body of Christ—it was not found, nor even searched for, because God had raised it from death. Even the high-priests and rulers seem to have been satisfied of this fact.

[1] Clarke's Comments on Matt. xxviii. 13. [2] Hebrews xi. 5.

When Elijah was translated, fifty men, who saw him ascend, searched three days for his body, supposing, as they said, that the Spirit of the Lord, which had taken him up, had dropped him upon some mountain, or in some valley;[1] but when the body of Jesus is missing, and it is alleged, as the best subterfuge his enemies can resort to, that the disciples had come, while the guard were asleep, and stolen the body, which, in such a case, might easily have been found,[1] no search is made, neither is the first step taken to arraign either the disciples or the guard—facts that show, even more clearly than words could, that the Jews did not believe either the soldiers or the disciples were guilty of any wrong.[2]

VII. *The account of the resurrection is in all respects consistent and natural; and for that reason has commended itself to the judgment and to the faith of mankind in all ages.*

Christ is dead and buried. The Shepherd is smitten and the sheep scattered.[3] The body is partly embalmed, and the pious females who loved him, and wept at the foot of the cross, have prepared spices to complete the embalming, having no idea whatever that it would arise from death.

[1] 2 Kings ii. 16.

[2] The case of Prof. Webster, who murdered Dr. Parkman, in Boston, a few years since, shows how difficult it is secretly to dispose of a human body, even by the aid of private rooms, and acids, and fire. How much more difficult would it have been for the disciples to have concealed the body of Jesus, even if they could have obtained possession of it.

[3] Zechariah, xiii. 7.

But let us read the account in the simple and unadorned language of the evangelists.

"In the end of the Sabbath, as it began to dawn toward the first *day* of the week, came Mary Magdalene, and the other Mary to see the sepulchre.

"And behold, there was a great earthquake: for the angel of the Lord descended from heaven, and came and rolled back the stone from the door, and sat upon it.

"His countenance was like lightning, and his raiment white as snow.

"And for fear of him the keepers did shake, and became as dead *men*.

"And the angel answered and said unto the women, Fear not ye: for I know that ye seek Jesus, which is crucified.

"He is not here: for he is risen, as he said. Come, see the place where the Lord lay.

"And go quickly, and tell his disciples, that he is risen from the dead, and behold he goeth before you into Galilee; there shall ye see him: lo, I have told you.

"And they departed quickly from the sepulchre, with fear and great joy; and did run to bring his disciples word."—Matthew xxviii. 1–8.

The account as recorded by St. Mark includes several particulars not mentioned by St. Matthew:

"And when the Sabbath was past, and Mary Magdalene, and Mary, the *mother* of James, and Salome, had bought sweet spices, that they might come and anoint him.

"And very early in the morning, the first *day* of the week, they came unto the sepulchre at the rising of the sun:

"And they said among themselves, Who shall roll us away the stone from the door of the sepulchre?

"(And when they looked, they saw that the stone was rolled away,) for it was very great.

"And entering into the sepulchre, they saw a young man sitting on the right side, clothed in a long white garment; and they were affrighted.

"And he saith unto them, Be not affrighted: ye seek Jesus of Nazareth, which was crucified: he is risen; he is not here: behold the place where they laid him.

"But go your way, tell his disciples and Peter, that he goeth before you into Galilee: there shall ye see him, as he said unto you.

"And they went out quickly, and fled from the sepulchre; for they trembled, and were amazed: neither said they anything to any *man;* for they were afraid."—Mark xvi. 1–8.

The narrative by St. Luke, though in substance the same, includes still other particulars:

"Now upon the first *day* of the week, very early in the morning, they came unto the sepulchre, bringing the spices which they had prepared, and certain *others* with them.

"And they found the stone rolled away from the sepulchre.

"And they entered in, and found not the body of the Lord Jesus.

"And it came to pass, as they were much perplexed thereabout, behold, two men stood by them in shining garments.

"And as they were afraid, and bowed down *their* faces to the earth, they said unto them, Why seek ye the living among the dead?

"He is not here, but is risen. Remember how he spake unto you when he was yet in Galilee,

"Saying, The Son of man must be delivered into the hands of sinful men, and be crucified, and the third day rise again.

"And they remembered his words,

"And returned from the sepulchre, and told all these things unto the eleven, and to all the rest."—Luke xxiv. 1–9.

The account by St. John is still more full and minute, and includes many things not mentioned by either of the other evangelists. But we must not take room here to cite a whole chapter.[1]

Taken together, however, these four narratives not only sustain each other, but furnish just such proof of the stupendous miracle, as all the circumstances required. Everything is *natural* and *credible,* without contradiction and without absurdity.

"Twice had the sun gone down upon the earth, and

[1] John xx.

all as yet was quiet at the sepulchre; death held his sceptre over the Son of God; still and silent the hours passed; the guards stood by their posts; the rays of the midnight moon gleamed upon their helmets and upon their spears; the enemies of Christ exulted in their success; the hearts of his friends were sunk in despondency and in sorrow; the spirits of glory waited in anxious suspense to behold the event, and wondered at the depth of the ways of God.

"At length the morning-star arising in the east announced the approach of light. The third day began to dawn upon the world, when suddenly the earth trembled to its centre, and the powers of heaven were shaken. An angel of God descended, the guards shrank back with terror from his presence, and fell prostrate on the ground; his countenance was like lightning, and his raiment was white as snow. He rolled away the stone from the sepulchre and sat upon it.

"But who is he that cometh from the tomb, with dyed garments from the bed of death? He that is glorious in his apparel, walking in the greatness of his strength. It is your Lord! He has trodden the wine-press alone—he has stained his raiment with blood, but now, as the first-born from the womb of nature, he meets the morning of the resurrection. He arises a conqueror from the grave; he brings salvation to the sons of men. Never did the returning sun usher in a day so glorious. It was the jubilee of the universe. The morning-stars sang together, and all the sons of God shouted aloud for joy. The Father of mercies looked down from his throne in heaven with complacency; he saw his world restored; he saw his work that it was good. Then did the desert rejoice; the face of nature was gladdened before him when the blessings of the Eternal descended as the dew of heaven for the refreshing of nations."[1]

Lives again our glorious king;
Where, O Death, is now thy sting?
Once he died our souls to save,
Where's thy victory, boasting Grave?

VIII. *The disciples aver that they* SAW JESUS ALIVE *after his burial, and* TALKED, *and* EAT WITH, *and* HANDLED *him, from time to time, for forty days; and at last saw him ascend to heaven.*

1. He was seen by Mary Magdalene.

"Now, when *Jesus* was risen early, the first *day* of the week, he appeared to Mary Magdalene, out of whom he had cast seven devils."—Mark xvi. 9.[2]

2. He was seen by the other women who had seen the empty tomb, and the vision of angels, and had started after Mary to tell his disciples.

"And they departed quickly from the sepulchre, with fear and great joy; and did run to bring his disciples word.

"And as they went to tell his disciples, behold, Jesus met them, saying, All hail. And they came, and held him by the feet, and worshipped him.

"Then said Jesus unto them, Be not afraid: go tell my brethren, that they go into Galilee, and there shall they see me."—Matthew xxviii. 8–10.

3. He was seen by Peter. St. Paul says, "He was seen of Cephas, then of the twelve."[3] At what pre-

[1] From a volume of sermons, entitled "*The Scotch Preacher.*"

[2] See also the detailed account, John xx. 1–18.

[3] 1 Cor. xv. 5.

cise time Peter saw him the Scriptures do not inform us; although it was evidently before he met the body of the disciples in Jerusalem. For, when they met in the evening, some said, "The Lord is risen indeed; and hath appeared unto Simon."[1]

4. He appeared to two of the disciples the same day, while on their way to Emmaus, walked and talked with them, eat with them, and finally vanished out of their sight.[2]

5. He appeared to ten of the disciples probably in their "upper room" at Jerusalem:

> "And as they thus spake, Jesus himself stood in the midst of them, and saith unto them, Peace be unto you.
>
> "But they were terrified and affrighted, and supposed that they had seen a spirit.
>
> "And he said unto them, Why are ye troubled? and why do thoughts arise in your hearts?
>
> "Behold my hands and my feet, that it is I myself: handle me, and see; for a spirit hath not flesh and bones, as ye see me have.
>
> "And when he had thus spoken, he shewed them his hands and his feet.
>
> "And while they yet believed not for joy, and wondered, he said unto them, Have ye here any meat?
>
> "And they gave him a piece of a broiled fish, and of an honeycomb.
>
> "And he took it, and did eat before them."—Luke xxiv. 36–43.

Judas had hanged himself, and Thomas was absent on this occasion.[3] On his return the other disciples informed him that they had seen the Lord, to which he replied:

> "Except I shall see in his hands the print of the nails, and put my finger into the print of the nails, and thrust my hand into his side, I will not believe."—John xx. 25.

Now let it not be forgotten that all five of these

[1] See Luke xxiv. 34. [2] Luke xxiv. 13–31. [3] John xx. 25.

manifestations were *upon the very day that he arose from the dead;* and that four of the five were in or very near Jerusalem itself—the very city through which the two statements were flying, one that he had risen from the dead, and the other that the disciples had stolen the body.

6. A week later he again appeared to the eleven in Jerusalem.[1]

> "And after eight days again the disciples were within, and Thomas with them: then came Jesus, the doors being shut, and stood in the midst, and said, Peace be unto you.
>
> "Then saith he to Thomas, Reach hither thy finger, and behold my hands; and reach hither thy hand, and thrust it into my side; and be not faithless, but believing.
>
> "And Thomas answered and said unto him, My Lord and my God.
>
> "Jesus saith unto him, Thomas, because thou hast seen me, thou hast believed: blessed are they that have not seen, and yet have believed."—John xx. 26–29.

7. He appeared at the sea of Tiberias, in Galilee, to Peter, Thomas, Nathaniel, James and John, and two others.[2] On this occasion also he talked and eat with the disciples, remaining some time with them, and giving them the most ample proofs of his identity as their risen Lord and Master.

8. He appeared to the disciples in a mountain in Galilee, where he had promised to meet them:

> "Then the eleven disciples went away into Galilee, into a mountain where Jesus had appointed them.

[1] The expression "the eleven" and "the twelve" are used by the apostles to represent *the body of the disciples* (as they were often so called collectively) without intending to indicate the precise number present.

[2] John xxi. 1–14. This is said to be *the third time* he showed himself to the disciples, that is, to the *apostles,* when they were assembled together.

"And when they saw him, they worshipped him: but some doubted."—Matt. xxviii. 16, 17.

Upon this occasion he was seen by over five hundred of the disciples, at one time:

"After that, he was seen of about five hundred brethren at once; of whom the greater part remain unto this present, but some are fallen asleep."—1 Cor. xv. 6.[1]

"This was *probably* in Galilee, where the Lord had spent the greater part of his public ministry, and where he had made most disciples. The place, however, is not designated, and, of course, cannot be known. . . . After his resurrection, Jesus said to the women who were at the sepulchre, "Go tell my brethren that they go into Galilee, and there shall they see me." And in verse 16, it is said, "The eleven disciples went away into Galilee, into a mountain where Jesus had appointed them."[2]

Jesus had spent most of his public life in Galilee. He had made most of his disciples there. It was proper, therefore, that these disciples, who would, of course, hear of his death, should have some public confirmation of the fact that he had risen. It is very probable, also, that the eleven who had went down into Galilee after he rose, would apprize the brethren there of what had been said to them, that Jesus would meet them on a certain mountain; and it is morally certain that they who had followed him in so great numbers in Galilee, would be drawn together by the

[1] Dr. Barnes enumerates these as two different manifestations (Notes, vol. i., p. 34,) but we see no reason for regarding them as otherwise than identical.

[2] Matt. xxvii. 10, 16.

report that the Lord Jesus, who had been put to death, was about to be seen there again alive. Such is human nature, and such was the attachment of these disciples to the Lord Jesus, that it is morally certain a large concourse would assemble on the slightest rumor that such an occurrence was to happen. Nothing more would be necessary anywhere to draw a concourse of people than a rumor that one who had been dead would appear again; and in this instance, where they ardently loved him, and when, perhaps, many believed that he would rise, they would naturally assemble in great numbers to see him once more. . . .

"What more conclusive argument for the truth of his resurrection *could* there be than that five hundred persons had seen him, who had been intimately acquainted with him in his life, and who had become his followers?

"If the testimony of five hundred could not avail to prove his resurrection, no number of witnesses could. And if five hundred men could thus be deceived, any number could; and it would be impossible to substantiate *any* simple matter of fact by the testimony of eye-witnesses."[1]

And though some twenty-six years had intervened, the apostle avers that "the greater part" of this five hundred who saw Jesus on this occasion, were still alive.

9. After that he was seen of James.[2] When and where this occurred we are not informed. "It is probable," says Dr. Barnes, "that the Lord Jesus appeared often to the disciples, as he was forty days on

[1] Barnes' Notes on 1 Cor. xv. 6.

[2] 1 Cor. xv. 7.

earth after his resurrection, and the evangelists have only mentioned the more prominent instances, and enough to substantiate the fact of the resurrection."

10. On still another occasion he was seen by all the apostles,[1] but upon what particular occasion, or under what circumstances, we are not informed.

11. Having thus been seen from time to time for forty days, he appeared to the disciples on Mount Olivet again, led them out as far as Bethany, and after addressing them in regard to the gift of power which they were to receive, he lifted up his hands and blessed them, and then was visibly "carried up into heaven."[2]

12. He was seen by Saul of Tarsus while on his way to Damascus. "And last of all," says he, "he was seen of me also, as of one born out of due time."[3] This was some two years after his ascension to heaven.

13. Finally, he appeared to St. John on the Isle of Patmos, A.D. 96, or 63 years after his ascension, saying: "I am he that liveth, and was dead; and behold, I am alive for evermore, Amen; and have the keys of hell and of death."[4]

Such is the number and the variety of the proofs that he had risen from the dead. Many were the witnesses "to whom also he showed himself alive after his passion by many infallible proofs, being seen of them forty days, and speaking of the things pertaining to the kingdom of God."[5]

IX. *Although great numbers saw the Lord after he arose, the apostles ever regarded themselves as the* SPECIAL WITNESSES *of his resurrection.*

[1] 1 Cor. xv. 7. [2] See Luke xxiv. 5, and Acts i. 8–11.
[3] 1 Cor. xv. 8, and Acts ix. [4] Rev. i. 18. [5] Acts i. 3.

1. Such seems to have been the divine plan, that there should be twelve special witnesses, to whom Christ should first appear, and upon whose testimony his resurrection should be proclaimed.[1] Christ had chosen twelve apostles, and as he was about to ascend had said, "And ye are witnesses of these things;"[2] from which the disciples doubtless concluded that he wished the number of witnesses to be kept the same as it was before his crucifixion. Hence when Judas fell and was dead, they elected from among those who had companied with them from the baptism of John to the ascension, Matthias, to be a witness with them of his resurrection.[3]

2. On the day of Pentecost Peter said: "This Jesus hath God raised up, whereof we are all witnesses;"[4] and so again, after the healing of the lame man,—"And killed the Prince of life, whom God raised from the dead; whereof we are witnesses."[5] Still again in the temple subsequently:—

> "The God of our fathers raised up Jesus, whom ye slew and hanged on a tree.
> "Him hath God exalted with his right hand to be a Prince and a Saviour, for to give repentance to Israel, and forgiveness of sins.
> "And we are his witnesses of these things."—Acts v. 30–32.

3. Again, while preaching at the house of Cornelius, Peter said:

> "Him God raised up the third day, and shewed him openly;
> "Not to all the people, but unto witnesses chosen before of God,

[1] It was the peculiar office of the apostles to be *witnesses of his resurrection*, on which the truth and certainty of the whole gospel, and all the promises of it did entirely depend.—*Sherlock on the Happiness of Good Men, etc. London*, 1726, p. 232.

[2] Acts i. 21, 22. [3] Luke xxiv. 48. [4] Acts ii. 32. [5] Acts iii. 15.

even to us, who did eat and drink with him after he rose from the dead."—Acts x. 40, 41.

4. St. Paul also refers to these special "witnesses" of Christ's resurrection in his discourse at Antioch:

"And when they had fulfilled all that was written of him, they took him down from the tree, and laid him in a sepulchre.

"But God raised him from the dead:

"And he was seen many days of them which came up with him from Galilee to Jerusalem, who are his witnesses unto the people."—Acts xiii. 29–31.

X. *The evidence of these witnesses of Christ's resurrection is as strong as could possibly exist to establish any event.*

Let us briefly enumerate the principal facts that go to establish their credibility as witnesses:—

1. So far as *knowing* Jesus was concerned, *they could not be deceived.* They had been with him day and night for three years, in public and in private, in Galilee, at Bethany, at Jerusalem, and wherever he had been; and if *they* were not prepared to infallibly identify him, if he arose and walked and talked and eat with them as he had been wont to do, then no body of men could identify a fellow human being.

2. They were *twelve in number*. To deceive one or two men for once, might have been possible; but to deceive twelve men, for forty days, and under such a variety of circumstances, on the road, in the house, on the sea of Galilee, and elsewhere, is absolutely incredible.[1]

3. They were not a set of credulous fanatics, who had predicted the event, and were expecting and

[1] It requires far greater faith in incredible things to doubt the resurrection of Christ than it does to believe it.

anxious for its accomplishment. On the contrary, notwithstanding all that Christ had said upon the subject, they *were not expecting* the resurrection of the Saviour, and were as much surprised and astounded by the fact, as the chief priests themselves. It cannot, therefore, be said of them that they were looking for a miracle, and therefore imagined that they saw it.

4. They could have had no hope of earthly advantage from declaring that Christ had risen. John, his forerunner, had first been imprisoned, and then beheaded. The Shepherd had now been smitten, dying as a malefactor on the cross, and now that he was buried, they had every motive, so far as their safety from persecution and their personal earthly comfort were concerned, for desiring that the agitation and their consequent trials and sufferings for his sake, should now come to an end. As they were situated, therefore, they had *no motive* for testifying falsely that Christ had risen from the dead.

5. Notwithstanding all these circumstances, they boldly declared *at the time*, and subsequently, *in Jerusalem itself*, and in the very presence of those who crucified him, that he had risen from the dead.[1] Despite the allegation that they had stolen the body, they publicly affirmed that it had been raised to life by the power of God, who had thus given to Israel "the sure mercies of David."[1]

6. So overwhelming was the evidence of the mighty fact, to those who heard the apostles preach it, that not less than three thousand souls were convinced at one

[1] Acts xiii. 34, and Isa. lv. 3.

time, and were baptized in the faith that Christ had risen.[1]

7. God himself endorsed the testimony of the apostles, "bearing them witness, both with signs and wonders, and with divers miracles, and gifts of the Holy Ghost, according to his own will?"[2] They speak with tongues on the day of Pentecost, and on their heads are seen the "cloven tongues of fire." At their hands the lame and the sick are healed,[3] and even the dead are raised to life.[4] Upon their bodies the poison of asps takes no effect,[5] and, to vindicate their testimony, earthquakes rock the world, prison doors and gates fly open, and the angels of God show themselves as their visible attendants and guardians.[5]

8. Though counted as the offscouring of the earth, and made a spectacle to men and angels on that account, they adhered firmly to their testimony through life, amid hardships, and persecutions, and perils, in almost every form, and finally, with a solitary exception, sealed their testimony with their blood![6]

[1] Acts ii. 41. [2] Heb. ii. 4.

[3] Acts iii. 4, and xiv. 9. [4] Ibid. xx. 9.

[5] Ibid. xxviii. 3–5, Mark xvi. 18, and Luke x. 19.

[6] According to tradition the following was the fate of the apostles:—*Matthew* is supposed to have suffered martyrdom, or was slain with a sword at the city of Ethiopia. *Mark* was dragged through the streets of Alexandria, in Egypt, till he expired. *Luke* was hanged upon an olive tree in Greece. *John* was put into a cauldron of boiling oil at Rome, and escaped death! He afterwards died a natural death at Ephesus, in Asia. *James the Great,* as he was called, was beheaded at Jerusalem. *James the Less* was thrown from a pinnacle or wing of the temple, and then beaten to death with a fuller's club. *Philip* was hanged up against a pillar at Hierapolis, a city of Phrygia. *Bartholomew* was flayed alive, by the command of a barbarous king. *Andrew*

Such are the evidences that Christ rose from the dead. The prophet had predicted it, and our Lord had distinctly and publicly announced that he would rise again. Having been sentenced to death, the law under which he was crucified required that he should hang upon the cross till he was dead. After hanging upon the cross for three hours, he bowed his head, and gave up the ghost. The executioners being fully satisfied that he was dead, assured Pilate of the fact, and the dead body was delivered to Joseph for burial. The body was embalmed and laid in a new tomb near the city, cut out of a solid rock, a great stone rolled to the door, a seal placed upon it, and a Roman guard mounted to see that the body was not removed, with the penalty of death overhanging them if they should sleep at their post. On the morning of the third day they come flying into the city, and declare that the body is gone! At the instigation of the rulers they accept a bribe, and a promise of protection, and report that while they were asleep, the disciples came and stole the body. But they are not arrested; neither are the disciples. Neither is any effort made to find the body. The disciples, however, who had no idea that he would arise, (such was their unbelief,) affirmed that he had risen and appeared to them on some twelve different occasions; that they talked and walked and

was bound to a cross, from which he preached to the people till he expired. *Thomas* was run through the body with a lance, at Coromandel, in the East Indies. *Jude* was shot to death with arrows. *Simon Zelotes* was crucified in Persia, and *Matthias* was first stoned and then beheaded. *Barnabas* was stoned to death by the Jews at Salina. *Peter* was crucified head downward, and *Paul* was beheaded at Rome, by the tyrant Nero.

eat with him, and even handled his body; that he appeared five times on the day that he arose; that as many as five hundred saw him at one time; and that finally, after having been seen in many places, for forty days, and under every circumstance that could enable them fully to identify him, he ascended visibly from Mount Olivet in the presence of them all. A few days afterward, these very disciples, who were so unbelieving, and were so astonished and affrighted at the report that he had risen, stand up in Jerusalem in the presence of thousands, and boldly preach his resurrection. God confirms their word by enabling them to speak in various languages unknown to them before, and crowning their heads with the symbol of his own presence—the "cloven tongues of fire." So overwhelming is the evidence to those who saw and heard them, that three thousand embrace the faith of Christ, and are baptized in a single day. Finally, with no hope of earthly advantage, and the sure prospect of persecution and ignominy, the twelve apostles continue to preach Jesus and the resurrection, through life, in spite of persecution, ignominy, and peril of every kind, till at length, with a single exception, (made such by a miracle,) they all seal their testimony with their blood.

Whence but from heaven could men unskilled in arts,
In different nations born—in different parts—
Weave such agreeing truths? Or how, or why
Should all conspire to cheat us with a lie?
Unask'd their pains, ungrateful their advice,
Starving their gains, and martyrdom their price.

Such are the proofs that Christ arose from the dead; and upon this testimony the Christian religion has spread from age to age, and from land to land, till nearly all nations have seen the salvation of the gospel.

When he first the work begun,
  Small and feeble was his day;
Now the word doth swiftly run;
  Now it wins its widening way;
More and more it spreads and grows,
  Ever mighty to prevail;
Sin's strongholds it now o'erthrows,--
  Shakes the trembling gates of hell.

But while some admit that in some sense Christ rose from the dead, they still deny that his was a physical resurrection. To this question we shall give attention in the next chapter.

CHAPTER VIII.

THE RESURRECTION OF CHRIST AND THE "NEW CHURCH" THEORY.

THE bearing of the resurrection of our Lord upon the question of the *nature* of the resurrection, is most obvious. If Christ literally rose from the dead, in the same body laid in the tomb, and is both a *proof* and a *pattern* of our resurrection, it follows that we also shall arise from the dead with the identical bodies laid in the grave.

But it is averred by a class of "spiritualists," who claim to believe the Bible, that, while it may be admitted that Jesus rose from the dead in some sense, his material body never arose. "It must, we conceive, be maintained," says Prof. Bush,[1] "that the body which hung upon the cross was miraculously dissolved or resolved into its primitive elements, like that of Elijah,[2] when he was translated," &c. To this "new church" theory, therefore, as applied to the resurrection of Christ, we think it well to devote a few pages in this connection. And, in order to do this, it will be necessary to recur again to some of the facts and Scrip-

[1] Anastasis, p. 166.

[2] There is no proof whatever of this assumption. On the contrary, all the circumstances go to show that Elijah ascended bodily to heaven. —See 2 Kings, chap. ii.

tures of the preceding chapter, that they may be viewed in the light of the above theory.

I. According to Emanuel Swedenborg and Prof. Bush, the resurrection is the development of a spiritual from the material body at the moment of death.

"Death in the word," says Swedenborg, "signifies resurrection and continued life."[1] "By resuscitation is meant the drawing forth of the spirit from the body, and its introduction into the spirit world, which is commonly called resurrection."[2]

"The true doctrine of the resurrection is the doctrine of the development of a spiritual body at death, from the bodies which we now inhabit."[3] "Let it be understood as a present event, or one that takes place with every individual believer as soon as he leaves the body."[4] If this is the true notion of the resurrection, it follows that Christ rose from the dead when he gave up the ghost, that is, while his body hung upon the cross. But, with all his boldness in criticism and theorizing, Prof. Bush does not dare to confront the gospel narrative, which so often asserts that he "rose again *the third day*." With strange inconsistency, therefore, he abandons his favorite theory, or, in other words, admits that, so far as the resurrection of Christ throws any light upon the subject, the resurrection is *not* the evolving of a spiritual from the material body at the hour of death. "The *fact* itself of his emerging from the sepulchre on the third day is of course admitted."[5]

II. This being granted, the theory of Prof. Bush is

[1] *Heaven and Hell*, p. 245, American edition. [2] Ibid. p. 246.
[3] *Anastasis*, by Prof. Bush, p. 84. [4] Ibid. p. 170. [5] Ibid. p. 151.

that the material body of Christ never was raised from death, but that a "spiritual body" was evolved from it on the third day, in which he subsequently appeared often to his disciples, and finally ascended to heaven.

But just here is the fatal assumption that vitiates the whole theory. It is *assumed* that there is such a thing as a "spiritual body," *distinct from the material;* whereas the doctrine of St. Paul is, that a spiritual body is none other than the present body made incorruptible and immortal, like unto Christ's glorious body.

"It is sown in corruption, it is raised in incorruption:

"It is sown in dishonor, it is raised in glory: it is sown in weakness, it is raised in power:

"It is sown a natural body, it is raised a spiritual body.

"For this corruptible must put on incorruption, and this mortal *must* put on immortality."—1 Cor. xv. 42–44, 53.

How obvious from these passages that the spiritual body is the same material body which is sown, invested with the attributes of incorruption and immortality; on which account alone it is called a "spiritual body." it is the sheerest assumption, therefore, to talk of a "spiritual body," as opposed to the *material*, when the Scriptures merely place it in contrast with the *corruptible* and *mortal*.

III. But it is said that Christ entered the room on two occasions, "the doors being shut." Very true; and for aught we know, or are entitled to assert to the contrary, every immortal body may have that capability after the resurrection; for "it is raised in power." Besides, the whole process is and must be supernatural. How absurd, therefore, to attempt to test its character by the principles of natural philosophy, or to object that our Lord's resurrection body was not material because it exhibited properties unknown to matter under ordinary circumstances.

VI. "He is not here," said the angel to Mary Magdalene, Matt. xxviii. 6, "for he is risen, as he said. Come, see the place where the Lord lay." He was visible, and walked and talked, and eat with the disciples after he arose, and as if to place the question of his material identity beyond all cavil for ever, he challenged them in two instances at least, to *handle* him and be fully satisfied that he had risen from the dead in the same body laid in the tomb.

At his first appearing in the upper room at Jerusalem, the disciples were terribly frightened, and "supposed that they had seen a spirit,"—the very thing which Prof. Bush insists they did see. Of course, then, Christ should have left them with their first impressions unchanged. Instead of this, however, he said,

> "Why are ye troubled? and why do thoughts arise in your hearts?
>
> "Behold my hands and my feet, that it is I myself: handle me, and see; for a spirit hath not flesh and bones, as ye see me have." —Luke xxiv. 38.

Thomas was not with them at this time, and when the other disciples told him that they had seen the Lord, he said,

> "Except I shall see in his hands the print of the nails, and put my finger into the print of the nails, and thrust my hand into his side, I will not believe."—John xx. 25.

When, therefore, our Lord next showed himself to

the disciples, Thomas being now present, and the Saviour knowing his former declaration, said to him,

> "Reach hither thy finger, and behold my hands; and reach hither thy hand, and thrust it into my side; and be not faithless, but believing."—John xx. 27.

Now what did our Lord mean when he said, "It is *I myself?*" Did he mean to assert that he was in a spiritual body in the Swedenborgian sense?—a body utterly unlike that laid in the tomb? If so, why virtually affirm that he had "flesh and bones?" Why labor to convince them that he was not a spirit, but had the same body? And so in regard to Thomas: why did Christ ask him to look at "the print of the nails," and thrust his hand into his side, if not to convince him that they were the very hands which had been nailed to the cross, and the very side pierced by the soldier's spear? It is impossible to conceive of stronger proof of our Lord's physical identity, than that which he himself has furnished by these facts.

VII. That the apostles *believed* and subsequently *preached* that the veritable body of Christ rose from the dead, is certain. This is admitted even by Prof. Bush. "We may admit, indeed," says he, "that the disciples *supposed* that the body which they saw and handled was the veritable body of their crucified Lord, and that in their preaching the resurrection of Jesus they had no other idea than that of the resurrection of his body of flesh. . . . All the phenomena addressed themselves in such a manner to their senses as to beget the belief of a material substance." [1]

[1] Anastasis, p. 165.

This being admitted, it follows either that what they "supposed" and preached was true, namely, "that the body which they saw and handled was the veritable body of their crucified Lord;" or else that they were *deceived* and *misled* by the Redeemer himself, and consequently preached gross error touching his resurrection all the days of their lives! Prof. Bush adopts the latter theory, and modestly intimates that he knows more upon that subject than did the apostles. "We know no reason why the measure of their intelligence on this point should be the limit of ours!"[1]

But let us see how they preached.

VIII. In the second chapter of the Acts, we find Peter insisting upon the resurrection of Christ, in proof of his Messiahship:

"Ye men of Israel, hear these words; Jesus of Nazareth, a man approved of God among you by miracles, and wonders, and signs, which God did by him in the midst of you, as ye yourselves also know:

"Him, being delivered by the determinate counsel and foreknowledge of God, ye have taken, and by wicked hands have crucified and slain:

"Whom God hath raised up, having loosed the pains of death: because it was not possible that he should be holden of it.

"For David speaketh concerning him, I foresaw the Lord always before my face; for he is on my right hand, that I should not be moved:

"Therefore did my heart rejoice, and my tongue was glad; moreover also, my flesh shall rest in hope;

"Because thou wilt not leave my soul in hell, neither wilt thou suffer thine Holy one to see corruption.

* * * * * * * *

"Men and brethren, let me freely speak unto you of the patriarch David, that he is both dead and buried, and his sepulchre is with us unto this day.

"Therefore being a prophet, and knowing that God had sworn

[1] Anastasis, p. 165.

with an oath to him, that of the fruit of his loins, according to the flesh, he would raise up Christ to sit on his throne:

"He, seeing this before, spake of the resurrection of Christ, that his soul was not left in hell, neither his flesh did see corruption.

"This Jesus hath God raised up, whereof we all are witnesses.

* * * * * * * *

"For David is not ascended into the heavens: but he saith himself, The LORD said unto my Lord, Sit thou on my right hand,

"Until I make thy foes thy footstool.

"Therefore let all the house of Israel know assuredly, that God hath made that same Jesus, whom ye have crucified, both Lord and Christ."

The argument of Peter based upon the passage cited from the sixteenth Psalm, is, (1) That he speaks of his *flesh* "resting in hope," and not seeing corruption, and of its being exalted to the right hand of God. (2) That this was not true of David in his own person, because he was dead and buried with them, and was not ascended into heaven, and, therefore, (3) That being a prophet, he was speaking not of himself but of the resurrection of Christ, that *his* flesh should not see corruption, &c. Now, the term "flesh" in this prophecy; the allusion to the body of David still in the tomb, as a proof that he had not risen or ascended; and the claim that the whole had been fulfilled in the resurrection of Christ, shows conclusively that though preaching under the miraculous promptings of the Holy Ghost, Peter fully believed that the "flesh" of Christ had risen from death, in accordance with the prophecy of David, in the sixteenth Psalm.

IX. The apostle Paul makes a similar use of the same prophecy, in the thirteenth chapter of the Acts of the Apostles:

"And when they had fulfilled all that was written of him, they took *him* down from the tree, and laid *him* in a sepulchre.

"But God raised him from the dead.

"And he was seen many days of them which came up with him from Galilee to Jerusalem, who are his witnesses unto the people.

"And we declare unto you glad tidings, how that the promise which was made unto the fathers,

"God hath fulfilled the same unto us their children, in that he hath raised up Jesus again; as it is also written in the second psalm, Thou art my Son, this day have I begotten thee.

"And as concerning that he raised him up from the dead, *now* no more to return to corruption, he said on this wise, I will give you the sure mercies of David.

"Wherefore he saith also in another *psalm*, Thou shalt not suffer thine Holy One to see corruption.

"For David, after he had served his own generation by the will of God, fell on sleep, and was laid unto his fathers, and saw corruption.

"But he, whom God raised again, saw no corruption."

Here it is insisted that Christ had risen from the dead—that it was in accordance with a promise made to the fathers—that the promise thou shalt not suffer thine Holy One to see corruption, could not have related to David in his own person, because he "saw corruption;" and therefore that it must have been a prophecy fulfilled in the resurrection of Christ, who "saw no corruption." And as in the previous citation of the same prophecy by Peter, and its application to Christ, the whole argument proceeds upon the supposition that the "flesh," or body of Christ was the subject of the "promise" or prophecy, and also of the resurrection from the tomb.

No wonder, therefore, with such passages as these in their sermons, that Prof. Bush admits that the Apostles believed in and preached the literal resurrection of the body of Christ.

VIII. But it is argued that Christ's material body was not raised, because he could not ascend to heaven in such a body. The form of the argument, properly stated is, (1) Christ must have ascended in the same body in which he was raised. (2) He could not ascend in his material body, therefore (3) He did not arise in his material body. In reply, we answer, (1) That it does not necessarily follow that he must ascend in the same body—that is, a body in the same *state*—in which he arose. Precisely when the body became "glorious," or incorruptible, we do not know. (2) We *deny* the second premise, namely, that a material body could not ascend to heaven. That "flesh and blood," in its present corruptible state, "cannot inherit the kingdom of God," or in other words, that "corruption cannot inherit incorruption," we freely admit; but when the "vile body" is "changed," and clothed upon;" when "this mortal puts on immortality," and "mortality is swallowed up of life," the body is no longer "flesh and blood" in the sense of the apostle; but a celestial, indestructible and glorious body, equal unto the angels,—a fitting abode for the blood-washed and happy spirit forever.

We have no doubt, however, that he ascended in the same body in which he arose; and is now before the mercy-seat on high, in the same "glorious body"—a perfect sample of humanity redeemed from the power of the grave, and a guaranty of the resurrection of the bodies of all the righteous dead to glory and immortality. Not only do all the circumstances of his resurrection and ascension point in this direction, but St. Paul distinctly asserts that the same that was buried ascended to heaven:

"Now that he ascended, what is it but that he also descended first into the lower parts of the earth?

"He that descended is the same also that ascended up far above all heavens, that he might fill all things."—Eph. iv. 9.

IX. The absurdity of the opposite theory is still further seen in the sorry expedients to which its advocates are obliged to resort, to give it even a semblance of consistency. In the first place, Prof. Bush admits that the apostles *supposed* that Christ's real body had risen, and so preached. All the phenomena were calculated to lead to this belief. But how so, if there was really no material body, that could naturally be either visible or tangible? Let Prof. Bush answer: "The phenomena indicating a material body to the senses of the disciples must have been assumed. In other words, they were mere appearances"—"a miraculous adaptation of the visible phenomena to the outward senses of the disciples."[1] His appearing to eat was also a mere "*optical* act," etc.

The substance, then, of the whole narrative, is, according to this highly "spiritual" theory, that the proper "body" of Christ never arose from death at all; that an ethereal or "spiritual body" was evolved from it, which was, in its very nature, invisible and intangible, and then that for some reason Christ "assumed" a visibility and tangibility, and all other physical phenomena necessary to such a result, misled the disciples into the belief that his body had risen from the dead, when nothing of the kind had occurred; and thus sent them forth to preach falsehood upon a point regarded even by Prof. Bush as of the utmost import-

[1] Anastasis, pp. 154, 162.

ance! Such is the alternative placed before us, then, by these modern theorizers, either to accept the ancient faith that Christ is risen indeed, or admit that he purposely deceived and misled his disciples, and that so far as this subject is concerned, the apostles were dupes and false teachers—blind leaders of the blind!

X. But there is yet another difficulty. If Christ's body never arose, *what became of it?* The manner in which Prof. Bush struggles with this question reminds one of the effort of Prof. Webster, of Boston, to dispose of the body of Dr. Parkman, whom he had murdered. He tries acids and he tries fire—anything to get rid of the tell-tale body. So with Prof. Bush—he seems to toil and sweat under the insupportable burden of the body of Christ. *It is gone;* and if not raised, where has it gone to? It will hardly do to unite with the guard in saying "the disciples came and stole it away." *What then became of the body?*

Our answer is, it rose from death to immortality and incorruption, was seen, and heard, and handled, and fully identified for forty days, and then ascended to heaven. So the apostles believed and preached, Prof. Bush being witness, and so we believe and preach. But denying this, the Swedenborgian answer is, "the body which hung upon the cross was miraculously dissolved or resolved into its primitive elements, like that of Elijah when he was translated!"[1] No proof of this, however, is even attempted; and the reference to the case of Elijah does not furnish even an analogy. His body went to heaven, and *was not* dissolved into its primitive elements. He "went up by a whirlwind

[1] Anastasis, p. 166.

into heaven," and though fifty men searched three days for his body, they failed to find it, *not* because it had been "resolved into its primitive elements," but, as in the case of Enoch, he "was not found because God had translated him."[1]

XI. Now if Christ's resurrection consisted of the raising again to life of the identical body that hung on the cross, that fact of itself goes far towards proving that our resurrection shall also be a physical and corporeal one. Even Prof. Bush acknowledges the force of this fact. "If," says he, "he actually rose in his *material* body—in the self-same body in which he was crucified—it doubtless affords some countenance to the idea that his people are also to rise in like manner in the bodies which they laid down at death.[2] But it does far more than merely to afford "some countenance" to the true doctrine. For,

1. There is not an intimation in all the Bible that the resurrection of the saints is to be different, in its nature, from that of Christ.

2. The apostles constantly pointed to him as a specimen of proper resurrection, which they could not logically have done had they known that the resurrection of others must be essentially different from his.

He is called "the first-fruits of them that slept," and the "first-begotten from the dead," implying that the residue of the harvest shall be like this first sheaf.

3. They "preached through Jesus the resurrection from the dead," or, in other words, argued the resurrection of others from the fact that *he* had risen,—thus assuming that he was a *sample* of proper resur-

[1] 2 Kings ii. 11, 17, and Heb. xi. 3. [2] Anastasis, p. 151.

rection, and implying that all other resurrections would be essentially like his.

4. They represent Christ not only as the *pledge* of our resurrection, but also as the *pattern* after which all the saints shall arise.

> "For if we have been planted together in the likeness of his death, we shall also be in the likeness of his resurrection."—Rom. vi. 5.

"When he shall appear, we shall be LIKE HIM;"[1] for he has promised to "change our vile body, that it may be fashioned LIKE UNTO HIS GLORIOUS BODY."[2] No language could be more explicit, and no number of additional texts could strengthen the testimony of these unequivocal passages.

It is indubitably clear, therefore, from the gospel history that our Lord arose in the same material body that hung on the cross, and that he is set forth as a pledge and pattern of our resurrection; and that when this corruptible shall put on incorruption, the bodies of the saints will be fashioned like unto Christ's glorious body. They must, therefore, be material and corporeal bodies, though incorruptible, powerful, glorious and immortal. With these attributes of spirit they may well be denominated "spiritual bodies."

The following sensible observations may appropriately close this chapter:—

"Some of the pagan philosophers," says Sherlock, "who lived since the times of Christianity, and were implacable enemies to Christ and his religion, such as *Celsus*, *Porphyry* and *Julian* the Apostate, knew not what to say to those many miracles which were attri-

[1] 1 John iii. 3.   [2] 2 Cor. iii. 21.

buted to our Saviour. They could not absolutely deny that such things were done, nor deny miracles to be a divine testimony. And therefore to lessen the authority of our Saviour's miracles they set up *Pythagoras* and *Apollonius* for his rivals, and tell a great many wonderful stories of what they did, but without any credible authority. And yet, as they tell their story, it is easy to see that all is owing to fiction or magic; that they were all either forged stories, or the cheats of wicked spirits: and not to be compared to the miracles of our Saviour, either for number, or nature, or quality, much less as to the evidence and certainty of them.

But here is one answer which will serve for all. Let them show us any man, that died, and rose again from the dead, in testimony of the doctrine which he preached; and then we will grant that this will weaken the authority of our Saviour, notwithstanding his resurrection from the dead. But this they can never do. For I suppose no man will think that *Pythagoras'* concealing himself for seven years, and then pretending that he had been in the other world, and returned again to teach men philosophy, is to be compared to the certain account we have both of the death and resurrection of our Saviour, who rose again with an immortal body, not to live in this world, and to die again, but to ascend in his glorified body up to heaven, there to live forever, and never to die any more: which is so peculiar to our Saviour that no man ever yet had the impudence to pretend to it."[1]

[1] Sherlock's "Discourse concerning the Happiness of Good Men," etc. 12mo., London, 1726, pp. 333, 334.

CHAPTER IX.

TEACHINGS OF THE APOSTLES.

FROM the teachings of Christ and the proofs of his own resurrection, let us now inquire what the "chosen witnesses" of Christ's resurrection, and the anointed preachers of his gospel, taught upon the subject of the future life of the body.

I. In recording the events that took place in connection with our Lord's resurrection, St. Matthew says:

> "And the graves were opened, and many bodies of the saints which slept, arose,
>
> "And came out of the graves after his resurrection, and went unto the holy city, and appeared unto many."—Matt. xxvii. 52.

Despite the Herculean effort of an unscrupulous criticism, to break the force of this unequivocal declaration, it is clear beyond all peradventure that "many *bodies* of the saints" arose—that those bodies "came out of the *graves*," where they had "slept;" and that being material, and therefore naturally visible, they "went into the holy city [Jerusalem] and *appeared* unto many," as additional witnesses of Christ's resurrection power, and of the completeness of his victory over death and the grave. It is of no force to inquire "what became of these bodies?" Suppose we answer, we do not know; does that change the clearly-stated fact that they arose? We may suppose it improbable that having been raised from the dust of the grave by the power of Christ, and shown themselves in Jerusalem, they would *die again* and be remanded back to corruption. It seems far more likely that they accompanied Christ to heaven as trophies of his victory. But be that as it may, what God has revealed stands sure—"many BODIES of the saints arose;" and that is the chief fact with which we are at present concerned.

II. It is admitted even by those who deny a physical resurrection, that the apostles *supposed* and *preached* that the body of Christ literally rose from the dead, and ascended to heaven. "We may admit, indeed, that the disciples *supposed* that the body which they saw and handled was the veritable body of their crucified Lord, and that in their preaching the resurrection of Jesus, they had no other idea than that of the reanimation of his body of flesh. Under the influence of those carnal apprehensions which they then cherished, it was scarcely to be expected that they should come to any other conclusion."[1] So far, therefore, as this writer is concerned, no further testimony is necessary as to the teachings of the Apostles. It is conceded that they supposed and preached the literal resurrection of Christ's body from the tomb, though Prof. Bush believed they were mistaken; and could see "no reason why the measure of their intelligence on this point should be the measure of ours."[2] Which would be most likely to be mistaken, the chosen

[1] Anastasis, p. 165. [2] Ibid. p. 165.

witnesses,[1] endued as they were with power from on high, or Prof. Bush, the reader will judge.

But if they believed and preached that Christ arose bodily from the tomb, and then "preached through Jesus the resurrection from the dead," as they certainly did,[2] is not the inference a fair one, without examining their sermons and writings, that they preached, and in their writings taught the resurrection of the bodies of all men? If not, how could the raising of Christ's body, (which we are told they erroneously imagined,) be a proof that others also would arise from the dead?

III. The Greek word used by the apostles to represent this change from death to life is ἀναστασις, *anastasis;* the primary meaning of which is *the raising up again of that which is fallen.* Take the following definitions from the Greek lexicographers: "a standing on the feet again, or rising, as opposed to falling—a rising or resurrection of a dead body;"[3] "the act of raising from a sitting or reclining posture, from a seat on the ground; the act of raising up, resuscitation—the erection or re-edification of walls, &c.;[4] "standing up, rising, resurrection," &c.;[5] "a rising up, as of walls," and in the New Testament, "the resurrection of the body from death, the return of the dead body to life."[6] Robinson then refers to Heb. xi. 35,—"women received their dead raised to life," as an instance in which the term occurs (ἐξ ἀναστάσεως, *ex anastaseos*) and where it relates to the literal raising to life of two dead bodies by Enoch and Elijah.

In Herodotus, the old Greek Historian, the term is

[1] Acts i. 3 & x. 41. [2] Acts iv. 2. [3] Parkhurst.
[4] Donnegan. [5] Groves. [6] Robinson.

used in the sense of "a removal or transportation of a people from their own to another country."[1] Others define it to mean "a rising up—the removal of a people from their abodes,—the raising of a wall—resurrection of the dead;"[2] "a making to stand or rise up; awaking, a restitution, for example, of the dead—a making to rise and leave their place, removal—a sitting up again, rebuilding."[3]

With these definitions all theological writers agree. "The very word *resurrection*, and the corresponding term *ἀναστάσις*, both signify the rising or standing up of something which had fallen or laid down; and if it is a different body from their present with which men will hereafter be clothed, a word has been chosen by the inspired writers which conveys a fallacious idea. This single argument I think conclusive.[4]

"*Ἀναστάσις* signifies etymologically 'a raising or rising up.' It is used in Scripture to designate the future general raising, by the power of God, of the bodies of all men from the sleep of death."[5]

"The word *resurrection* signifies the raising again of that which is fallen."[6] "Its original and literal meaning is, to stand up, or to stand again."[7] "The literal signification of the word *resurrection* implies a repeated existence of the same thing."[8] "The word plainly implies a fresh production of what was before."[9]

[1] Cary's Lexicon of Herodotus. [2] Jones. [3] Liddell & Scott.

[4] Lectures on Theology, by Dr. John Dick, of Glasgow, Cincinnati, 1858, p. 439.

[5] Outlines of Theology, by Rev. A. A. Hodge, p. 440.

[6] Dr. Gill, p. 963. [7] Dwight's Theology, Sermon CLXV.

[8] Bishop South, Sermon XLIII.

[9] John Wesley, Works, Vol. II., p. 507.

"The identity of the body raised from death is so necessary that the very name of the resurrection doth include or suppose it."[1] "The leading idea conveyed by this word is undoubtedly that of *raising* in a *physical* sense; and if we have no reason from other sources for supposing that the resurrection implied anything but the *resurrection* of the body, this would unquestionably be the import which we should naturally assign to it when used in reference to that subject."[2]

IV. From the foregoing concessions as to the *belief* and *design* of the apostles, and these etymological definitions of the *term* employed by them in representing the change the nature of which we are investigating, let us now pass to a consideration of their *preaching*, as recorded by Luke in the Acts of the Apostles. And remember, the question is not whether or not they taught *a* resurrection from the dead, but rather *what kind* of a resurrection their teachings authorize us to look for.

1. Let us notice the *sermon of Peter* on the memorable day of Pentecost, as recorded in the second chapter of Acts:—

> "Ye men of Israel, hear these words; Jesus of Nazareth, a man approved of God among you by miracles and wonders and signs, which God did by him in the midst of you, as ye yourselves also know:
>
> "Him, being delivered by the determinate counsel and foreknowledge of God, ye have taken and by wicked hands have crucified and slain:

[1] Pearson on the Creed, American Ed., p. 568.

[2] Prof. Bush, Anastasis, p. 145,—a very remarkable concession for one who professes to believe the Scriptures, and yet denies a physical resurrection.

"Whom God hath raised up, having loosed the pains of death: because it was not possible that he should be holden of it.

"For David speaketh concerning him, I foresaw the Lord always before my face; for he is on my right hand, that I should not be moved:

"Therefore did my heart rejoice, and my tongue was glad; moreover also, my flesh shall rest in hope:

"Because thou wilt not leave my soul in hell, neither wilt thou suffer thy Holy One to see corruption.

"Thou hast made known to me the ways of life; thou shalt make me full of joy with thy countenance.

"Men and brethren, let me freely speak unto you of the patriarch David, that he is both dead and buried, and his sepulchre is with us unto this day.

"Therefore being a prophet, and knowing that God had sworn with an oath to him, that of the fruit of his loins, according to the flesh, he would raise up Christ to sit on his throne;

"He seeing this before, spake of the resurrection of Christ, that his soul was not left in hell, neither his flesh did see corruption.

"This Jesus hath God raised up, whereof we all are witnesses."

We have already quoted this remarkable argument once before, the object then being to show (what Prof. Bush admits) that Peter believed the "flesh" of Christ had risen from the dead; and we now cite it again as a sample of the preaching of Peter, while the "power from on high" was resting upon him. Referring the reader to our comments elsewhere,[1] it is sufficient to observe here that, according to the argument, when David said "my flesh shall rest in hope," he had reference to the flesh of Christ, which, by being raised from the dead, saw no corruption. But if the flesh of Christ did not rise, but was "miraculously dissolved into its primitive elements," as Prof. Bush avers,[2] what relevancy has this prophecy of David to Christ's resurrection? The "new church" theory not only

[1] Chapter VII., Section 8. [2] Anastasis, p. 166.

convicts the apostles of holding to and preaching essential error upon this vital point, but of misquoting and misapplying the Scriptures to support their false teachings! How much more reasonable the belief that the doctrine which the inspired apostles believed and preached touching a corporeal resurrection is the true doctrine of the Bible.

2. In his discourse after healing the lame man at Jerusalem, Acts iii., Peter said:

> "But ye denied the Holy One, and the Just, and desired a murderer to be granted unto you;
>
> "And killed the Prince of life, whom God hath raised from the dead; whereof we are witnesses."
>
> * * * * * * * *
>
> "Unto you first, God having raised up his Son Jesus, sent him to bless you, in turning away every one of you from his iniquities."—Vs. 14, 15, 26.

So again in chapter iv.:

> "Be it known unto you all, and to all the people of Israel, that by the name of Jesus Christ of Nazareth, whom ye crucified, whom God raised from the dead, even by him doth this man stand here before you whole."—Ver. 10.

3. After the miraculous release of the apostles from prison, Acts v., he said:

> "The God of our fathers raised up Jesus, whom ye slew and hanged on a tree:
>
> "Him hath God exalted with his right hand to be a Prince and a Saviour, for to give repentance to Israel, and forgiveness of sins."—Vs. 30, 31.

4. In his discourse at the house of Cornelius at Cesarea, Acts x., he said:

> "And we are witnesses of all things which he did, both in the land of the Jews, and in Jerusalem; whom they slew and hanged on a tree:

"Him God raised up the third day, and shewed him openly:

"Not to all the people, but unto witnesses chosen before of God, even to us, who did eat and drink with him after he rose from the dead."—Vs. 39–41.

Three things are worthy of note in these quotations: First, the language clearly implies that the same "Prince of life" who was "slain" and "hanged on a tree," was also "raised from the dead," "exalted," or "raised up" the third day. Second, the speaker lays great stress upon the fact that the apostles then present, whose heads were crowned with tongues of fire, were "chosen before of God," to be witnesses of his resurrection; and third, that the proof of the fact was, that he had been "shown openly," and they had eat and drank with him after he rose from the dead." No language could more clearly inculcate the doctrine of a corporeal resurrection.

V. *St. Luke* and *St. Stephen* seem to have believed and preached the same doctrine. Hence the former, Acts i. 3;

"To whom also he showed himself alive after his passion, by many infallible proofs, being seen of them forty days, and speaking of the things pertaining to the kingdom of God."

As Stephen was about to yield up the ghost, Acts vii., he said, "Behold, I see the heavens opened, and the Son of man standing on the right hand of God:" thus virtually asserting that Christ had risen and ascended to heaven.

VI. In all his preaching and defences before both Jews and Greeks, *St. Paul* makes the resurrection of Christ equally prominent, and is equally specific as to its corporeal character.

1. In his sermon at Antioch, Acts xiii., he thus reasoned:

> "Men *and* brethren, children of the stock of Abraham, and whosoever among you feareth God, to you is the word of this salvation sent.
>
> "For they that dwell at Jerusalem, and their rulers, because they knew him not, nor yet the voices of the prophets which which are read every Sabbath-day, they have fulfilled *them* in condemning *him.*
>
> "And though they found no cause of death *in him,* yet desired they Pilate that he should be slain.
>
> "And when they had fulfilled all that was written of him, they took *him* down from the tree, and laid *him* in a sepulchre.
>
> "But God raised him from the dead:
>
> "And he was seen many days of them which came up with him from Galilee to Jerusalem, who are his witnesses unto the people.
>
> "And we declare unto you glad tidings, how that the promise which was made unto the fathers,
>
> "God hath fulfilled the same unto us their children, in that he hath raised up Jesus again."--Acts xiii. 26–33.

Here again we have the same reference to the character of the apostles as "witnesses," and also to the physical proof—"he was seen many days, &c."

2. Of his labors in Thessalonica, Acts xvii., it is said:

> "And Paul, as his manner was, went in unto them, and three Sabbath-days reasoned with them out of the Scriptures.
>
> "Opening and alleging, that Christ must needs have suffered, and risen again from the dead; and that this Jesus, whom I preach unto you, is Christ."—Acts xvii. 2, 3.

3. At Athens, the Epicureans and Stoics said:

> "He seemeth to be a setter forth of strange gods: because he preached unto them Jesus, and the resurrection."—Acts xvii. 18.

And in his speech on the same occasion, he said:

> "He hath appointed a day, in the which he will judge the world in righteousness, by *that* man whom he hath ordained: *whereof* he hath given assurance unto all *men,* in that he hath raised him from the dead.

"And when they heard of the resurrection of the dead, some mocked: and others said, We will hear thee again of this *matter*." —Acts xvii. 31, 32.

4. In his noted defence at Jerusalem, he declared that he had seen Jesus alive on his way to Damascus, and had heard him speak, Acts xxii. 7–14; and before the Council, Acts xxii. 6; he cried out,

"Men *and* brethren, I am a Pharisee, the son of a Pharisee: of the hope and resurrection of the dead I am called in question;"

plainly implying that he was a Pharisee in his views of the resurrection; or, in other words, that he held to the literal resurrection of the body.

Before Felix, and in allusion to this declaration, he said:

"Except it be for this one voice, that I cried, standing among them, Touching the resurrection of the dead I am called in question by you this day."—Acts xxiv. 21.

5. Before Agrippa, he said:

"And now I stand, and am judged for the hope of the promise made of God unto our fathers:

"Unto which *promise* our twelve tribes, instantly serving *God* day and night, hope to come. For which hope's sake, king Agrippa, I am accused of the Jews.

"Why should it be thought a thing incredible with you, that God should raise the dead?"—Acts xxvi. 6–8.

And after relating how the Lord appeared to him in the way to Damascus, and how he had been persecuted for preaching Christ, he adds:

"Having therefore obtained help of God, I continue unto this day, witnessing both to small and great, saying none other things than those which the prophets and Moses did say should come.

"That Christ should suffer, *and* that he should be the first that should rise from the dead, and should show light unto the people, and to the Gentiles."—Ver. 32, 33.

6. In the eighteenth chapter of Acts, we have an account of Paul's first visit to Corinth; but nothing is there said of the substance of his preaching, beyond the general statement that "he reasoned in the synagogue every Sabbath, and persuaded the Jews and the Greeks." In the fifteenth chapter of his first epistle to that church, written some seven years afterwards, he tells us distinctly what was at least *one* of the prominent doctrines in his ministrations.

> "For I delivered unto you first of all that which I also received, how that Christ died for our sins according to the Scriptures:
>
> "And that he was buried, and that he rose again the third day according to the Scriptures:
>
> "And that he was seen of Cephas, then of the twelve:
>
> "After that, he was seen of above five hundred brethren at once; of whom the greater part remain unto this present, but some are fallen asleep.
>
> "After that, he was seen of James; then of all the apostles.
>
> "And last of all he was seen of me also, as of one born out of due time."—1 Cor. xv. 3–8.

Here we have not only the fact that the resurrection of Christ was the doctrine taught at Corinth also, "first of all," but we again have a summary of the *evidence* by which that doctrine was supported—the various physical manifestations of Christ to himself and others after he had risen from the dead.

These numerous passages, we think, fully establish these three points:

(1.) That in the apostolic ministry, the *resurrection of Christ* was always put in the fore-ground, as of vital importance, and the very pivot upon which the whole gospel turned. (2.) That they always spoke of it in such a manner as to carry the idea that his *body* had actually risen from death; and (3.) That by thus preaching his resurrection, and then "preaching through Jesus the resurrection from the dead," they virtually preached that in the general resurrection the bodies of all men would arise from their graves, as the body of Jesus the "first-fruits" had risen.

It is not strange, therefore, that Prof. Bush felt obliged to concede that the apostles both believed and preached that his material body actually arose from the tomb; and that consequently the "new church" theory is "another gospel," than that preached by the apostles.

VII. In harmony with the conceded belief and preaching of the apostles, is their *written* teachings from the first of Romans to the last of Revelation.

> "Concerning his Son Jesus Christ our Lord, which was made of the seed of David according to the flesh;
>
> "And declared to be the Son of God with power, according to the Spirit of holiness, by the resurrection from the dead."—Rom. i. 3, 4.

Here note, it is "the resurrection *from the dead*," upon which the apostle insists, and which he sets forth as the proof that Christ is "the Son of God." Again,

> "Know ye not, that so many of us as were baptized into Jesus Christ were baptized into his death?
>
> "Therefore we are buried with him by baptism into death: that like as Christ was raised up from the dead by the glory of the Father, even so we also should walk in newness of life.
>
> "For if we have been planted together in the likeness of his death, we shall be also in the likeness of his resurrection:
>
> "Knowing this, that our old man is crucified with him, that the body of sin might be destroyed, that henceforth we should not serve sin.
>
> "For he that is dead is free from sin.
>
> "Now if we be dead with Christ, we believe that we shall also live with him:

"Knowing that Christ being raised from the dead dieth no more: death hath no more dominion over him.

"For in that he died, he died unto sin once: but in that he liveth, he liveth unto God."—Rom. vi. 3–10.

It will scrcely be denied that in this passage the apostle alludes to baptism as representing the believer's faith in the death and resurrection of Christ.[1] But if Christ's *body* never arose, what pertinency is there in these allusions? Observe, also, the expression, "Christ was raised up *from the dead*,"—"being raised *from the dead*,"—"he died," "he liveth," etc.; all of which clearly teach the literal resurrection of his body.

"But if the Spirit of him that raised up Jesus from the dead dwell in you, he that raised up Christ from the dead shall also quicken your mortal bodies by his Spirit that dwelleth in you. . .

"And not only they, but ourselves also, which have the first-fruits of the Spirit, even we ourselves groan within ourselves, waiting for the adoption, to wit, the redemption of our body."—Rom. viii. 11, 23.

In the first of these passages the subjects of quick-

[1] See Wesley's Notes, and Clarke, Macknight, and Barnes on the passage. Of the Relation of Baptism to the Doctrine of the Resurrection, Bishop Hobart thus speaks:

"Applying the word 'baptized' literally to the Christian sacrament of baptism, we shall arrive at the true meaning of the passage. 'Baptized for the dead' refers to those who have secured Christian baptism in testimony of the doctrine of the resurrection of the dead.

"But how, it may be asked, was this testimony given in baptism? It was denoted in the rite itself; it was given in the profession then made.

"The rite itself holds forth the doctrine of the resurrection. 'Buried with him,' says the apostle, 'by baptism into death: that like as Christ was raised from the dead by the glory of the Father, even so we also should walk in newness of life. For if we have been planted in the likeness of his death, we shall be also in the likeness of his resurrection.' . . . Thus, then, they who were baptized, were 'baptized for the resurrection of the dead.' They received a rite which most forcibly denoted this fundamental truth."—*Hobart's Works, vol. ii. pp.* 368, 369.

14

ening or resurrection are our "mortal bodies,"[1] and in the other the adoption for which our spirits wait is the redemption of the body from the dominion of the grave—both evidently inculcating the doctrine of a corporeal resurrection.

4. In his first epistle to the Corinthians, St. Paul furnishes us with the most logical and sublime argument for the resurrection of the dead, that was ever constructed. Upon that subject the fifteenth chapter of this epistle stands amid the chapters of the New Testament even, like the sun in the midst of the heavens.

As was his custom in preaching, so in this epistle, the first point made is to assert the resurrection of Christ in the most explicit and emphatic manner.

> "For I delivered unto you first of all, that which I also received, how that Christ died for our sins according to the scriptures;
>
> "And that he was buried, and that he rose again the third day according to the scriptures:
>
> "And that he was seen of Cephas, then of the twelve:
>
> "After that, he was seen of above five hundred brethren at once; of whom the greater part remain unto this present, but some are fallen asleep.
>
> "After that he was seen of James; then of all the apostles.
>
> "And last of all he was seen of me also, as of one born out of due time."—1 Cor. xv. 3–8.

[1] We follow *Benson* and *Clarke,* rather than *Macknight, Wesley,* etc., as to the true import of this text. Benson's paraphrase of the passage is as follows:

"*If the Spirit of him that raised up Jesus*—our great covenant head—*from the dead, dwell in you; he*—God the Father—*that raised up Christ from the dead*—the first-fruits of them that slept—*shall also quicken your mortal bodies*—though corrupted and consumed in the grave—*by his Spirit*—or on account of his Spirit—*which dwelleth in you*—and now communicates divine life to your souls, and creates them anew.'

In his letter to the Galatians he tells them that he received this gospel from Christ himself:—

> "But I certify you, brethren, that the gospel which was preached of me was not after man.
>
> "For I neither received it of man, neither was I taught it, but by the revelation of Jesus Christ."—Gal. i. 11, 12.

And not only does he claim to be divinely taught in what he was about to write, but the recital of the instance, in which Christ was seen after his resurrection, shows conclusively that he believed that the same body that was "buried," "rose again the third day," and was visible and tangible because it was the same body that hung upon the cross of Calvary.

This first point being asserted and proved, he proceeds to argue the resurrection of all men from the resurrection of Christ.

> "Now if Christ be preached that he rose from the dead, how say some among you that there is no resurrection of the dead?
>
> "But if there be no resurrection of the dead, then is Christ not risen;
>
> *　*　*　*　*　*　*
>
> "But now is Christ risen from the dead, and become the first-fruits of them that slept.
>
> "For since by man came death, by man came also the resurrection of the dead.
>
> "For as in Adam all die, even so in Christ shall all be made alive.
>
> "But every man in his own order: Christ the first-fruits; afterwards they that are Christ's at his coming."—1 Cor. xv. 12–23.

Here the relation of Christ to the dead is put in contrast with that of Adam—as death came upon all by Adam's sin, so all shall have a resurrection by virtue of the atonement and resurrection of Christ, who sustains the same relation to the general resurrection, as "the first-begotten from the dead," that the first-fruits sustain to the general harvest. And inasmuch as he taught the literal resurrection of the body of Christ, as a sample and pledge, and argued the resurrection of all men therefrom, it is undeniable that the resurrection for which he was contending, was that of the *bodies* of men from the dominion of death and the grave.

Having proved the resurrection of Christ, and from that the resurrection of all men, the next step is to vindicate this doctrine by answering objections :—

> "But some man will say, How are the dead raised up? and with what body do they come?
>
> "Thou fool, that which thou sowest is not quickened except it die:
>
> "And that which thou sowest, thou sowest not that body that shall be, but bare grain; it may chance of wheat, or of some other grain:
>
> "But God giveth it a body as it hath pleased him, and to every seed his own body."—Verses 35–38.

The import of this passage depends upon the nature of the objection it was designed to answer. That objection is two-fold,—"how are the dead raised up;" that is, how can life be evolved from death?" and "with what body do they come?" The first of these objections is effectually answered by the appeal to the well-known fact in nature, that the kernel of grain or nut, or whatever seed it may be from which the new plant is to come, usually dies, and goes to decay, in the process of reproduction; so that nature herself might teach the caviler that the fact of the *death* of the body furnished no ground for doubting its future life. "That which thou sowest is not quickened except it die."

Then follows an answer to the second question—"with what body do they come?" Continuing the illustration drawn from the sprouting of a kernel of wheat, and the subsequent development of the new grain, it is said:

"And that which thou sowest, thou sowest not that body that shall be, but bare grain, it may chance of wheat, or of some other grain:

"But God giveth it a body as hath pleased him, and to every seed his own body."—Ver. 37, 38.

Whatever may be the import of this passage, as bearing upon the question of the *amount* or *proportion* of the old body that enters into the new at the resurrection—whether the whole of it, or only an inconsiderable germ—one thing is certain, and that is, that in either case the apostle is clearly speaking of a physical resurrection; for to no other can his illustration be in any respect applicable. Whether much or little, if the resurrection is like the germination and growth of grain in any respect, the new body must have at least a *portion* of the matter contained in the old; or, in other words, there must be, to a certain extent, a *material identity*.

Leaving what relates to the *nature* of the resurrection body for consideration in a future chapter, observe in the next place how clearly the apostle teaches, as he proceeds, that the physical identity implied in the illustration extends to the whole body laid in the grave; that is, that the body "raised," and the body "sown," are one and the same:—

"It is sown in corruption, it is raised in incorruption.

"It is sown in dishonor, it is raised in glory: it is sown in weakness, it is raised in power:

"It is sown a natural body, it is raised a spiritual body."—Ver. 42–44.

In all these contrasts the physical identity is invariably maintained; "IT is sown—IT is raised, etc."

"This corruptible must put on incorruption, and this mortal put on immortality."

Observe, it is not another body, constructed of common elements, or a mere germ of the old body that is to be the subject of this change, but "THIS CORRUPTIBLE" and "THIS MORTAL" is to "PUT ON" incorruption and immortality.

The promised translation of the saints who are alive when Christ shall come again, furnishes a strong analogical argument for a corporeal resurrection:—

"Behold, I shew you a mystery: We shall not all sleep, but we shall all be changed,

"In a moment, in the twinkling of an eye, at the last trump: for the trumpet shall sound, and the dead shall be raised incorruptible, and we shall be changed.

"For this corruptible must put on incorruption, and this mortal must put on immortality."—Verses 51–53.

Here the closing sentence, "for this corruptible, etc.," applies as well to those who do not "sleep," that is, are yet alive, as to the dead. They are *all* to put on incorruption and immortality.

In his first epistle to the Thessalonians the apostle gives us still further light upon the subject:—

"For this we say unto you by the word of the Lord, that we which are alive and remain unto the coming of the Lord shall not prevent[1] them which are asleep.

[1] This term "prevent" originally signified to *assist*, or *help on*, and is here used in the sense of *go before*, *anticipate* or *outstrip*,—shall not go before or outstrip the dead, whose bodies are in the graves.

"For the Lord himself shall descend from heaven with a shout, with the voice of the archangel, and with the trump of God; and the dead in Christ shall rise first:

"Then we which are alive and remain shall be caught up together with them in the clouds, to meet the Lord in the air: and so shall we ever be with the Lord."—1 Thess. iv. 15–17.

It is plain from these scriptures that the bodies of the saints who live when Christ re-appears, will be changed, made incorruptible and immortal, and then translated to heaven with the risen dead, to be forever with the Lord. But what an anomaly will their bodies be in heaven, if the bodies of their brethren who sleep in Jesus are not raised and made glorious and immortal!

To say nothing, therefore, for the present, upon the numerous other interesting points discussed in this chapter, nothing can be more certain than that its entire scope and phraseology, as well as its illustrations and allusions, point unmistakably to a resurrection of the identical body laid in the grave at death.

5. The same idea is conveyed by the apostle, Phil. iii. 21: "Who shall change our vile body," etc. It is not a new body, or a spiritual or ethereal body, which is to be the subject of the change from corruption to incorruption, but "OUR VILE BODY." To what body can this language apply if not to the corruptible body in which we have dwelt during our mortal life-time?

6. The manner in which the Scriptures of both Testaments point to the *places* where the bodies of the dead repose, strongly implies that in the reconstruction the elements of which the new body shall be composed, will be gathered from the places where the ashes of the dead slumber under the power of death. Take

the following as examples: "God will redeem my soul from the power of *the grave*." Ps. xlix. 15. "Thy dead men shall live, together with my dead body shall they arise. Awake and sing, *ye that dwell in dust:* for thy dew is as the dew of herbs, and *the earth shall cast out* the dead;" Isa. xxvi. 19. "And many of them *that slept in the dust of the earth* shall awake," etc.; Dan. xii. 2. "I will ransom them from *the power of the* grave." Hosea xiii. 14. "O *grave*, where is *thy victory?*" 1 Cor. xv. 55. "The hour is coming when all that are *in the graves* shall hear his voice, and shall come forth;" John v. 28. "And the sea gave up the dead which were in it;" Rev. xx. 13.

Now if it were true that the resurrection takes place at death, and consisted of the evolving of an ethereal body from the physical at that moment, how obviously misleading would all these Scriptures be, which point to the "graves," "dust," "sea," etc., as the places from which the new bodies shall emerge in the resurrection. And so upon the hypothesis that the new body shall be composed of common elements gathered anywhere, without reference to the substance of the former body —such allusions to "the graves," the "dust of the earth," etc., would be both superfluous and deceptive.[1] Upon no hypothesis whatever can they be fully justified, except upon that which involves the raising again to life of the same body laid in the grave.

These passages must suffice under this head, as we

[1] If nothing is derived from the grave, or from the body once laid there, for what possible reason does the Bible constantly speak of a resurrection from the grave? It could serve no purpose but to mislead the reader. Nor can any reason be alleged for the use of such language.—*Hitchcock's Religious Lectures*, p. 12.

wish to avoid repetition, and shall have occasion to cite others in discussing other branches of the subject in subsequent chapters. But they are quite sufficient to show, not only that the apostles believed (as Prof. Bush admits they did) that Christ's body literally rose from death, but that they *preached* a physical resurrection, and no other; and described that transition by the use of a term which necessarily implies the raising up again to life of the same body laid in the grave at death.

We have now given the substance of the *direct* testimony bearing upon the question of the *nature* of the resurrection. We have shown that the Jews, both before and at the time of our Lord's ministry, believed in a physical resurrection and no other—that the early Christians held to the same faith with scarcely an exception—that such has been the current creed of the Christian Church for eighteen centuries, with but here and there an inconsiderable exception—that the Old Testament Scriptures fully justify the belief of the Jews, founded upon the writings of Moses and the prophets, that the bodies of men should rise again—that Jesus of Nazareth, the Great Teacher, taught the same doctrine, and demonstrated it by his own resurrection,—and that the apostles of Christ, endowed with power from on high, and preaching and writing as they were moved by the Holy Ghost, both preached and wrote that the corruptible and mortal bodies of men, which are cast off at death, and dissolved in the grave, shall be raised up again by the power of God, be made incorruptible, immortal, powerful and glorious, like unto Christ's glorious body; and, re-inhabited by their former souls, shall be their undecaying and indestructible abodes forever.

This we believe to be the plain and obvious teaching of the Sacred Writings. And not one in ten thousand into whose hands the inspired volume is placed, without any bias or intimation to the contrary, would ever dream of any other resurrection. In this faith the learned and devout of all ages, with very few exceptions, have lived and died; and if, (even the opponents of this doctrine being judges,) it was the faith of the apostles, and early martyrs, it behooves the modern church, and especially the ministry of our times to see to it that this glorious doctrine be not obscured, or perverted, or lost in the mazes of "philosophy," falsely so called. Let us rather contend earnestly for the faith once delivered to the saints.

CHAPTER X.

VARIOUS THEORIES CONSIDERED—DOES THE RESURRECTION TAKE PLACE AT CONVERSION?

BEFORE the close of the first century, there were those even among the professed Christian believers who denied the doctrine of the resurrection as generally held by the church, and explained it as having no reference to the reconstruction of the material body. Such were the *Gnostics*. "Their belief that matter is eternal, and the source of all evil, prevented them from admitting the doctrine of the future resurrection of the body."[1] Speaking of a certain false teacher at Corinth, whose heresies led to the writing of St. Paul's first epistle to that church, Macknight says: "Because the learned Greeks regarded the body as the prison of the soul, and expected to be delivered from it in a future state, and called the hope of the resurrection of the flesh, the hope of worms;—a filthy and abominable thing—which God neither will nor can do, (Celsus ap. Origen, lib. v. p. 240;) and because they ridiculed the doctrine of the resurrection of the body, Acts xvii. 32, this new teacher, to render the gospel acceptable to them, flatly denied it to be a doctrine of the gospel, and affirmed that the resurrection of the

[1] Mosheim's Eccl. Hist. vol. i, p. 90.

body was neither desirable nor possible; and argued that the only resurrection promised by Christ, was the resurrection of the soul from ignorance and error, etc."[1] On this ground they affirmed that the resurrection was past, and thereby overthrew the faith of some.[2]

The same view is entertained by some in our own time.[3] Because the Scriptures speak of the unrenewed as in a state of spiritual death, and of their recovery therefrom as a resurrection, they erroneously argue that there is *no other* resurrection. It may therefore be worth the space to devote a brief chapter to this very singular theory.

I. It is admitted that there is such a thing as moral or spiritual death, and a spiritual resurrection. Such was the import of Ezekiel's vision of the valley of dry bones, and their resurrection to life.[4] The whole house of Israel were in a state of apostacy from God, and void of spiritual life; and the prophet was to prophesy or preach to them till they arose from the dead, or, were recovered from their backsliding, and restored to spiritual life and the divine favor.

And so in the New Testament—all men are represented as by nature in a state of spiritual death—"dead in trespasses and sins."[1] Hence the exhortation, Awake

[1] Preface to 1 Corinthians, Sec. 4. [2] 2 Tim. ii. 18.

[3] We fear this is the view of a laxge portion of the Friends or Quakers. Barclay wholly ignores the subject in his Apology, but Dr. Cox avers in his work entitled "*Quakerism not Christianity,*" that the Friends do not believe in the resurrection of the body. See page 137, and onward. Many Unitarians and Universalists if not most of them utterly deny the resurrection of the body.

[4] Ezekiel, xxxviith chapter. [5] Eph. ii. 1.

thou that sleepest, and arise from the dead, and Christ shall give thee light."[1] To this species of resurrection our Lord refers, when he says, "The hour is coming and now is, when the dead shall hear the voice of the Son of God; and they that hear shall live."[2] Again, "and you, being dead in your sins—hath he quickened together with him."[3] That there is, therefore, such a thing as a spiritual resurrection, or, in other words, that the quickening of the soul of man by the Holy Spirit is described in the Scriptures under the figure of a resurrection, is obvious, and is not denied by the advocates of a physical resurrection.

II. But while the Scriptures speak of the renewal of the soul as a resurrection, they also speak of *another* resurrection, namely, that of the body. How, for instance, could John v. 28, 29, be understood of the conversion of souls?

> "The hour is coming, in the which all that are in the graves shall hear his voice,
>
> "And shall come forth; they that have done good, unto the resurrection of life; and they that have done evil, unto the resurrection of damnation."

In the first place, our Lord had just spoken of conversion from sin as a resurrection.

> "The hour is coming, and now is, when the dead shall hear the voice of the Son of God: and they that hear shall live."

This resurrection was then transpiring, as the people heard, and believed on the only begotten Son of God. And if the 28th and 29th verses mean precisely the same thing, it is an instance of flagrant tautology, to say the least. In the next place, if the resurrections

[1] Eph. v. 14. [2] John v. 27. [3] Col. ii. 13.

spoken of are the translation of souls from the kingdom of darkness, into that of Christ in this world, how is it that "they that have done good," or the righteous, have *such* a resurrection? or in other words are converted? And still worse, how is it that "they that have done evil"—the wicked—are converted "to damnation?"

III. Take the resurrection of Christ, and the fact that throughout the New Testament it is made both the proof and the pattern of our resurrection—the first-fruits of the coming harvest. Surely no one will pretend to say that Christ, the spotless Lamb of God, was ever depraved or sinful, or was ever pardoned or regenerated. He, therefore, never experienced a spiritual renewal; and cannot be an example for us, or a proof of our future spiritual resurrection. To attempt so to interpret all that is said about Christ's resurrection, and of ours as a consequence, would be to wrest the Scriptures from their most obvious meaning, and turn the whole New Testament into a myth or an allegory. Even Origen, with all his mysticism, never indulged in so idle a dream.

IV. If anything more is necessary to convince the reader that the resurrection taught in the Scriptures is not an intellectual or moral phenomenon; but pertains to the physical man, let him turn to the fifteenth chapter of First Corinthians, and attempt to explain it upon the former hypothesis. Mark how the apostle bases his whole argument upon the resurrection of Christ, so clearly described in the gospels as being the raising of his body from the tomb. If a spiritual change only is here spoken of as a resurrection, what does St. Paul mean by the different kinds of "flesh" —by something "sown"—by the "body," etc., of which he speaks? Any man who can read that chapter, and understand it to relate to the conversion of men from sin to righteousness, rather than to the raising up of the bodies of men, is too far gone in mysticism to be taught through the medium of human language; or to be influenced by any arguments addressed to the human understanding.

V. Take, also, Phil. iii. 21: "Who shall change our *vile body*," etc., and how absurd to aver that by "vile *body*" the apostle means the depraved *soul*, and that *this* is to be fashioned like unto Christ's glorious body! And still worse, that this event, (viz., conversion,) which had long before taken place with the apostle and those to whom he wrote, was, nevertheless, an object of future hope and desire! We must handle the word of God very "deceitfully"[1] indeed, to make it teach any such doctrine.

VI. Equally impossible is it to reconcile the various allusions to the *places* from which the dead are to come, cited in a previous chapter, with the idea of a merely spiritual resurrection. To do so, the "dust of the earth," the "graves," the "sea," etc., must be made to represent our depraved propensities, or our mortal bodies, out of which we are to be raised by conversion—a license of exegesis or stretch of fancy in which no sober and candid expositor will ever indulge.

VII. Finally, all figures used to represent or illustrate spiritual things, are based upon material phenomena.

[1] See 2 Cor. ii. 17, and iv. 2.

Hence the very idea and figure of a spiritual resurrection, is based upon and presupposes a literal resurrection of the body. The fact, therefore, that the Scriptures describe the renewing of the soul of man by the Spirit of God as a resurrection from death, is in itself a proof of a literal resurrection. Had there never been a literal fall of a human body, we had never read of the "fall" of Adam or of Judas. Had no literal birth ever occurred, we should never have read of the new birth. And so of the resurrection; if there was no such thing as a physical resurrection, Ezekiel would never have seen his wonderful vision in the valley, and we should never have read in the New Testament of a spiritual resurrection. The latter necessarily presupposes the former, and is built upon it; and to mistake the spiritual for the physical resurrection, is like mistaking the spire of a cathedral for its corner-stone.

So utterly at variance with the Scriptures, therefore, and with every principle of interpretation, is this "spiritual" idea of the resurrection, that we dismiss it with these brief remarks, as unworthy of further argument.

CHAPTER XI.

THEORIES CONSIDERED—DOES THE RESURRECTION TAKE PLACE AT THE DEATH OF THE BODY?

A SECOND theory, intended, like that of the Gnostics, to obviate the supposed philosophical difficulties of a physical resurrection, is that the resurrection takes place *at the death of the body*, and is simply the departure of the soul, or the evolving of an ethereal body from the corporeal, in the act of dying. This theory was first formally promulgated by Emanuel Swedenborg, a Swedish baron, about the middle of the last century; and has been re-produced by Prof. Bush and others of our own times. "Death, in the Word," says Swedenborg, "signifies resurrection and continued life."[1]

"By resuscitation is meant the drawing forth of the spirit from the body, and its introduction into the spirit world, which is commonly called resurrection."[2]

That he might not be in error as to the process, he professed to have died, and returned to life again. "How resuscitation [or the resurrection] is effected, has not only been told me, but also shown by living experience. The experiment itself was made with me, in order that I might fully know how it is done."[3]

[1] Heaven and Hell, p. 245, Amer. Ed. [2] Ibid. p. 246. [3] Ibid.

Prof. Bush sets forth and defends the same doctrine in his elaborate work on the resurrection. "The resurrection body," says he, "is that part of our present being to which the *essential life* of man pertains. We may not be able to see it, to handle it, to analyze it, to describe it. But we know that it exists, because we know that we ourselves exist. It constitutes the inner essential vitality of our present bodies, and it lives again in another state, *because it never dies.* It is immortal in its own nature, and it is called a *body*—a spiritual body—because the poverty of human language, or perhaps the weakness of the human mind, forbids the adoption of any more fitting term by which to express it. It is, however, a body which has nothing to do with the gross material particles which enter into the composition of our present earthly tenements."[1] "The true doctrine of the resurrection, is the doctrine of the development of a spiritual body at death, from the bodies we now inhabit."[2] Of the nature of this "spiritual body," he says,—"By *spiritual* in this connection, we mean refined, subtle, ethereal, sublimate. By the development of a spiritual body, we mean the disengagement—the extrication—of that physical part of our nature with which vital and animal functions are, in the present life, intimately connected, and which differs from the pure spirit, the intellectual principle, as the Greek *ψύχη* or *sensitive principle*, differs from *νοῦς*, the *self-conscious intelligence.* It is *tertium quid*—an intermediate something between the cogitative faculty and the gross body. It is indeed, invisible; but so are many of the mightiest agents in

[1] Anastasis, p. 70. [2] Ibid. p. 84.

nature, and so are many of the noblest entities in the ranks of created beings."[1]

"The true resurrection takes place at the death of every individual believer, when he emerges from a material into a spiritual body."[2]

The same doctrine is still more beautifully though less clearly inculcated by another modern writer:—

"Man's resurrection is the putting forth at death of a new existence, just as the decaying seed puts forth the blade. Its decay is necessary in order to release the life and the beauty that were imprisoned within its foldings. . . . The spiritual body is included elementally in our present mode of existence, with its perceptive powers all ready for the enlargement. The soul is not a metaphysical nothing, but a heavenly substance and organism, fold within fold. The material falls off, and the spiritual stands forth and fronts the objects and breathes the ethers of immortality. The future is wrapped up within us, and waiting to be unrolled. Death will not transfer us; it will only remove a hindrance and a vail. We receive with our present being the germ of all we are to become hereafter."[3]

These views will readily be identified as nothing more nor less than the Scriptural doctrine of the soul's separation from the body at the hour of death, with the hypothesis of its semi-materiality, and that it constitutes a spiritual body. And *this* we are asked to

[1] Anastasis, p. 78. [2] Ibid. p. 190.

[3] Foregleams of Immortality, by Edmund H. Sears, p. 85. Published by the American Unitarian Association, 1858.

believe is "the resurrection of the dead," taught in the Scriptures.[1]

The process by which this conclusion is reached, is, first to determine from "philosophy," falsely so called, what kind of a resurrection is *possible*, and then to extort from the Scriptures a meaning in accordance with the predetermined hypothesis. Hence Prof. Bush begins his chapter on "the true Body of the Resurrection," by saying, "We trust it may not be forgotten that we are prosecuting exclusively the *rational* argument in respect to the resurrection. The conclusions derived from the Scriptural view of the subject will be matter of subsequent consideration. At present we take philosophy for our guide, just as a geologist takes the earth for his theme, and from its own phenomena endeavors to ascertain its past and future history." Who cannot see that by this process, "reason," so called, becomes the instructor, and the Bible the pupil, sitting at the feet of a crude and half-instructed philosophy? It is well, however, that this is conceded by the votaries of the "New Church" theory. It is a virtual admission that their interpretations of Scripture are a constant effort to bend them to a predetermined theory, or, in other words, that their theory is not in accordance with the legitimate and obvious import of the Sacred Writings.

It is not strange, therefore, that very little effort is made to sustain this theory by affirmative proofs from the Bible. Very few scriptures are cited for that purpose. The great effort is to show that the vast number of passages in both testaments which seem and are

[1] Anastasis, pp. 67, 68.

usually understood to teach a corporeal resurrection, are capable of another construction, in harmony with the Swedenborgian idea.

1. The following passages are urged as directly favoring this doctrine:—

> "Jesus saith unto her, Thy brother shall rise again.
>
> "Martha saith unto him, I know that he shall rise again in the resurrection at the last day.
>
> "Jesus said unto her, I am the resurrection, and the life: he that believeth in me, though he were dead, yet shall he live."
>
> "And whosoever liveth and believeth in me shall never die. Believest thou this?"—John xi. 23–25.

The argument based upon this passage is that our Lord desired to lead Martha off from her gross conceptions of the resurrection as a future and distant event, to the more spiritual idea that it takes place at death; and that the expression, "I am the resurrection, etc.," is equivalent to a declaration that the resurrection is a present and not a future event. Let us examine the passage, then, through the medium of this hypothesis.

(1.) What did Jesus mean by the statement, "Thy brother shall rise again?" Upon this theory he had already risen when he died four days before. Is it not obvious that he spoke of the raising up of his body to life? (2.) Martha responds, "I know that he shall rise again in the resurrection at the last day." (3.) Christ replies, "I am the resurrection and the life," as if he had said, the power that shall raise all the dead at the last day, is present with you now, and can raise your brother now as well as then; and then he proceeded to fulfil the promise, ("thy brother shall rise again,") by crying, "*Lazarus, come forth,*" and raising his half putrid body from the tomb. How utterly incongruous and misleading was all this, if our Lord designed to teach the Swedenborgian theory of the resurrection; to teach and promise a *spiritual* resurrection, and illustrate the doctrine and fulfil the promise by raising the gross and half decayed *body* to life.

2. A second affirmative proof-text is the following:

> "Now that the dead are raised, even Moses showed at the bush, when he calleth the Lord the God of Abraham, and the God of Isaac, and the God of Jacob.
>
> "For he is not a God of the dead, but of the living: for all live unto him."—Luke xx. 37, 38.

Here, it is said, we are plainly taught that Abraham, Isaac and Jacob had experienced their resurrection; otherwise how could they be cited as examples and proofs of a resurrection? And if they were examples of resurrection while their bodies were still in the grave, then the resurrection has no reference to the body; and must be an event transpiring at death. This, in our view, is the most plausible argument founded upon the Scriptures that we have anywhere met with; and yet it is altogether fallacious.

We have already considered this passage at length in another chapter;[1] but we may add in this connection,

(1.) That the Sadducees, with whom our Lord was arguing, not only denied the resurrection of the body, but also the existence of souls distinct from the body. Having answered their question, it was proper that he should carry the argument further, and endeavor to convince them from their acknowledged oracles, that

[1] See page 77.

they were equally in error as to the future life of the souls of men. Hence the quotation to prove that Abraham, Isaac and Jacob were still alive, in another state, long after their natural death. "Our Lord combats and confutes another opinion of the Sadducees," says Dr. Clarke, "viz., *that there is neither angel nor spirit;* by showing that the soul is not only immortal, but lives *with God,* even while the body is detained in the dust of the earth, etc."

(2.) It is not denied that the word *ἀναστάσις*—*anastasis*—usually rendered resurrection—is sometimes used comprehensively in the sense of a general future existence; and in this sense it is no doubt used here, or rather in the parallel passage, Matt. xxii. 31. Taken in this sense, the transition from the specific subject of the resurrection of the body, to the more general subject of a future life, is both easy and natural. "But as touching the *anastasis*—the future state—have ye not read?" etc.

(3.) That the argument was *understood* by the Sadducees to reach much further than the question of the future life of the body, is very evident. They were "put to silence" upon the whole subject of their heresy, and "durst not ask him any questions at all."

From all this it is most obvious that, although at first view, the passage might seem more than any other in the Scriptures to favor the idea of a death-bed resurrection, it affords no real support to that hypothesis.

The expression in the same connection that in the resurrection the saints shall be "equal unto the angels," is claimed as favoring the new theory. Matthew reports the remark thus—"For in the resurrection they neither marry nor are given in marriage, but are as the angels of God in heaven;" and Luke—"but are as the angels," etc. How evident that the resemblance affirmed of the angels is not in their being without material bodies, but solely in their *not marrying* or being given in marriage. In this respect alone they are "as" or "equal unto the angels."

3. The following is also cited as favouring the theory under consideration:

> "For we know that, if our earthly house of this tabernacle were dissolved, we have a building of God, a house not made with hands, eternal in the heavens.
>
> "For in this we groan, earnestly desiring to be clothed upon with our house which is from heaven:
>
> "If so be that being clothed we shall not be found naked.
>
> "For we that are in this tabernacle do groan, being burdened: not for that we would be unclothed, but clothed upon, that mortality might be swallowed up of life."—2 Cor. v. 1–4.

The argument is that the apostle expected to occupy an ethereal body immediately upon the death of his earthly house; or, in other words, to experience his resurrection at the moment of death. But we are told that the spiritual body is included elementally in our present body, and is evolved from, or drawn out of it at death. How, then, is it "our house" "which is from heaven?" and "eternal in the heavens?" And if, as the new theory teaches, the soul is not disrobed of its spiritual vehicle in the act of dying, but merely glides out of the material body, still enwrapped in its immortal vestments, how is it "clothed upon" with a "building of God?"

The truth is that the passage has no reference to the resurrection in any sense, unless it be in the very general one of a future life. It is merely a contrast between our present abode on earth—a "tabernacle," in which we tarry for a day, and our everlasting home in heaven. The paraphrase of Dr. Macknight has hit its trne meaning precisely. "*We know that our earthly house, which is only a tent,* a temporary habitation, *is destroyed, we* shall *have a building* from God, a house not made, like our present houses, *with* the *hands* of men; nor of a temporary duration, but *eternal,* and *in the heavens,* or heavenly country. *But* though we are sure of a building from God, *yet,* while in this tent, this earthly house, *we groan,* as *earnestly desiring to go permanently into our habitation, which is* the *heavenly* country promised to Abraham, and to his spiritual seed. *And surely, if we go into it, we shall not be destitute* of a habitation, when this earthly is destroyed, as the wicked undoubtedly shall be. *But, yet,* as I said before, (Ver. 2,) *we who are in this tent groan, being burdened; not because we desire to go out, but to go permanently into* our heavenly habitation, *that sin,* and misery, and weakness, and *whatever* in this world *accompanies mortality, may be swallowed up in* an eternal *life* of happiness."[1]

Because the apostle elsewhere speaks of the body as a tabernacle, it has been erroneously supposed that by the "earthly house of this tabernacle," in this passage, he must have meant his mortal body, and by the "building of God," his celestial body; whereas, the contrast is evidently between the earth, our present temporary abode, and the everlasting city of our God in the heavenly country. The passage yields no sup-

[1] See Literal Translation of the Epistles, etc.

port, therefore, to the idea that the resurrection takes place at the death of the body.

From these brief notices of proof-texts urged by the New Church theologians, we shall now pass to state somewhat at length the *objections* to which their theory is liable.

I. *It is confessedly a* THEOLOGICAL NOVELTY.

Prof. Bush admits at the outset, that the doctrine of a physical resurrection has been "the current creed of the church, for the space of eighteen centuries."[1] If, therefore, the presumption is, that the apostles and early martyrs and confessors, and the church of Christ in all subsequent ages, have correctly understood the sacred oracles upon the great subject of the life to come, to the same extent does the presumption exist that this avowedly new theory is erroneous.

So thorough and candid have been the research into the meaning of the Bible, that it has long since come to be admitted that its true meaning is understood, at least upon all the great and fundamental doctrines; and consequently it has passed into an axiom among all candid and competent students of the Scriptures, that "whatsoever is *new* in theology is *false*." So far, therefore, as the voice of the church of Christ in all ages is concerned, the Swedenborgian theory is a novelty, having no foundation in the word of God.

II. *It is virtually conceded that upon their face, the Scriptures teach the doctrine of a literal resurrection.*

To find any other doctrine in the Bible, the reader's mind must pass through a process of supernatural illumination, by which he can get at the "internal sense"

[1] Preface to Anastasis, p. 5.

of the Scriptures—a sense that no one else can discover, and one by which "body" means "spirit," and spirit body, light darkness, and darkness light. Put the Bible into the hands of ten thousand sane men, who have no theory upon the subject, and let them read it carefully from beginning to end, either in English or in Greek, and Hebrew, with a view to ascertaining what it teaches touching the resurrection, and not one of the ten thousand would ever think of the notion of Prof. Bush and the "New Church." Indeed, no intelligent Swedenborgian will ever *claim* that his doctrine is the obvious doctrine of the Bible. Unless, therefore, the Scriptures are adapted to mislead the masses and instruct a chosen few only, their obvious teaching is the real truth; and the new, and occult, and hard to be understood, is erroneous.

III. *This theory confounds death* and the *resurrection as one and the same event; whereas the Scriptures always speak of them as distinct events.*

It will be seen by the passages cited from Swedenborg and others at the commencement of this chapter, that in their view the resurrection not only takes place at death, but is identical with it—is the going forth of the spirit from the body, which we call death. Now, if this be the true doctrine, how shall we understand such Scriptures as these—"and that he died—and rose again,"[1] —"for since by man came death, by man came also the resurrection from the dead,"[2] etc.?

If death and the resurrection are the same event, how shall we account for this strange tautology? Such

[1] 1 Cor. xv. 2. [2] 1 Cor. xv. 21.

an idea degrades these and numerous other similar passages, into the most unintelligible jargon.

IV. *This theory contradicts all those Scriptures that teach that Christ was the first who rose from the dead.*

> "Having therefore obtained help of God, I continue unto this day, witnessing both unto small and great, saying none other things than those which the prophets and Moses did say should come:
>
> "That Christ should suffer, and that he should be the first that should rise from the dead," etc.—Acts xii. 22, 23.
>
> "But now is Christ risen from the dead, and become the first-fruits of them that slept."—1 Cor. xv. 20.
>
> "But every man in his own order: Christ the first-fruits."—Ver. 23.
>
> "And he is the head of the body, the Church: who is the beginning, the first-born from the dead; that in all things he might have the pre-eminence."—Col. i. 18.
>
> "And from Jesus Christ, who is the faithful Witness, and the First-begotten of the dead."—Rev. i. 5.

Others had been raised, but not to immortality. Theirs was not the "better resurrection" of which St. Paul speaks,[1] and they all died again like other mortals, and await the general resurrection. But Christ was the first who arose "to die no more." So say the Scriptures. But the New Church theory tells us that death and the resurrection are one and the same thing. If so, as Abel was the first who died, *he*, and *not* Christ, was the first who rose from the dead; and in the experience of such a transition *he* has "the preeminence," and not our Lord and Redeemer.

V. *The Scriptures represent the dead as all rising* AT THE SAME TIME, *in obedience to the voice of the final trumpet.*

[1] Heb. xi. 35.

"Marvel not at this: for the hour is coming, in the which all that are in the graves shall hear his voice,

"And shall come forth; they that have done good, unto the resurrection of life; and they that have done evil, unto the resurrection of damnation." John x. 28, 29.

The same doctrine is also inculcated in this passage:

"Behold, I shew you a mystery; We shall not all sleep, but we shall all be changed,

"In a moment, in the twinkling of an eye, at the last trump: for the trumpet shall sound, and the dead shall be raised incorruptible, and we shall be changed."—1 Cor. xv. 51, 52.

These and other similar Scriptures show that the resurrection is an event of the "last day," as Martha said to Jesus, and not of all the ages. But if Swedenborgianism be true, it is constantly occurring, and has been occurring in every instance of death since the world began.

VI. *The Scriptures constantly speak of the resurrection of* THE DEAD.

"There shall be a resurrection of the dead, both of the just and unjust."—Acts xxiv. 15.

"For since by man came death, by man came also the resurrection from the dead."—1 Cor. xv. 21.

"So also is the resurrection of the dead."—1 Cor. xv. 42.

"Why should it be thought a thing incredible with you that God should raise the dead?"—Acts xxvi. 8.

Now who are meant by "the dead" in these passages? Most obviously those who have passed through the change of death, and whose bodies slumber in the dust. Of all such there is yet to be a resurrection. But if the new theory be true, the resurrection is *past* with all such—they had their resurrection at the moment of death. How then say the Scriptures that "the dead" are yet to experience a resurrection?

VII. *This theory denies the resurrection of the body of Christ, which the Scriptures so explicitly and constantly insist upon.*

As the apostles "preached through Jesus the resurrection from the dead," or, in other words, constantly set forth his resurrection as a specimen, proof, and pledge of the resurrection of all men, our "New Church" expositors are sorely pressed by the fact of the resurrection of the Saviour's body. Prof. Bush admits that the apostles *believed* and *taught* that his body had risen, but were mistaken![1] And as Christ *had* a body on the cross, which was laid in the tomb of Joseph; was missing and could not be found; we are told that it was miraculously dissolved in the tomb, and thus disappeared forever! To such straits and such reckless assumptions are they driven, in their efforts to disprove the doctrine of a corporeal resurrection.

VIII. *If the Swedenborgian theory be correct, our Lord experienced his resurrection when he died on the cross.*

"The true resurrection," says Prof. Bush, "takes place at death, etc." Then Christ's resurrection took place from the cross at the moment of death. How, then, came he to teach that *after three days* he would rise again? And how came the inspired apostles so utterly to misunderstand the true doctrine as not only to suppose that his body arose, when it was not the case, but always to affirm that he rose "the third day" after his crucifixion, when in fact his resurrection took place when he "gave up the ghost?"

[1] So says Prof. Bush, Anastasis, p. 165.

IX. Finally it may be stated in general terms, that the idea that the resurrection takes place at death, or in other words, that it is nothing more nor less than the emerging of the spirit from the body, is contrary to the teachings of Moses and the prophets upon the subject, the teachings of Christ and the apostles, and to all the analogies of divine truth. If this doctrine be true, what mean the bodily translations of Enoch and Elijah to heaven? What the resurrection of the bodies of many saints at Christ's resurrection? and what his corporeal ascension to heaven in the presence of all the disciples? Upon this theory the whole Bible is incoherent, inexplicable, contradictory and misleading. And to give it the slightest air of plausibility, it becomes necessary not only to wrest the Scriptures without scruple, but to brand the apostles themselves as the dupes of a cunningly devised fable, and to charge them with preaching and writing heresy all their lives as the result of their own stupidity! And all this while professing to speak and write by the inspiration of the Holy Ghost!!

The logical result of the whole is, that the maintenance of the "New Church" idea requires a license of criticism which will completely override the meaning of the inspired writers, and in the end virtually reject the Scriptures as an inspired record. If I may so wrench and torture the Bible as to make it teach that the resurrection takes place at death, and that all its descriptions and declarations and examples of a bodily resurrection mean nothing of the kind; that very liberty which I take with that Holy Book, shows that I have ceased to respect its teachings as either infallible or authoritative, and that I am already far down in the dark abyss of Deism. If Swedenborgianism be true, the Bible is false; but if the Bible be true, this phantom of a bewildered imagination is false and to be rejected.

CHAPTER XII.

THEORIES CONSIDERED—THE "GERM THEORY" OF SAMUEL DREW AND OTHERS.

IN order to obviate the supposed difficulties of a literal resurrection of the body, a new theory of bodily identity has been proposed, which makes the body proper to consist of an inappreciable portion of what we usually regard as our body—a minute *germ* or *stamen* which preserves its place and maintains its identity through all the changes to which the body is subject during life; continues its peculiar vitality after death; and will either eventually expand into the resurrection body, or will constitute the nucleus around which other elements shall gather to build up the new body at the last day.

1. Probably the most noted advocate of this theory is Samuel Drew, the distinguished metaphysician of St. Austell, England, who wrote a very able treatise upon the subject in 1809; and as it is important that we understand as nearly as possible precisely what the theory is, it is due to Mr. Drew to state it at length in our pages in his own words.

"By the term *germ* or *stamen* I understand a certain portion of immovable matter, which was lodged in the human body at its primary formation, and which, as a principle, to which the floating particles of flesh and blood have occasionally adhered, and which in all probability is immediately united to the immaterial spirit, and has remained permanent through all the intermediate stages of life. It is a portion which constitutes perpetual sameness; which shall remain forever as a radical and immovable principle; which shall form the rudiments of our future bodies; and shall either collect matter around it, which collected matter shall adhere forever, or contain within it all those particles which are necessary to constitute those bodies which we shall perpetually possess."[1]

Of the probable minuteness of this supposed germ, Mr. Drew says:

"To know the dimensions, the texture, the configuration, and the place of residence of this portion of immovable matter, might perhaps be highly gratifying to the curiosity of man; but that such knowledge would be of any real use to us, may well admit of considerable doubt. Perhaps the acuteness of those organs, which would enable us to become intimately acquainted with the internal constitution of its nature, together with those adhesive powers by which its various parts are connected, would deprive us of their utility in practical life," etc.[2]

"It is perhaps in a manner somewhat analogous to air, that those permanent principles of the human body exist, in which I have supposed its identity to consist; but which, on that account, can be no more

[1] Essay on the Identity and General Resurrection of the Human Body, etc. London, 1822, pp. 263–4.

[2] Ibid., p. 177.

liable to dissolution than the atmosphere, to which, in modes of existence, it may probably be allied. And though to this portion of immovable matter, the different particles of flesh and blood occasionally adhere, during the various stages of our natural lives; yet, as they are in a state of perpetual fluctuation, adhering to the system, retiring from it, and then adhering anew, they can form no part of that immovable portion, in which identity or sameness must consist.

"And since these accessory particles which are in a state of perpetual mutation, can form no part of that portion which is permanent, it is highly probable that, when the hour of death shall be succeeded by dissolution, these floating particles will drop off: and resuming their primary state, leave at last this portion unclothed and totally separated from all extraneous matter.

"Divested of all extraneous matter, it is probably in its own nature so constituted, that it becomes incapable of incorporating with any other animal substances; incapable of affording any nutrition, or of filling up any vacuity in the animal systems of other bodies. In this state of separation it may lie reposing in the grave in an apparently dormant condition, equally inaccessible to all violence, and removed from all decay. The accidents, indeed, which float on the stream of time, may tend to disturb its tranquility, and dislodge it from its gloomy mansion; in this case, it may float in the breeze for a season, or it may be wafted into distant regions with the adverse winds of heaven;—but change of station can never affect the permanency of its nature.

"Removed from the influence of gravitation through

the elementary principles of its constitution, it will be able to make no resistance to external bodies; and rendered too subtile for our organs of vision, it may elude all discernment; becoming at once imperceptible to sight and touch. And, while in this naked state, abandoned by its immaterial partner, and separated from all those cumbrous particles of flesh and blood, which now clothe and adhere to it; it must remain without affording any evidences of its existence, till the arrival of the great day of retribution, when resuming its medium office, or new condition, it shall be re-united to its immortal partner, never to be separated from it again through eternity.[1]

"Having admitted that this portion of matter may probably possess a contracting and expansive power, it may perhaps be inquired, 'To what extent is it capable of expanding? and to what minuteness is it capable of contracting itself?'

"To these questions the most rational reply perhaps that can be given is, that the compages of the body form the exterior confines of its active elasticity, and beyond these boundaries it cannot possibly pass through the limitation of its nature and its name. While, on the contrary, it may, when actually separated from its immaterial partner, and from all adhesive matter, be capable of contracting itself to such minuteness as may forever elude our researches, and become totally invisible to all discernment, except that of God."[2]

"It is therefore not improbable to conjecture, that the specific quantity of matter which is included in

[1] Essay, pp. 180–182.

[2] Ibid., p. 183.

that portion which constitutes the identity of the human body, may be, when divested of pores, and reduced within the confines of the least possible space, too minute for our discernment, our comprehension, or even our conception."[1]

"The continuance of this principle of bodily identity amidst the shocks of life, and the desolations of surrounding parts, is not the decision of theory, but of fact; and its preservation amidst the ravages of death may be inferred from just analogy. And though from hence it will follow, that it is capable of a separate state of existence, when perfectly disunited from all other matter and from spirit, yet it will not follow, that it will possess any active energy, or be capable of locomotion. In this state of total separation, it can have nothing more than a kind of *vegetative existence*, totally destitute of animal power."

"Shrivelled and folded in itself, it must retire to mix with common matter, and continue in a torpid state; in which it may undergo in a way and manner which surpass our comprehension; a passive process somewhat analogous to that of a germinating atom, which is included in grain. And in this state it may ripen towards the grand result of things, when it shall come forth in a matured state,—unfold all its latent powers,—put forth all its bloom,—and flourish throughout eternity."[2]

These extended extracts embody a fair and full statement of Mr. Drew's theory, usually denominated the "germ theory," of the resurrection. The *germ* or *stamen* in which the essential identity of the body con-

[1] Essay, pp. 183, 184. [2] Ibid., p. 186.

sists, is an imaginary atom, deposited at the beginning of our corporeal being, which is incapable of mixing, so to speak, with other elements in the body, remain unchanged through all physical vicissitudes, is so minute or subtile as to be invisible, intangible, inconceivable; retains its independent identity after death, though blown over the earth by the winds of heaven; is capable of indefinite expansion, and is either to expand to the proper dimensions for the resurrection body, or to be the nucleus around which the remaining elements necessary to the new body shall be collected. If to this we add the idea that this germ is unchangeable even by death, that it is "inaccessible to dissolution and decay," and consequently does not die with the body, we believe we have every principle and element of this singular though ingenious hypothesis.

2. Dr. Edward Hitchcock, late President of Amherst College, seems to have at least partially adopted this germ theory.

"If," says he, "only a millionth part, or a ten thousand millionth part, of the matter deposited in the grave, shall be raised from thence, it justifies the representations of Scripture, that there will be a resurrection of the dead. And why may we not suppose, that amid all the transmutations which the dead body will undergo, some infinitesimal germ may be watched over by omniscience, and by omnipotence at length be made to constitute the germ of the spiritual body."[1]

Such being the theory, let us now proceed to show why we cannot accept it as the Bible doctrine of the resurrection.

[1] Religious Lectures, p. 17.

I. *It is a mere hypothesis or supposition, without warrant in the Holy Scriptnres.*

The only passage we have ever known to be cited in its support, is 1 Cor. xv. 36–38, which we have elsewhere shown to have no reference to any such corporeal vegetation."[1]

Mr. Drew dwells at length upon this passage, as teaching his theory. But if we are to take this illustration of another point, as we claim, as teaching the real process of the resurrection, what shall we do with the same illustration when used by our Lord, and applied to his own resurrection? "Except a corn of wheat fall into the ground and die, it abideth alone: but if it die, it bringeth forth much fruit.[2] Now, will any advocate of this theory affirm that Christ's resurrection body was not the *whole* of the veritable body which hung on the cross? Was *it* developed from an inappreciable germ which never had died? He himself declared after his resurrection,[3] that his body which then lived "was dead;" and the gospel narative is conclusive upon the point that the *whole body* of Christ arose.

The truth is, that both our Lord and the apostle used this illustration merely to show that the death of the body furnished no ground for doubt as to its living again by resurrection, after the change of death.

II. *This theory obviates none of the supposed difficulties in the way of a corporeal resurrection.*

"If by this hypothesis it was designed to remove the difficulty of conceiving how the scattered parts of one body could be preserved from becoming integral parts

[1] Chr. viii. p. 161. [2] John xii. 24. [3] Rev. i. 18.

of other bodies, it supposes that the constant care of Providence is exerted to maintain the incorruptibility of those individual germs, or stamina, so as to prevent their assimilation with each other. Now if they have this by original quality, then the same quality may just as easily be supposed to appertain to every particle which composes a human body; so that though it be used for food, it shall not be capable of assimilation, in any circumstance, with another human body. For if these germs or stamina, have not this quality by their original nature, they can only be prevented from assimilating with each other by that operation of God which is present to all his works, and which must always be directed to secure the execution of his own ultimate designs."

"If this view be adopted, then, if the resort must at last be to the superintendence of a Being of infinite power and wisdom, there is no greater difficulty in supposing that his care to secure this object shall extend to a million rather than to a thousand particles of matter. This is, in fact, the true and rational answer to the objection that the same piece of matter may happen to be a part of two or more bodies, as in the instances of men feeding upon animals which have fed upon men, and of men feeding upon one another. The question here is one which simply respects the frustrating of a final purpose of the Almighty by an operation of nature. To suppose that he cannot prevent this, is to deny his power; to suppose him inattentive to it, is to suppose him indifferent to his own designs; and to assume that he employs care to prevent it, is to assume nothing greater, nothing in fact so great, as many instances of control, which are always occurring; as, for instance, the regulation of the proportion of the sexes in human birth, which cannot be attributed to chance, but must either be referred to superintendence, or to some original law."[1]

Thus this theory affords no relief to the only real difficulty involved in the orthodox view, but leaves the whole case still to be resolved into the almighty power of God.

III. *According to this theory there is no resurrection of the "body," as the Scriptures plainly teach.*

In what sense can an impalpable germ, perhaps smaller than a grain of mustard seed, be called "*the body?*" As Mr. Watson has well inquired, "If a finger, or even a limb is not the body, much less can these minute parts be entitled to this appellation." All those Scriptures, therefore, which speak of the resurrection of the "vile body," the "flesh," etc., are plainly in conflict with this theory of the resurrection.

IV. *This hypothesis virtually denies that the germ from which the future body is to spring, ever dies at all.*

The germ of an acorn or a grain of wheat from which the tree or the new stalk of wheat grows, does not die. And so of this imaginary fleshly germ—it is supposed to retain, not only its *identity*, but also its peculiar *vitality*, through the vicissitudes of the present life, and the change of death; and then to germinate and to live on forever. When, then, is it *dead?* And in what possible sense can this living germ be called

[1] Watson's Theological Institutes, Part II., Chap. xxix.

"the dead?" And yet the Bible is emphatic that "the dead shall be raised."[1]

V. *According to this theory there is no resurrection whatever.*

"For if the preserved part be a germ, and the analogy of vegetation be adopted; then we have no longer a *resurrection* from death, but a *vegetation* from a suspended principle of secret *life*."[2]

There is, therefore, no resurrection whatever—no raising up again of that which has fallen down.

VI. *This notion of the resurrection is contrary to all the examples and analogies of the Bible.*

As we have had occasion so often to remark, the apostles constantly referred to Christ as a *pattern* of the resurrection of his saints. But his was a veritable resurrection to life of the identical body laid in the tomb—no inconsiderable germ, merely, but the *entire body*, with "all things pertaining to the perfection of man's nature."[3] And so of the saints which arose after his resurrection, and came into Jerusalem. They were not mere "*germs*" or "stamina," which arose, but the "*bodies* of the saints." So, also, of Enoch and Elijah—their entire bodies were carried up into heaven. All these specimens of resurrection and translation are therefore but so many refutations of the idea that the resurrection of the Scriptures is merely the germination of an infinitesimal portion of the original body.

[1] 1 Cor. xv. 52. [2] Watson.
[3] Articles of Religion of the M. E. Church, Art. iii.

CHAPTER XIII.

THEORIES CONSIDERED—A NEW BODY OF COMMON ELEMENTS.

A FOURTH theory, and one that is worthy of distinct consideration, is that promulgated by Archbishop Whately, Dr. Hitchcock, and others, namely, that bodily identity does not consist in identity of substance, even to the extent of the minutest germ, but in *sameness of chemical elements, form and structure*, though composed of materials gathered anywhere, without reference to the substance of the former body. This theory is thus set forth by Archbishop Whately:

"Let it be remembered, then, that even for a *body* to be the *same*, it is not at all necessary that it should consist of the same particles of matter." . . . "With respect to the *sameness of our bodies*, it seems clear enough, that a man's body is called *his*, from its union with his soul, and the mutual influence of the one on the other." "So that if, at the resurrection, we are clothed with bodies which we, in this way, perceive to belong to us, and to be ours, it signifies nothing, of what particles of bodily substance they are composed."[1]

[1] Future State, American edition, pp. 97, 99.

The same doctrine is clearly taught in the following illustration:

"If any one's house, for instance, be destroyed, and another man promised to *re*-build it for him, he would not be considered, as failing in his promise because he did not put together all the former materials. If the materials were equally good, and if the man were put in possession of a house not less commodious and beautiful than he had before, *that* would be to all practical purposes sufficient. It would be thought idle caviling to contend that this was not, strictly speaking, the re-building of the *same* house, but the building of a different one; because the materials were new; and that therefore the promise was not fulfilled. No one would attend to such frivolous distinction, when all practical purposes were completely answered."[1]

Dr. Hitchcock thus sets forth the same idea:

"The identity of the body consists, not in a sameness of particles, but in the same kinds of elementary matter, combined in the same proportion, and having the same form and structure. Hence it is not necessary that the resurrection body should contain a single particle of the matter laid in the grave, in order to be the same body; which it will be if it consists of the same kinds of matter combined in the same proportions, and has the same form and structure. For the particles of our bodies are often totally changed during our lives; yet no one imagines that the old man has now the same body as in infancy."[2]

"Sameness of chemical composition and peculiarity

[1] Future State, pp. 100, 101.

[2] Religion of Geology, p. 8.

of form and structure are all that is essential to personal corporeal identity. . . . It matters not whence the elements of a compound are derived, whether from China or the United States; if they are only united in the same proportion, they will constitute exactly the same substance. Thus, it can make no difference from what source the oxygen and hydrogen are obtained, that form water. It will be identically the same substance, though its elements come from the antipodes. So it is with the oxygen, hydrogen, carbon, nitrogen, phosphorus, and lime, that make up the human system. The essential thing that makes them the flesh and bones of a man, is their combination in a certain definite proportion, etc."[1] Again:

"By this view, it is not necessary that the resurrection body should contain a single particle of the body laid in the grave, if it only contain particles of the same kind, united in the same proportion, and the compound be made to assume the same form and structure as the natural body. For all this is what often happens to men in this world, without exciting a suspicion that the identity of the individual is endangered. God may give to the man raised from the grave, such a body as pleases him, just as he does to the plant: but if it be only composed of the same elements, in the same proportion, and have a peculiarity of form and structure, its identity with the individual buried will be preserved."[2]

These extracts contain a full and explicit statement of the theory under consideration—a theory that is

[1] Religious Lectures, pp. 24, 25. [2] Ibid., pp. 26, 27.

supposed to meet all the requirements of the Scriptures, while it obviates all the supposed difficulties of a physical resurrection.

That it obviates the alleged "difficulties" in the way of a resurrection of the identical body laid in the grave, is admitted. So does the Swedenborgian theory. And so does the theology of the Sadducees and of the avowed deists, who deny that there will ever be a resurrection of any kind. That fact, therefore, in itself considered, is no proof that the theory is either Scriptural or philosophical. For while it obviates certain alleged difficulties, it may encounter others far more formidable; and even if it were not perceptibly in conflict with philosophy, it might be directly opposed to the teachings of the Holy Scriptures. Let us, therefore, examine this bold hypothesis, in its relations to philosophy and revelation.

I. Is it good "philosophy" to call two different bodies "the *same* body," merely because they are of the same *form* and *chemical elements?* Suppose one crossing the Atlantic were to promise that if a fellow-passenger would drop his watch into the sea, he would bring it up from the bottom and restore it to him again; and after the watch had sunk, should present him with another watch *exactly like* the one thrown overboard, in material, size, form and workmanship, and should insist that he had restored to him the same watch; would "philosophy" or common sense decide that identity of chemical elements, form and proportions is all that is necessary to constitute the latter the same watch that was thrown overboard? One must have strange ideas of "sameness" to decide that the promise to restore the sunken watch had been fulfilled.

And suppose the watch was one that had been presented by some cherished friend, and the owner had carried the precious keepsake for many years, could you satisfy him by saying, "This watch is *just like* the one your friend gave you, and which you dropped overboard—keeps just as good time, and is worth just as much,—and therefore, for all practical purposes, is *the same watch?*" By no means. Not only is it *not* the same watch, but it fails to answer all the ends which the first watch answered. To answer all these ends, and carry with it all the attachments and precious memories that gather around it, the *identical watch itself* must be reproduced—the same mainspring, and drum, and chain, and face, and hands, and case. In a word, it must be the same watch in all its essential elements, or there is no sameness or identity worthy of the name. It may lack a hand or a crystal, but its substance must be unchanged. What, then, becomes of the theory that sameness of chemical elements and form is all that is necessary to constitute a body made of new or common elements, the same body laid in the grave?

II. Take another illustration: suppose a father and mother living in Vermont had a son starved to death at the Andersonville Prison, and buried with the thirty thousand who perished there. After a time they visit the scene of his death, recover the body, as they suppose, have it enclosed in a leaden coffin, and conveyed to his former home; and the neighbors and friends are assembled for funeral rites, preparatory to final burial.

Just then it comes to light that in looking for the body they have taken the *wrong number* from the books, and have consequently brought home the *wrong body!* What would be the feelings of those stricken parents? Would it relieve the difficulty to say, "Bodily identity does not consist in identity of *atoms* or *substance*, but in *sameness of chemical components and structure*, and as this body and that of your son are alike decomposed, this is for all practical purposes the same as your son's body?" Would *such* an identity satisfy them? Would they go on with the funeral services, weep as they laid the body in the tomb, plant flowers over it, rear a tablet and inscribe upon it the name of their lost son, and ever afterward call that his grave? The very idea refutes itself to the judgment and the heart of every reader. "*It is not my son*," says the half-distracted mother. "Away with your far-fetched theories of bodily identity. I want *the body of my son* brought home, and buried amid his native hills." The search is renewed till the *identical body* is found, and conveyed to its former home. And so it is: no other kind of identity will at all answer the demands of reason, philosophy or affection.

III. The illustrative argument of Bishop Whately, given on a previous page, is inapplicable to the question under discussion, and consequently fallacious; for

1. To rebuild a house that had been destroyed, and use only the materials of the old house, would be impossible to man; but to assume that it is impossible for God to restore the elements of the old body, in a new and more glorious one—to "change our vile body," etc.—is to beg the very question in dispute.

2. The promise to "*rebuild*" the house is not a fair representation of the promise of the resurrection. If that promise extended only to the production of *a* body, without reference to that laid in the grave, the illustration would be pertinent; but we deny that such only is its scope.

3. To conform the illustration to the real question, the contractor should engage to renovate and restore the old house itself—to raise up out of the ashes, and brick, and broken glass, and nails, and other debris that fill the cellar, a new house—the same house that was consumed by fire; and should claim that he had fulfilled his promise by gathering materials here and there, and building a house *just like* the first and equally serviceable. Had the promise been that he would build a house *like* the first, or as *good* as the first, the obligation would have been met; but such a promise, fairly stated, would have misrepresented the promise of the resurrection. And yet that is the real import of the promise in the illustration, and all that the supposed contractor has fulfilled. The whole argument based upon this illustration, therefore, is fallacious, not only because it assumes the very question in dispute, viz., that God has not engaged to raise up the same body, but because it takes that which is impossible with man to represent that which *is* possible with God.

IV. Such a production of a future body would not be a *resurrection* in any sense, any more than was the creation of the body of Adam. Neither would it be a *re*production; but the simple *creation* of a *new body*. By what principle can such an act be called a resurrection—the raising *again* of that which has fallen down? And still worse, in what sense can it be called the resurrection of *the dead?* Would such a new body ever have been "*dead*," either in its organic form or its constituent elements? The idea is incompatible with every notion of the resurrection, as gathered from the New Testament.

V. Christ is not only the first-begotten from the dead, but is constantly set forth as a proof and a specimen of the resurrection of the dead. This fact no candid reader of the Acts of the Apostles, and of the Epistles, can deny. "They preached through Jesus the resurrection from the dead." But how was it with this illustrious sample and forerunner? Was *his* resurrection body made of common elements? or was it the identical body laid in the tomb? If the theory of Archbishop Whately be correct, nothing is better calculated to mislead us, than the contemplation of our Lord's resurrection as a pledge and proof of our own. *His* was a veritable raising up again to life of the identical body laid in the grave; while this theory is that of the creation of a new body, of elements that perhaps were never in any animal body, or under the power of death at all. Where, then, is the triumph, the victory over death and the grave? Where the appropriateness of the saying that is written, "O death, where is thy sting? O grave, where is thy victory?"

VI. The fact that the bodies of Enoch and Elijah were translated to heaven, furnishes an argument from analogy against the theory we are opposing. And so of the case of the saints who arose after our Lord's resurrection. "And the graves were opened; and many bodies of the saints which slept arose, and came out of the graves after his resurrection, and went into the holy city, and appeared unto many."[1] Were *these* bodies constructed of common elements gathered at random? Why, then, were the graves opened? And especially why is it stated so specifically that these "bodies of the saints" "came out of the graves?" Is it not plain beyond all cavil, that in all these cases, (and they were "many,") the very body laid in the grave, was raised out of it? And if this be true, we have not only the case of Christ the great Pattern in opposition to the theory under consideration, but "many" other instances of actual resurrection, not one of which was modeled after this theory. It must, therefore, be "another gospel," and not the Scriptural doctrine of the resurrection of the dead.

VII. As we have elsewhere shown:[2] the early saints certainly expected a resurrection of the very body laid in the grave. It was this very point that made the doctrine of the resurrection so offensive to their enemies. Not that they should have a *new body* at some future time, but that *the same body* laid in the grave, should be raised to life again.

Could they have modified the doctrine of the resurrection as Bishop Whately and Dr. Hitchcock have done, many of them might thereby have escaped the edge of the sword, or the fires of martyrdom; but they adhered to what we have shown to have been the early faith, even unto death. The whole weight, therefore, of their example as Christian believers of the purest age of the church; and their heroic death, in attestation of

[1] Matt. xxvii. 52. [2] Chapter iii. pages 28–44.

their faith; is against the idea of substituting a new creation for a legitimate resurrection.

VIII. It is impossible to make this theory harmonize at all with the general language of the Scriptures upon the subject. "In my flesh shall I see God." "My flesh also shall rest in hope." "Thy dead men shall live, together with my dead body shall they arise. Awake and sing ye that dwell in dust." "And many of them that sleep in the dust of the earth shall awake." "O, grave, I will be thy destruction." "This corruptible shall put on incorruption, and this mortal shall put on immortality." "Shall also quicken your mortal bodies"—"the redemption of our body;"—"it is sown in corruption, it is raised in incorruption,"—"who shall change our vile body, etc.?"

All such language points to the material identity of the body, and is incompatible with the idea that the construction of a new body irrespective of the substance of the old one, will satisfy the requirements of a Scriptural resurrection. How shall we explain the expression, "my flesh," "in my flesh," "my dead body," "ye that dwell in dust," "this corruptible," "the dead," "our vile body," "your mortal bodies," etc., in harmony with the idea that the resurrection body is to have no physical relation to the former body beyond that of a sameness of chemical proportions?

No ingenuity of interpretation can divest such language of its bearing upon the question at issue. Despite all criticism and philosophy falsely so called, all such passages point to the grave where the body rests, and teach beyond all cavil that the idea of a new body, constructed of elements that constituted no part of the former body, concedes more to the half-taught philosophy and skepticism of the times, than it does to the oft-repeated and unequivocal declarations of the word of God.

For all these reasons, then, the theory of Bishop Whately, is to be rejected, as both unphilosophical and unscriptural. It is based upon an erroneous theory of sameness or identity; and one at which both reason and affection revolt. The illustration by which he endeavors to sustain it is inapplicable and fallacious. It virtually denies that "the dead" shall rise at all, or that there shall be any resurrection whatever. It is contradicted by all the examples of resurrection with which the Scriptures furnish us; by the faith and hopes of the saints of the apostolic age; and is in conflict with the language and general tenor of the Sacred Writings. However satisfactory it may be, therefore, as a compromise with Rationalism, so called, it is not "the resurrection from the dead," taught by the prophets and apostles, and illustrated and made sure by the resurrection of Christ, the Lord of life and glory.

"The blessed in the new covenant, shall rise up quickened each one from his grave, wearing again the garments of the flesh, ministers and messengers of life eternal."

CHAPTER XIV.

TRUE THEORY OF THE RESURRECTION.

It has been shown in the last few chapters that neither the restoration of the fallen spirit of man to moral life; the going forth of the soul from the body at the hour of death; the aggregating of a new body around some minute germ of the old one; nor the constructing of a body out of common elements, irrespective of the former body; can possibly be "the resurrection from the dead," taught in the Scriptures. And yet, beyond all question, the Bible teaches a physical resurrection.

Just here then arises a question: how shall we understand the doctrine of a corporeal resurrection? What does it include or exclude?

Upon the answers given to these questions will depend, in a greater or less degree, the pertinency or otherwise of many of the objections urged against the orthodox view.

1. Some conjecture that the future body will include the substance of limbs that have been amputated, if not of all the matter that has ever been connected with the body. So extreme is their construction of the language of Scripture, that "*the body*" shall rise again. But such theorists seem to forget that the Scriptures

always speak of "the body," *which is laid in the grave*, and never of any former body or parts of the body. The soldier who has lost an arm or leg in defence of his country's flag, no longer regards the decayed limb as a part of his body. That only is *his* which his conscious spirit still pervades and controls. And so with the substance which has come and gone from the body, by the process of waste and supply—now a part of the muscular tissue, or glands or bone, and in a short time thrown from the structure altogether—it has ceased to be a part of our physical selves, and we have ceased to regard it as such. Consequently the promise that "the dead" shall rise, and the idea of a corporeal resurrection, no more includes lost limbs and animal substance thrown from the body year by year, than the sentence that one should be hung, would require the hanging with the body of an arm lost years before; or the collection of every atom that was ever connected with the body, to be suspended with it upon the gallows.

Besides, this singular conjecture draws after it several very embarrassing consequences.

Suppose it to be true, as physiologists affirm, that every part of the human body is changed once in seven years, by the process of waste and nutrition. Suppose, also, that a man dies at the age of seventy, who, so far as matter or substance is concerned, has had seven different bodies during his life. What kind of a resurrection would *his* be if all this matter was included? And what resemblance could there be between *such* a body, and the body laid in the grave?

True, it has been said in reply to this objection, that

all this unwieldy mass may be condensed in the resurrection within due limits; or that only the solid portion may be preserved. But one of these hypotheses is but a supposition, and the other is an abandonment of the very theory it is designed to relieve. And as such a retrospective application of the promises of a future life for the body, is a palpable violence to their obvious scope and meaning, we leave the conjecture without further comment, as upon its face too fanciful, and too much at variance with the Bible, to be accepted by any enlightened Christian.

II. Others have understood the doctrine of a physical resurrection to be that every particle of matter composing the body at the hour of death, will be raised up and reconstructed into a new body, and become the future home of the spirit forever. Perhaps, so far as the great mass of Christians are concerned, this is the prevailing belief. Such seems to have been the idea of Montgomery, when he wrote:

"Grave, the guardian of our dust,
Grave, the treasury of the skies,
Every atom of thy trust
Rests in hope again to rise."

And so, also, Dr. Watts:

"God my Redeemer lives,
And ever from the skies,
Looks down and watches *all my dust,*
Till he shall bid it rise."

Dr. Blair has the same idea:

"The time draws on
When not a single spot of burial earth,
Whether on land, or in the spacious sea,

> But must give back its long-committed dust
> Inviolate; and faithfully shall these
> Make up the full amount; not the least atom
> Embezzled or mislaid of the whole tale."

And yet, perhaps, it would be wrong to infer from these passages that their respective authors believed that "every atom" of matter included for instance within the skin of the body at the hour of death, would be raised again, and enter into the composition of the resurrection body. Something is no doubt due to poetic license and fervor. But as many have the idea that a literal resurrection of "the body" requires the raising up of *every particle* belonging to it or included within it at the moment of death, it is not improbable that the above extracts were intended to teach this doctrine.

So far as any imaginary difficulty in its accomplishment is concerned, we have no objection to such a statement of the doctrine of the resurrection. It is just as easy for an omnipresent, omniscient and almighty Being to watch over and finally to collect and form into a new body every particle of the body laid in the grave, bones and sinews, muscles and tendons, veins and arteries, blood, brain, nerves, skin, solids and fluids, as it is to raise up the substance of the bones merely. And yet it may well be doubted whether the doctrine of a physical resurrection ought to be thus understood and insisted upon. For,

1. If *most* of the matter included within the limits of the body at the hour of death be re-collected, and formed into a new body, it may properly be regarded as a resurrection of the body, and promised and spoken of as such. If *no part* of the old body was raised,

as Bishop Whately supposes, or if only a *few particles* of its substance were raised, as Mr. Drew imagines, it would be absurd to talk of the resurrection of the dead. But if three-fourths or two-thirds of the matter of the body laid in the grave, be raised out of it, and formed into a new and immortal body, the language of the Scriptures and every description of the resurrection are fully justified.

2. In most instances of death, there is at the moment of death no small amount of matter within the limits of the corporeal system, that is not yet fairly incorporated as a part of the body. The blood, for instance, may be charged with the substance of digested food, not yet secreted by the glands and converted into muscle, bone, etc. So also the fluids that are thrown out in perspiration—they are *in* the body, perhaps, and passing through it, but, properly speaking, they are no part of it, any more than the fluid in a sponge is a part of the sponge itself. If, therefore, the doctrine of the resurrection of the body is to be taken in its most literal sense, it by no means necessitates the resurrection of all the matter connected with the body at the time of burial; since there is at all times matter connected with every human body, which in point of fact is no part of the body itself.

3. The same may be said of diseased persons whose bodies are swollen and filled with watery substance, as in cases of dropsy, etc. Such a person may be "tapped," as it is called, and large quantities of water drawn from the system. Is such water, properly speaking, a part of the body? Is it not rather a foreign element introduced among the healthy tissues

by the defective action of certain organs? Is it really incorporated, or any more a part of the body while within the skin, than it is after it is drawn from it and thrown into a river?

4. While the body is in a healthy state, the different substances composing it bear certain general proportions to each other—the bones, muscles, blood, brain, etc. But suppose by diseased action a mass of flesh called a wen, should accumulate on the neck, for instance, weighing forty or fifty pounds, more or less; does that excrescence belong to the body proper, merely because diseased action of the system has developed it? And so of all other abnormal developments; they are, strictly speaking, no part of the body proper.

It is not, therefore, a wresting of the Scriptures from their legitimate import, nor a mere expedient to obviate difficulties, to say that by "the body" of which the resurrection is predicated, we are to understand the body of man *in its normal state*, and not as disfigured and burdened by abnormal appendages, or distended by dropsy or inflammation. Any other hypothesis, it seems to us, necessitates the raising up again of *every thing* included within the limits of the body at the moment of death, even to the *poison* by which the death may have been caused. This idea must therefore be excluded as erroneous.

5. But if the above view be correct (and we can but think it is,) has it not a further application? A person is bloated, for instance, by the use of intoxicating drinks—becomes abnormally corpulent. Stop his beer or brandy, and in a short time he contracts to his normal dimensions. This shows that a *foreign element*

had been injected among the tissues of his body, which did not properly belong to it, and was in no wise essential to its health or physical integrity. Why, then, should it be regarded as legitimately a part of the physical man?

Take another case: here is a person of ordinary stature, (like several who have been on exhibition in New York,) who weighs perhaps six or seven hundred pounds. Her skin is as white as alabaster, and almost semi-transparent; and everything shows that the collection of such an amount of adipose matter, is an anomaly in the operations of digestion and secretion. Is that body in its normal state? or are here hundreds of pounds of substance that has no business there, and justly speaking, is no part of the body?

All these may be regarded by some as fanciful and useless speculations; but in our view they not only belong to the subject, but are questions upon the settlement of which the whole controversy depends. It is not enough to affirm that we believe in the resurrection of the body; we should as far as possible define what we mean by "the body." Prof. Bush understands by it the mind; Mr. Drew, an atom; and Archbishop Whately, a body *like* the one laid in the grave, in form and chemical composition. If none of these views are regarded as Scriptural, of what, in our opinion, shall the resurrection body be composed?

Because neither an inappreciable germ, nor a body composed wholly of foreign matter, will answer the demands of the Scriptures, are we therefore obliged to accept as the only remaining alternative the doctrine that every particle of the old body, including all that is connected with it in any and all conditions, must be raised and incorporated into the new body? This does not seem by any means to follow. And for the reasons already stated in the last few pages, we cannot see that the orthodox belief, as based upon the language of the Scriptures, requires anything more than the raising up again of that which legitimately belongs to the body, in its normal and healthy condition—the substance of the natural body.

III. We have shown in the early chapters of this work, that the doctrine of the "resurrection of the flesh," in some sense has been the faith of God's people in all ages. It is also obvious from the language of both the Old and New Testaments, that the substance of the body cast off at death, will be raised again to life, and enter into the new and immortal structure.

But as Mr. Watson has well said, "it cannot fail to strike every impartial reader of the New Testament, that the doctrine of the resurrection is there taught without any nice distinctions."[1] The subjects and substance of which the resurrection is predicated, are "my flesh," "the dead men," "my dead body," "them that sleep in the dust of the earth," "ye that dwell in dust," "all that are in the graves," "the dead," "this mortal," "this corruptible," "our vile body," the "bodies of the saints," "the dead small and great," etc.; all of which expressions point unmistakably to the *grave*, or rather to the *body* laid there, as the subject of resurrection. And whatever interpretation or hypothesis ignores or overrides this fact, (as do the several theories examined in the preceding chapters,)

[1] Institutes, Part II. ch. xxix.

should be rejected as "another gospel," and at war with the sure word of prophecy, the word of God.

IV. But it will be asked, "if a corporeal resurrection is insisted upon, and yet it is not made to include every particle of matter connected with the body at the hour of death, to what extent may we suppose the substance of the two bodies will be identical?" Or, in other words, what portion of the mortal body *will* enter into the composition of the new or resurrection body? We answer.

1. In general that while it may not and probably will not include *all* that in every case stands connected with, or seems to be part of the body at death, it must and will include *most* of the substance of the body,—enough to justify the Scriptures in calling it our "body," "this corruptible," the "bodies of the saints," etc.

2. Not only do the teachings of revelation require that *most* of the substance of the present body enter into the composition of the new one, but that it include that which has been most permanently connected with the soul during life, and is most legitimately and properly a part of the mortal body at the hour of death. We thus reach the conclusion embodied in the definition in chapter first, that "*all that constituted or properly belonged to the body at the hour of death, and is essential to its corporeal identity and integrity*, will be raised again to life; and will go to constitute the new or resurrection body."[1]

[1] This seems to be the theory of the Evangelical Lutherans in this country, as laid down in their Catechism.

V. This we believe to be the true theory of the resurrection, and for the following reasons:

1. It is a *physical* or *corporeal* resurrection, such as all the teachings and examples of the Bible imperatively demand.

2. It includes enough of the former bodies fully to justify the language of the Scriptures in pointing to the "graves," the "dust of the earth," and the "sea;" and enough to constitute the ground-work of a real physical identity.

3. It is eminently *philosophical* as well as Scriptural; in that while it includes all that properly belongs to the body in its normal state, it excludes all that does not properly belong to it—thus, restricting the scope of the resurrection to the *real* rather than to the adventitious or the merely apparent.

4. It obviates the difficulties that lie in the way of other theories. Not that it is at all difficult for God to raise up every atom that was *ever* connected with the body; but the idea that the substance of all excrescences that grow upon the body, with all the water or adipose matter collected within it by diseased organic action, or during the last sickness, is part of the body proper, and to be raised up with it, is not only repulsive to the judgment and the affections, (for we love the body in its normal condition) but is more than the Scriptures require. Moreover, it rather implies physical anomalies and disabilities in the life to come, cor-

" Q. 315. *Will the body that is raised be the same which was deposited in the grave?*

A. All that is essential to the identity or sameness of the body, will be raised; while its unessential particles will remain mingled with the mass of earth." *Catechism by S. S. Schmucker, D.D.,* Article xxvi.

responding to those under which we labor and suffer in the present world.

5. As the resurrection is, to the just at least, a complete triumph over death and hell, why should not the resurrection power ignore all the effects of sin and its curse, in deforming, or unduly expanding the body; and, taking the perfect body of Adam before the fall as the standard of legitimate physical identity, rebuild the new body, not of the elements which disease and death have protruded from or injected into the fallen and corruptible body, but of that only which would have belonged to it had man never sinned.

"Those who accept the commonly received opinion, do not contend that just the same amount of gross matter, neither more nor less, which was deposited in the grave, is essential to the resurrection. But they do believe that that which constitutes the essential identity or sameness of the body shall be raised again, not indeed in gross matter, but refined, purified, and made glorious. Our bodies, during life-time, may vary very considerably, so far as the amount of gross matter contained in them is concerned, and that, too, in a very short space of time; but who supposes that the essential identity of the body is thereby destroyed?"[1]

VI. It is no valid objection to this view of the extent of the physical resurrection, to say, that it does not definitely trace the boundary line between that which is to be raised and that which is excluded.[2]

[1] Bishop Kingsley's Treatise, pp. 34, 35.

[2] "God has not told us how much of our present body goes into the composition of the new on the morning of the resurrection."—*Nelson on Infidelity*, p. 71.

The same is true of the general statement that "every atom of the old body" will be raised. For the question still remains undetermined as to *what constitutes* or *is included in* "the old body." The truth is, as Mr. Watson has said, that a resurrection of the body is taught in the Scriptures without any nice distinctions as to what constitutes "the body." He, and *He only*, who made the body of man at the first, knows what is and what is not essential to its perfection and integrity. *We* do not; as the body in its best estate here, is in an abnormal condition, that is, mortal and corruptible, and very different from the body of Adam in Eden, or the body that shall be beyond the restoration. It is enough that "the body" shall be raised and live again; which must include all that which properly belongs to it in its normal state, and need not, and we think, *cannot*, include anything more. Precisely *how much* that is, we might not be capable of understanding, even if God were disposed to inform us. And as such a question is of no possible importance, either to our faith or practice, God has left it with a thousand other hidden things that belong to him, instead of placing it with revealed things that belong to us and our children.[1]

VII. From all these considerations we can but regard the views set forth in the preceding pages as the correct theory of the resurrection. We cannot accept the "spiritual resurrection" of the Friends, nor the Swedenborgian notion, as having the least countenance in the Scriptures. If language has any meaning, the resurrection is a physical phenomenon—the raising up

[1] Deut. xxix. 29.

and rebuilding of the decayed body of man. But a physical resurrection being granted, the germ theory of Mr. Drew, and the "common elements" theory of Archbishop Whately, are so wide of the mark as to be a virtual denial of the very doctrine they proposed to elucidate. We are thus shut up to the idea of physical identity beyond that embodied in a mere germ or atom of the former body, or a resemblance of chemical proportions and structure; and are thus turned back to the Scriptures, which still point us to the graves, and insist that "this corruptible shall put on incorruption." Looking, then, at the notion that every atom that is in any sense connected with the body at the hour of death shall be raised again, we see first, that the Scripture idea of the resurrection does not require such an extreme physical reproduction, and still further, that reason and analogy seem to limit the resurrection power to that which properly belongs to the body in its normal condition, if not to that which might properly have belonged to it in an unfallen and sinless state.

We thus reach our final conclusion already stated—that physical identity in the resurrection need not of necessity include all the particles of the mortal body as abandoned by the soul at death, but will include most of its substance—all that is really essential to its corporeal identity and integrity. We therefore repeat our theory or belief again, in the language of our first definition, that ALL THAT CONSTITUTED OR PROPERLY BELONGED TO THE BODY AT THE HOUR OF DEATH, AND IS ESSENTIAL TO ITS CORPOREAL IDEN-

TITY AND INTEGRITY *will be raised again to life; and will go to constitute the new or resurrection body.*

Such, in our view, is the true theory of a physical resurrection; and such is the theory we shall endeavor to defend and illustrate in the succeeding chapters.

CHAPTER XV.

OBJECTIONS TO A CORPOREAL RESURRECTION CONSIDERED.

THAT the doctrine of the resurrection of the dead was from the first discredited and opposed by persons outside of the Jewish and Christian Churches, is conceded. The Sadducees of our Lord's time denied it, and the Epicureans and Stoics to whom Paul preached at Athens, mocked or scoffed when they heard of the resurrection of the dead.[1] But among the orthodox Jews and the early Christians, there was but one faith upon this subject, from the time of Moses to the days of Origen in the early part of the third century. So far as we have knowledge, he was the first Christian writer who promulgated or held any other view of the resurrection than that of the literal raising up of the material body. From his time onward, and especially during the last two centuries, various objections have been urged against the orthodox belief, the consideration of which will next engage our attention.

I. The objection of Origen, and of the Platonists generally, was based upon the idea that *matter* is the seat of moral corruption; and that consequently whatever is in any way connected with it, is necessarily con-

[1] Acts xvii. 18, 32.

taminated. Having a strong attachment to the Platonic philosophy and a peculiar relish for mystical and allegorical interpretations, he very naturally fell into the error of discarding the doctrine of a physical resurrection; and in many other respects "greatly corrupted the simplicity of the gospel." He held to the pre-existence of souls, that they were condemned to dwell in bodies as a punishment for sins committed in a former state, and that after long periods of time, lost souls will be released from torment, and allowed another state of probation. It requires but little effort to see the resemblance between his views and the doctrine of the metempsychosis or transmigration of souls held by the ancient Pythagoreans and Platonists, and still taught by the Budhists of our own times.

Upon the subject of the resurrection he is said to have taught, that "at the resurrection all mankind will be again clothed with ethereal bodies: for the elements of our terrestrial composition are such as must fatally entangle us in vice, passion and misery."[1]

That matter, in itself considered, has any moral character, or can be the seat or source of moral evil, few perhaps would affirm. How can iron, or lime, or phosphorus have any moral character? The idea is absurd upon its face; and probably has few if any advocates in our own time and country. And yet there are those who, while they would perhaps discard the sweeping axiom of the Platonic philosophy, cherish a secret prejudice against matter, especially as it is found organized in the human body. Understanding the phrase "the flesh," as used in the New Testament to

[1] Encyclopædia of Religious Knowledge, article, *Origen*.

represent our carnal propensities, to mean the literal body, they believe that the physical system of man is the seat and source of moral evil. But even granting this, it is enough to say that Christ has promised to "change our vile body," so that we are not to infer future moral defilement in connection with the body, even if it were both the seat and source of all moral evil.

II. To the kindred objection that our bodies are gross, corruptible and mortal, and the source of much *suffering* in the present life, and consequently could be no blessing in the life to come, the same answer is sufficient. The objector is bound in candor and justice to take *the whole doctrine* of the resurrection, and not a single point only. Now it is a part of the doctrine that our bodies are to be *changed* from corruptible to incorruptible, and from mortal to immortal. What, then, becomes of the objection founded upon the unfavorable condition of our present bodies? Are not all such objections effectually disposed of by the promise that "the dead shall be raised incorruptible, and we shall be changed?" Because a house is inconvenient, cold, and uncomfortable after having been wrecked by a whirlwind, and beaten by storms and tempests for a generation, shall we aver that it will be an untenantable structure,—an abode of wretchedness and misery,—after it has been rebuilt from foundation to roof, and restored and beautified in every part? Why, then, should any object to the future body as a clog and impediment, merely because it is such to some extent here, since it is to be restored, and made like unto Christ's glorious body? But of this more at length in a future chapter.

III. Perhaps the strongest popular objection to the doctrine of a corporeal resurrection, is that founded upon its supposed *impossibility*. "There always have been," says Whately, "as there are now, not a few who seem to measure the power of God by the standard of their own minds; and are loth to admit, even on the authority of his assurance, the truth of anything which they cannot explain. Such persons would be very likely to start the question—'How are the dead raised up, and with what body do they come?'"[1]

In most cases the body is soon dissolved in the grave, and mingled with common dust. But such is not always the case. Some bodies are consumed by fire. Others decay slowly in water, or on the land, and their constituent particles are thus widely scattered. Others again are devoured by wild beasts or birds, or by fishes in the sea, and their substance thus passes, as it would seem, into the composition of other animal bodies. In other cases the matter of human bodies may be taken up by the roots of plants and trees, and may become part of the golden harvest, or of the waving forest trees.

Now the difficulty with some is, *how can God watch over all these atoms for ages, and finally collect them all again in the resurrection?*

Flavius Josephus, the Jewish historian from whom we have already quoted in chapter second, encountered this objection among the Greeks, even before the death

[1] Lectures on a Future State, p. 94.

of St. John. Hence in his Discourse to them concerning Hades, he says:

"He will make a resurrection of all men from the dead; not procuring a transmigration of souls, from one body to another, but raising again these very bodies, which you Greeks, seeing to be dissolved, do not believe [their resurrection.] But learn not to disbelieve: for while you believe that the soul is created, and yet is made immortal by God, according to the doctrine of Plato, and this in time, be not incredulous, but believe that God is able, when he hath raised to life that body which was made as a compound of the same elements, to make it immortal; for it must never be said of God, that he is able to do some things and unable to do others.

"We have therefore believed that the body will be raised again, for although it be dissolved, it is not perished; for the earth receives its remains, and preserves them; and while they are like seed, and are mixed among the more fruitful soil, they flourish, and what is sown is indeed bare grain, but at the mighty sound of God the Creator, it will sprout up, and be raised in a clothed and glorious condition, though not before it has been dissolved and mixed [with the earth.]

"So that we have not rashly believed the resurrection of the body; for although it be dissolved for a time on account of the original transgression, it exists still, and is cast into the earth, as into a potter's furnace, in order to be formed again, not in order to rise again such as it was before, but in a state of purity, and so as never to be destroyed any more. And to every body shall its own soul be restored."

The objections and difficulties, therefore, which we are called to meet in modern times, are not new; but in their substance are as old as the opposition of "philosophy falsely so called." Though reiterated and refuted a thousand times, they are reproduced in various forms from age to age, must be met by the friends of truth from generation to generation.

But before coming to the true answer to all such difficulties, let us look at a few facts that may serve measurably to relieve our embarrassment.

1. Our bodies are now composed of atoms collected from almost every clime and land. Think of the variety of food taken into the system, say in the space of seven years, and the sources from which it has been derived. The tea and coffee, and chocolate, and sugar—the figs and raisins, and dates, and nuts of various kinds—the fish and birds, and quadrupeds and grains—have been gathered by commerce from the four quarters of the globe, and have become more or less incorporated into our present systems.[1] Why, then, if they become scattered again by death, even as widely as they were twenty years before, should it be thought impossible or even difficult for God to re-collect them?

2. Though our present bodies are to be dissolved, and go back again to dust, not one particle of their present substance can ever go out of existence. "Whatsoever God doeth, it shall be forever: nothing can be put to it, nor anything taken from it: and God doeth it, that men should fear before him.[2] There is no such thing as the annihilation of matter. It may be changed into a thousand different forms and combi-

[1] Nelson on Infidelity, p. 75. [2] Eccles. iii. 14.

nations, but it will still exist.[1] "A mass of atoms may be separated and changed from one form to another by chemical and mechanical forces, but not one of them can ever be lost; for in all cases where a body is apparently destroyed, it can be shown experimentally that the parts are only separated, and can be collected again."[2] Burn a candle in a glass receiver, and when the mass of tallow and wicking are consumed, the weight of the receiver and contents remain the same. Gunpowder may be so exploded that all its parts may be collected again. The dispersion of the elements of our present bodies is not therefore, to be regarded as an obstacle to a corporeal resurrection, much less as making such a resurrection impossible. For, as Tupper has well said,

> Corruption, closely noted, is but a dissolution of the parts,
> The parts remain, and nothing lost, to build a better whole.

3. Whatever theory we may hold upon the subject, all will admit that the resurrection of the dead, is the work of God,—an infinite omniscient and omnipresent spirit, who is present with and knows and controls every particle of matter in all the universe. It cannot, therefore, be difficult for *him*, if for any reasons he desires such a resurrection, to watch over, and finally to collect again the very atoms of which our mortal bodies are composed, and to construct therefrom the resurrection body.

4. Look at the wonders that even man, with his limited knowledge and power, can perform, in the

[1] See Immortality of the Soul, pp. 245–247.

[2] Gray's Elements of Natural Philosophy, p. 22.

matter of collecting and identifying scattered atoms. Mix an ounce of steel-filings with a quart of sand, and one can separate every atom of the steel dust from the sand in a very short time, and that too in the profoundest darkness. The magnet will attract every atom of the steel to itself, if it be left free to move, no matter in what part of the sand it may be. Why, then, should it be thought difficult for God to collect the dust of which one or ten million human bodies are composed, though mingled with the sands of every shore, and with the floods of every sea? And who can say that we have not foreshadowed in this mysterious action of the magnet, the true philosophy of the resurrection? Here we have a mineral (the natural magnet) possessing the power of attracting certain other substances to itself. *Why* it attracts them, no philosopher can tell, beyond the simple fact that God has given it this attracting power. Nor is this power general as to the substances upon which it acts, but elective. It will attract steel or iron, but will not attract lead, or silver, or gold. Now, suppose God were to give to each human soul a similar power, in reference to the elements of its former body—to draw them around itself in the morning of the resurrection, as a magnet collects the steel dust from a heap of sand; would not all the above "difficulties" be at once obviated? And if God can give such attributes to a piece of iron ore, can he not, if he choose, give a similar elective attraction to every *soul*, and thus gathering about it the elements of its former body in the last day?

5. A person dies suddenly and mysteriously, and the body is handed over to a chemist for analysis, to see

if the subject has not been poisoned. The fatal arsenic has gone into the stomach, intestines, blood, lungs, liver, muscles, glands, brain and bones, and yet the chemist will not only detect it, but will collect and reproduce it, almost, if not quite atom for atom.[1]

6. Go to the assay office,[2] and you may be shown hogsheads of gold and silver in solution; and will find that one way of purifying gold of all alloy when it has but little, is to alloy it still more heavily, and then take all out together. No matter what the state of the gold is, solid or fluid, or however mixed up with other substances, they can easily find and collect it to the very last atom.

Give a good practical chemist a new golden eagle: he can reduce it to a fluid state, mix it with clay, and make a globe of the composition, and holding it in his hand before you, challenge you to detect the least particle. It is diffused through every part of the ball of clay, and to all appearance has passed from human sight forever. And suppose the eagle were the property of some poor unlettered laborer, who knew nothing of chemistry, how easy it would be to persuade him that his money was irrecoverably lost.

But wait a short time, and the chemist will reproduce its substance so perfectly that there shall be no appreciable loss of weight; and when it has been passed again under the dies of the mint, its eagle and

[1] This feat of chemistry was admirably performed, a few years since by Prof. Derœmus of New York, in the case of Mrs. Stephens, supposed to have been poisoned by her husband.

[2] There is one corner of Nassau and Wall streets, New York City, to which visitors are admitted, we believe, every Wednesday.

legend, or its "image and superscription" will all reappear, even more bright and perfect, perhaps, than before the dissolution.

7. Now take this very principle of chemical affinity, by which substances are separated, though found in the closest combination, and it ought to silence every doubt as to the possibility of a physical resurrection, even bone for bone, muscle for muscle, and atom for atom. Only let each soul have the same affinity for the matter of its former body that some substances have for others, chemically, and it might gather to itself every particle of its dissolved house of clay, and rebuild it, without further miracle, as chemistry performs its wonders of analysis and crystalization.

But our purpose in this section is merely to call attention to a few things that appear impossible to the ignorant, but are quite easy of accomplishment to the scientific and the skillful. Such are some of the phenomena described in the preceding paragraph.

All this *man* can do. Why, then, should any stagger at the promises of God? If poor, ignorant, finite man can perform such wonders, in the way of collecting and restoring the scattered particles of matter of any given kind, why should any doubt the ability of the omnipresent and infinite God to restore to every human spirit its own body, in all its material identity and integrity in the morning of the resurrection?

IV. But there is another, and, as many suppose, a still greater difficulty than the mere dispersion of the elements of which the body is composed, and their becoming incorporated in plants and trees and in other

20 *

animal systems. A decayed body nourishes the grain, or the lower animal, and another man partakes of the grain, or of the flesh of that animal, and thus a portion of the matter of another human body becomes part of his own body also. Or, as in the case of cannibalism, one human being feeds upon the body of another human being, incorporates that flesh into his own system, and then dies. In such a case it is claimed that the same identical particles have been part of two different bodies at the moment of death, and that consequently their reproduction as part of two different bodies at the same time, is simply a physical impossibility! [1]

"Philosophy shows us," says Dr. Hitchcock, "that the identity between the present and the resurrection body cannot be an identity of particles or of organization. The chemist can demonstrate, that the body laid in the grave is decomposed into its ultimate elements, and that these, by almost endless transmutations, pass through, or rather constitute, a part of other bodies; so that the successive races of men that appear on the globe, consist, at least in part, of the same particles which entered into the composition of their progenitors. This makes it physically impossible that the identical particles or atoms, which constitute the body laid in the grave, should belong to the resurrection body as a whole."

[1] Dr. Luther Lee, for whose power as a thinker and writer we entertain a very high respect, seems to have evaded or ignored this objection in his Elements of Theology, instead of stating and refuting it. This is a very unusual course for him. He discusses the subject without mooting the question of the presence of the same particles of matter in two different bodies at the hour of death."—See page 295.

[2] *Religious Lectures,* pp. 23, 24.

The following is perhaps a still more formidable statement of this "philosophical difficulty."

"Let it be proposed to construct one hundred vases, each of one hundred pennyweight, on one hundred successive days, each vase, after it shall have served its day, to be reduced to dust, and each succeeding vase to be constructed of one pennyweight of gold from each preceding vase, the balance to be made up of new gold; and after all the vases shall have been constructed, and have served their day and been reduced to dust, then let it be proposed to reconstruct at the *same moment of time*, the entire one hundred vases, each of which shall be composed of one hundred pennyweight, and of the identical particles of gold of which it was at first composed."[1]

"Now if the matter of the bodies of the dead may seek new affinities, and become component parts of other organic bodies, and by implication parts of other human bodies, and thus the material of one generation may be worked in for the construction of all succeeding generations; I am at a loss to think from whence, at the resurrection, shall come the material of the new and immortal edifice; and *especially urgent* is the dilemma in the case of the *living;* how the integrity of *their* bodies is to be preserved, (which may contain particles of matter that have helped form the bodies of men and women of every generation between the creation and the resurrection,) when the loadstone of

[1] How forcibly this supposititious dilemma reminds one of the question of the Sadducees, Matt. xxii., respecting a woman supposed to have had seven husbands, and concerning which they so foolishly inquired, "In the resurrection, whose wife shall she be of the seven, for they all had her?"

the Almighty shall ransack their tissues and make requisition for particles and parts, to which they have no original claim, and which they hold only by the slight tenure of appropriation."[1]

In the case of the vases, as above stated, the thing proposed is simply impossible—just as impossible as it is that an ounce of gold should be in a hundred different places at the same time. But the illustration assumes that in regard to the gold, which is not proved and never can be proved in regard to the substance of the human body; namely, that the same particles of matter ever *have* been or ever *will* be connected with two or more human bodies at the moment of their death. The illustration is therefore inapplicable to the subject under consideration, since the very question in dispute, (viz., whether the same portion of matter actually has belonged to two different bodies at the moment of death,) has to be *assumed* as a fact; whereas we have no evidence whatever that such a state of things ever existed, or ever will exist.

The following from Bishop Kingsley's admirable work, is a sufficient answer to all such objections:

"In regard to the first—namely, where the decomposed body goes to the support of vegetation, and this vegetation goes to the nourishment of human beings, it may be remarked, that but a small part of earth actually becomes part of vegetation at all. This is demonstrated by the growth of plants and trees, where the entire amount of earth to which their roots had access has been weighed, both before and after their

[1] This extract is from an anonymous letter received by the author after a sermon upon the resurrection in New York, October, 1863.

growth. In this manner plants and trees have increased many pounds in weight, while the earth to which their roots had access had diminished but a few ounces, showing that the atmosphere and water contribute very largely to the growth of vegetation.

"Now, suppose a human being to have eaten grain that had grown upon soil enriched by the decomposition of a human body: allow that he has consumed *one hundred pounds* of such grain; not more than one part in twenty-five of this grain ever becomes actually a part of the human body, that is, four pounds. But not more than one part in twenty of the grain is converted earth, that is, one-fifth of a pound. But probably not more than one part in a *thousand*, to which the roots of grain had access, was human dust, which, by the previous calculation, would give to the second human body but one part in five thousand of a single pound, that is, the one three-hundred-and-twelfth part of an ounce of matter which had ever been possessed by another human being. And even this small fraction of an ounce might go to the grosser parts of the system, not at all necessary to the resurrection body. And where an animal has intervened, the ratio is immensely diminished.

"Again: but a small part of the vegetation concerned in the growth of grain is actually grain itself; and how easy for God, who is not inattentive to anything he has made, and who has adapted means to ends, with infinite skill, throughout every part of nature, to have so ordered, in his providence, that this small part of human dust that actually becomes part of vegetation should lodge in the *roots*, and *stalk*, and leaves, without ever becoming a part of the grain at all! I say, cannot HE DO IT?

* * * * * *

"But let us take the case of cannibalism itself. Now, no considerable portion of the sustenance of any human being has been human flesh. But a small fraction of the entire food, even of those who occasionally indulge in this dreadful practice, has been of this kind. And but a small fraction, even of this small fraction, ever becomes part of the human body, allowing, for the present, that the flesh of one human being may become part of another human being. And even this small fraction may go to the grosser parts of the system, not at all necessary to the resurrection body. So that there is nothing absurd, even here, in the commonly received doctrine of the resurrection.

"But I have a more weighty argument to offer against this position. We have already seen that the resurrection of the body, belonging to the nature of miracles, must be studied in the *light* of miracles. The question, then, is simply this: If the God of infinite power and wisdom set himself to the accomplishment of this work, can he perform it? But it may be said, 'This is the very thing we deny, namely, that God *has* set himself to the accomplishment of this work.' But let it be remembered that it is admitted on all sides that this is the obvious meaning of the Scriptures; and a meaning which all would receive, but for these 'rational deductions,' which we are now examining, and which allege that the thing is absurd and self-contradictory. I say, then, we have a right to repeat the inquiry, "If the God of infinite power set himself to accomplish this work, cannot he perform it?" and to answer, as above, He may so order, in his providence, that no human being at death shall possess a single particle of another human being at death, even allowing cannibalism to be ever so much practiced. There are many ways of which *we* can conceive in which this can be done, and no doubt many more are open to the view of infinite wisdom. This may most easily be accomplished by controlling the circumstances of the death of those who have been guilty of this inhuman practice; and by other methods which have already been enumerated, even upon the supposition that one part of a human body may become, at some period, a portion of another body.

"But we will now admit, for the sake of the argument, what is claimed in the third proposition, that the resurrection of the identical body requires the resurrection of all the gross materials of which the body is composed; not indeed in gross materials; and *then* show that the doctrine implies nothing contradictory or absurd. For then, examining the subject in the light of miracles, we have only to consider the Supreme Being as undertaking the task of raising every human body, *entire*, as it respects the amount of matter possessed by it at death. And is it not infinitely easy for him so to order, in his power and wisdom, that no part of one human body after death shall ever become a part of another human body, under any circumstances? Is it not as easy that a law shall be stamped upon the matter composing the human body, by which it cannot become amalgamated with another human body, as that a similar law should exist in regard to *oil* and *water*, or *iron* and *clay?* And cannot he who could cause *five loaves* and *two fishes* to nourish *five thousand men*, besides *women and children*, also cause the other food that has been eaten, to be entirely sufficient for the nourishment of the human body, no matter how much the practice to which we have alluded has prevailed? And will he not *do* it before his ultimate purposes in this respect shall be thwarted? Are the divine resources so *feeble* and scanty; are the ultimate designs of the eternal Jehovah so circumscribed, that a mere pigmy can throw them into confusion? "Well, but this could not be done without a miracle." Well, what then? The whole subject of the resurrection belongs to miracles. Why will men, professing to believe the Bible, identify themselves with rationalists and infidels, in their abhorrence of anything miraculous? Who shall stand up to "limit the Holy One of Israel?" We have seen, then, that this last and most plausible objection interposes no serious obstacle in the way of the sublime and *Scriptural* doctrine of the resurrection of the body.

* * * * * *

"I have bestowed the more attention upon these positions, because they contain the whole strength of the argument against the resurrection of the body. It is admitted that the plain letter of inspiration teaches another doctrine. 'But this doctrine,' it is said, 'encounters insuperable difficulties.' So then, if these 'insuperable difficulties' have been fairly removed, the argument is yielded at once; inasmuch as these 'difficulties' are all that have prevented the Scriptural doctrine from being received."[1]

These copious extracts do indeed contain and fully meet "the whole strength of the argument against the resurrection of the body," drawn from the wide dispersion of its elements, or their supposed incorporation with other human bodies.

He who has said "the dead men shall live," is everywhere present, of infinite wisdom, and knowledge, and Almighty power; and lives on from age to age, and forever and ever. He *created* every particle of matter in all the universe, has given it all its *properties* and *affinities*, and knows well its *nature* and its *name*. Can it be even *difficult* for such a being to collect again, if need be, every atom of the former mortal body, even though scattered from pole to pole, and to re-build from the corruptible and mortal, the incorruptible and the glorious? "Is anything too hard for the Lord."[2] "Hath he said, and shall he not do it? or hath he spoken and shall he not make it good?"[3]

"The question here is one which simply respects the frustrating a final purpose of the Almighty by an operation of nature. To suppose that he cannot prevent this, is to deny his power; to suppose him inattentive to it, is to suppose him indifferent to his own designs; and to assume that he employs care to prevent it, is to assume nothing greater, nothing in fact so great, as many instances of control, which are always occurring; as, for instance, the regulation of the proportion of the sexes in human births, which cannot be attributed to

[1] Treatise on the Resurrection of the Dead, pp. 36–42.

[2] Gen. xviii. 14. [3] Num. xxiii. 19.

chance, but must either be referred to superintendence, or to some original law."[1]

If necessary to the grand and glorious consummation, God will dissolve all forms of material existence into their primal elements, thus literally fulfilling the poet's vision of the resurrection morning—

> "Before the ploughman fell,
> His steers; and in midway the furrow left.
> The shepherd saw his flocks around him turn
> To dust. Beneath his rider fell the steed
> To ruins."[2]

But it is not necessary to dwell longer upon this objection. The wonder is that ever any person who believed in an all-wise and infinite God should be perplexed by it or even name it.

A late writer has thus expressed his astonishment at such doubts. After stating some of the facts set forth in the preceding pages, he says:

"Here is a man who is acquainted with all these facts. He knows that the body he is to have, if he lives, is now diffused and commingled through all the elements of earth, air, and water; but his belief is, that when he dies, if his body should go back into these elements, and be scattered abroad once more, God cannot collect it again! Well might heaven mourn, earth be astonished, and hell rejoice. I never could have believed this if I had not seen and heard it. The scientific man is fully aware that for the twentieth time he has had a body gathered from the corners of the world; but his prop for eternity is, that God can-

[1] *Watson's Theological Institutes,* Part 3, ch. xxix.

[2] Pollok, Book vii. p. 336.

not do this once more on the morning of the resurrection!"[1]

How many thus err, not knowing the Scriptures, nor the power of God. With men the raising of a Lazarus would have been impossible, but "with God all things are possible."[2] And how weighty, in view of such groundless and yet to some perplexing speculations, is the counsel of the apostle, "Beware lest any man spoil you through philosophy and vain deceit, after the tradition of men, after the rudiments of the world, and not after Christ."[3] And yet, perhaps it ought not to be thought strange that one who has no faith in God, and no just conception of his character, should stumble at the doctrine of a corporeal resurrection. But that a *Christian* should ever be perplexed or thrown into doubt by such speculations, may well be regarded as inexplicable.

It is *not* a thing incredible, therefore, that God should raise the dead, if need be, bone for bone, muscle for muscle, ounce for ounce, and atom for atom. It is God who has promised to effect the mighty miracle, and IT WILL BE DONE!

Take, then, my body as the soul departs,
Burn, pulverize, dissolve, and scatter wide,
Till all its substance, every particle,
Is mingled with the sands of every zone,
And with the floods of every sea and clime;
And as I leave the fast-dissolving form,
And spread my spirit-wings for brighter skies,
One single thought my every doubt shall quell—
The promise is that "God shall raise the dead,"
And in my flesh I yet shall see the Lord.

[1] *Nelson on Infidelity,* pp. 75, 76. [2] Matt. xix. 26. [3] Col. ii. 8.

V. But we are not yet done with objections, extended as our remarks under this head have already been. It has been alleged that if all the dead who have ever lived, and who ever shall live and die, were raised again to life, there would not be room for them all to stand upon the surface of the globe. We answer,

1. That we are nowhere taught in the Scriptures that the risen dead are ever to stand upon the surface of our planet.

2. If such ever should be the Divine will, there is room enough on any *one* of the continents, to say nothing of the others, and the surface of the mighty oceans, to accommodate many times the population of our globe, of all ages and lands, as the following calculation will show:

"The vast number of inhabitants who now live, and have lived upon the earth, appears at first sight to defy the power of calculation. But if we suppose the world to have existed six thousand years; that there are now one thousand millions of human beings living upon its surface; that a generation passes away every thirty years; that every past generation on an average equals the present; and that four individuals can stand upon a square yard of the earth's surface, we find that all the human beings who now live and have lived on the earth would not occupy a space equal to one-half of the state of New York."

Six thousand years, and a generation every thirty years, will give us two hundred generations, which at a thousand millions to a generation, gives two hundred thousand millions. Divide this number by four, and the result is, fifty thousand millions—the number of square yards necessary to accommodate the whole race of man up to the present time.

Now, there are in a square mile three millions, ninety-seven thousand six hundred square yards, by which, if the former sum be divided, it will give sixteen thousand one hundred and forty-one square miles, as the space necessary to accommodate the entire race. But the State of New York, has forty-seven thousand square miles of surface; so that it could accommodate the whole race of man, down to the present time, and have more than thirty thousand square miles to spare; or, in other words, they would only cover about one-third of the area of this one state of the Union."[1]

This estimate shows how largely those persons draw upon their imaginations who deny the possibility of a physical resurrection, on the ground that the earth would not afford room for its resurrected inhabitants.

VI. It has been objected that if our theory of a material resurrection is ever carried out, it will remove so much of the matter of our globe, as to destroy the equilibrium of the planetary system, change the orbit of the earth, reverse the seasons, and perhaps bring on a wide-spread catastrophe, and a general wreck. A few words must suffice, in reply to this objection.

1. If half the globe were removed, no such catastrophe as is supposed would follow. The earth might revolve in the same orbit it now does, with its axis inclined to the ecliptic as it now is, though it were reduced to the dimensions of an asteroid.

2. Even if such a result as is supposed were to fol-

[1] We regret our inability to give credit for this extract, as we have forgotten whence it was obtained.

low the general resurrection of the dead, it would not exceed what St. Peter tells us *shall* occur, when "the heavens shall pass away with a great noise, and the elements shall melt with fervent heat, the earth also and the works that are therein shall be burned up."[1] Granting, therefore, all that is predicted, as a consequence of a physical resurrection, the above objection is of no force whatever, and needs no further consideration.

VII. It has often been urged by the disciples of Emanuel Swedenborg, and others, as an argument against the orthodox belief, that a material body would be *of no use* in a future state; and therefore that such a resurrection would be *superfluous*, and the idea absurd. This objection involves the whole question of the *nature* and *uses* of the resurrection body; and should therefore be the subject of a distinct chapter.

[1] 2 Peter, iii. 10.

CHAPTER XVI.

NATURE AND CHARACTERISTICS OF THE RESURRECTION BODY.

HAVING now gone over the history of the doctrine of the resurrection for the last three thousand years, and ascertained the true nature of that event, the next question in order is, What are the nature and characteristics of the resurrection body? Happily the Sacred Writings shed no small amount of light upon this interesting question.

I. *It will be a* MATERIAL BODY, *and not a mere spirit or shadow.* This, we believe, is admitted in substance by all the theories reviewed in the preceding chapters, that of the Gnostics and Quakers excepted. Even Emanuel Swedenborg and Prof. Bush accord materially to the very subtle and attenuated form that they suppose is evolved from the natural body at the hour of death. The only difference between them and the orthodox belief, so far as this particular point is concerned, is, that they seem to regard the "spiritual body," which they imagine is raised out of the natural body at death, as matter in an etherealized or very refined state.

The theories of Mr. Drew and Archbishop Whately

admit the materiality of the resurrection body, in its fullest and strongest sense; and the Scriptures are so explicit and full upon the subject as to render their citation a superfluity and a weariness. Adam's body was material before the fall. Death, by sin, stripped that body from the spirit, and laid it in the grave; and if ever man is restored through grace and the power of God, he must stand complete, like Adam in Eden, in a material body. Enoch and Elijah and Christ ascended to heaven in their material bodies. The bodies of the saints who live at Christ's second coming are to be changed and then taken to heaven, and it is the "vile *body*" of the deceased Christian that is to be the subject of the great and glorious change of the last day, and to be crowned with glory and honor and immortality.

1. It is described as a *body*, and not a *spirit*. "It is raised a—*body*." God is to quicken "our mortal *bodies*," to "change our vile *bodies*," etc.

"It is then *body*, and not *spirit*, to which the reasoning of the apostle in this instance relates. He is treating of the transition which human nature is destined to pass through, from one condition of corporeal existence to another; and he speaks of the laying down a body that is gross, or at least infirm, and the taking up a body that shall be potent, illustrious, and permanent."[1]

"The substance to be raised is the "*flesh*," as so happily expressed in the Greek and Latin copies of the Apostles' Creed. "The Greeks," says Bishop Pearson, "always used *σαρκος ἀναστασιν*, the Latins,

[1] *Taylor's Physical Theory of Another Life*, p. 15.

carnis resurrectionem;" both of which literally signify the resurrection of *the flesh.*

2. No other idea is compatible with the apostle's reasoning in the fifteenth of first Corinthians, where he says:

> "All flesh is not the same flesh; but there is one kind of flesh of men, another flesh of beasts, another of fishes, and another of birds.
>
> "There are also celestial bodies, and bodies terrestrial; but the glory of the celestial is one, and the glory of the terrestrial is another.
>
> "There is one glory of the sun, and another glory of the moon, and another glory of the stars; for one star differeth from another star in glory.
>
> "So also is the resurrection of the dead."—1 Cor. xv. 39–42.

Here the obvious design is to show that while all these bodies are alike material, they differ greatly in their properties, "as one star differeth from another star in glory." And by applying these illustrations to the resurrection—("so also is the resurrection of the dead")—he plainly teaches that the difference between the present and future body is not in their *substance* or essential elements, but in their *properties*; as the flesh of a fish and of a quadruped may differ in taste and texture, though both are alike material.

"What the Christian Scriptures, then, and St. Paul specifically affirm, is not any abstruse metaphysical doctrine, concerning mind and matter; but the simple physiological fact of two species of corporiety destined for man: the first, that of our present animal and dissoluble organization, which we share, in all its conditions, with the irrational sentient tribes around us; and the second—a future spiritual structure, imperishable and endowed with higher powers and many desirable prerogatives."[1]

Our prejudice, therefore, against matter, as unsuited to the more spiritual future of man, is no reason why we may not have material bodies in a future state. Our connection with the body, and with other forms of matter in the present life, has been under circumstances calculated to mislead the judgment and becloud the reason. The whole earth is under a curse. The blight of sin and death rests upon the entire planet from pole to pole. We know nothing of the attributes of matter in a sinless world. On the contrary we know it only in connection with moral evil, and with death and corruption. It is natural, therefore, that we should come to regard it as unadapted to that more spiritual and more holy state of existence that awaits the Christian in the life to come. And yet it is easy to perceive that all such conclusions are founded more in prejudice than in unbiased reason.

That the resurrection body will be in many respects different from our present corruptible bodies is certain; and yet they will be "*bodies*"—literal, tangible and visible *bodies*, with form, dimensions, etc., precisely as the body of our Lord exhibited all these attributes of matter after it rose from the dead.

"Handle me and see," said he, "for a spirit hath not flesh and bones as ye see me have." And so we doubt not it will be with all, beyond the resurrection. Each will be able to say in truth, "I am not a mere phantom or shade, or ethereal vapor—a something be-

[1] *Taylor's Physical Theory*, p. 23.

tween matter and spirit—but a spirit in a body; a real visible, tangible and substantial *body*.

It is no objection to this view that "flesh and blood cannot inherit the kingdom of God;"[1] for the context shows that by "flesh and blood," the apostle meant merely the body *as it now is*,—mortal and corruptible. Hence, having made this general statement, he proceeds at once to speak of the *change* that must take place before the body can enter the heavenly world. Take the whole passage in its connections:—

> "Now this I say, brethren, that flesh and blood cannot inherit the kingdom of God; neither doth corruption inherit incorruption.
>
> "Behold I show you a mystery; we shall not all sleep, but we shall all be changed.
>
> "In a moment, in the twinkling of an eye, at the last trump: for the trumpet shall sound, and the dead shall be raised incorruptible, and we shall be changed.
>
> "For this corruptible must put on incorruption, and this mortal must put on immortality."—1 Cor. xv. 50–53.

Is it not obvious that the apostle only meant to affirm that "flesh and blood" as it now is, must be changed, and made incorruptible and immortal, before it enters the heavenly land. As Dr. Barnes has well said, "flesh and blood" denotes such bodies as we have here—"bodies that are fragile, weak, liable to disease, and subject to pain and death;" but when changed and made incorruptible and immortal, they will be perfectly adapted to a spiritual and eternal world.

II. *The resurrection body will be a* SPIRITUAL BODY. "It is sown a natural body, it is raised a spiritual body."[2] What the term "spiritual" imports, as descriptive of the resurrection body, we may not fully

[1] 1 Cor. xv. 50. [2] 1 Cor. xv. 44.

understand in this life; and yet we may "know in part" from a careful study of the connections of this comprehensive declaration.

It is very obvious that "spiritual" is not put in contrast with *material*,—as if it had been written "a *spirit* body;" for that would have been a contradiction. It is a *spiritual* or *spirit-like* body—a body having some of the attributes of spirit, as had just been specified.

"The term '*spiritual body*,' says Dr. Hitchcock, "is peculiar to Paul, and chosen probably because it comes as near to giving an idea of the resurrection body, as human language admits; not because it gives a full idea of that body. Numerous attempts have been made to define this term. It cannot mean that the future body will be spirit; for then it would not differ from the soul. It must be material, therefore, unless there be in the universe a third substance, which is neither matter nor spirit."[1]

And yet it is clear that the apostle meant to convey these two ideas by the use of this term; first, that the resurrection body will be very unlike our present mortal bodies; and second, that the difference will consist of the investing of the new body with some of the characteristics of spirit, namely, incorruption, and glory, and immortality. Hence it is called a spiritual or spirit-like body.[2]

[1] *Religious Lectures*, pp. 19, 20.

[2] The Scriptures represent the spiritual body as possessing a specific and individual identity. By this I mean, that it will possess characteristics which mark it off distinctly from every other created thing: as the different species and individuals of animals and plants are marked off

But although we believe this one term—"spiritual" comprehends all the particulars specified by the apostle, in this chapter and elsewhere, we shall nevertheless consider them one by one, in distinct sections, as worthy of distinct notice in such an investigation.

III. *The new or resurrection body will be* INCORRUPTIBLE. "It is raised in *incorruption.*" "This corruptible must put on *incoruption.*" "The dead shall be raised *incorruptible.*" We know what corruptible and corruption are, but what are incorruptible and incorruption? Obviously the latter are the opposite of the former, a superiority to putrefaction and dissolution. Now a wound or ulcer may become corrupt and loathsome while we still inhabit the body, and at death the whole body dissolves and crumbles back to dust. But the resurrection body will not be thus liable to inflammation, ulceration, or decomposition, more than were the bodies of Adam and Eve before the fall. As pure gold may remain unaffected through a thousand changes that would dissolve our corruptible bodies, and the brilliant diamond may bid defiance to cold and heat and acids, and shine on for ages a changeless emblem of incorruption, so our bodies, having put on incorruption, shall shine on, in their undecaying perfection and beauty, indestructible and changeless forever.

IV. *The resurrection body will be immortal.* "This mortal must put on *immortality.*" "Mortality" must be "swallowed up of life," and "death swallowed up in victory." "Neither shall they die any more," for

from one another in this world. This very important principle appears to me in a very great degree, to have been overlooked by commentators."—*Religious Lectures,* p. 18.

"there shall be no more death, neither sorrow, nor crying; neither shall there be any more pain, for the former things are passed away." The body, being incorruptible, can no more fall into such a state of derangement as to dislodge the soul from its occupancy. It has "put on immortality!"

Of course we cannot fully conceive of such a body. All we know is, that being superior to death, that is, incorruptible and immortal, it can never be affected by cold or heat, or hunger or thirst, or sickness or decay. Hence, "they shall hunger no more, neither thirst any more; neither shall the sun light on them nor any heat;" and "God shall wipe away all tears from their eyes."

V. *The new body will be raised up* IN POWER. "It is sown in *weakness*, it is raised in *power*." Not *by* power, but *in* power, having reference not to the *agency* by which it is raised, but to the *condition* it shall be in when raised. In our best estate here, there is much of "weakness." The best eye does not suffice for all the purposes of knowledge or enjoyment, and we must therefore supplement it by the microscope on the one hand, and the telescope on the other. Moreover, the eye and ear, and touch and taste, and smell may grow weary, or partially or wholly fail us, and the whole body at length break down under the strain of continued exertion or the weight of years. Glorious as it is, and much as we owe to it as the instrument of the Spirit and the medium of our knowledge of the external world, it is nevertheless insufficient to answer all the purposes of its immortal proprietor.[1] And as

[1] How strikingly is this fact illustrated in the case of the lamented

sometimes in life, so much more in death: the eye is sightless, the ear deaf, and all their powers are dead. But in contrast with this "weakness" in which the body is buried, it is to be raised in "power," or as some render the term, *sufficiency*, to answer all the demands of the soul perfectly and forever.

If the body as a whole is to be raised "in power," its various organs must be "in power" also, for these are necessary to make up the aggregate of the corporeal system. The stomach, we are told, is to be destroyed, as the body will no longer be sustained by the digestion and assimilation of food; and as in that world they "neither marry nor are given in marriage," the organs of reproduction may also be wanting, as unnecessary in the immortal state. But not so with eye and ear and voice and hands. These, though of inestimable value here, may be of infinitely more service to us in the future state than they have ever been in this world.

1. Take the EYE, for instance. There are birds and insects which have microscopic eyes. Others can adjust their eyes to a longer or shorter range, like changing the focus of a refracting telescope. Others again have eyes adapted to vision under water; while others still, both birds and quadrupeds, if not fish and reptiles and insects, can see in the night as well as we can in the daytime. Now suppose the human eye to be so restored and perfected in the resurrection as to include all these adaptations; to be microscopic or telescopic at will, to be equally serviceable in any medium, and

Hugh Miller, and also in the case of Hon. Preston King, late Collector of the port of New York, who committed suicide in Dec. 1865.

with any degree of light. Add to this, if you please, the power of the prism to resolve the rays of light into their original components, and gild any scene at will with the colors of the rainbow. If birds and fish and beasts and insects have most of these visual powers even in this world, some one and some another, is it too much to suppose that when the human eye is raised incorruptible and immortal it may possess *all* these powers? We have known a hunter who could see the satellites of Jupiter with the naked eye. A few years ago the papers gave an account of a boy in Kentucky whose eyes were telescopic, so that he could see the rings and satellites of Saturn without artificial aid. What, then, may be the "power" of the eye when the curse has for ever passed away, and the whole body is raised in "power?" Shall we still be obliged to help out vision with microscopes and telescopes? Shall we do without the knowledge attained in this life only by the aid of these artificial helps, or shall we have eyes that will be sufficient to answer all these ends?

2. And so of the EAR. Many of the lower animals can hear sounds to which the ear of man is deaf. The air is full of sounds, or atmospheric undulations, which make no impression upon this sense in man. And it is well that it is so in this world of discord, otherwise the ear, which is now the source of so much knowledge and happiness, might become the source of perpetual wakefulness and misery. All the senses are, in this respect, adapted to our present abode and circumstances.

But let us go where no discordant notes are to be heard; where "fragrant flowers immortal bloom," and where the greatest conceivable delicacy of touch and taste and smell and hearing and sight could but waft to the soul a perpetual tribute of delight, and what a blessing would such a body be.

We are not as fearful as some of "getting up a Mohammedan Paradise," by including the pleasures of sense among the joys of the immortal life. Such timidity is, in our view, too much like rejecting all natural illustrations and corroborative proofs of the wisdom, power, and goodness of God, merely because we have a written revelation. As Adam, in his primeval holiness, enjoyed all the pleasures brought to the soul through his unfallen senses, and as such enjoyments, properly regulated and restricted, are compatible with the highest communion with God in this present world, so in the future life, the pleasures of sense may be added to and forever mingle with the streams of spiritual bliss that flow unceasingly from God and the Lamb.

3. The VOICE, too, shall be "raised in power." For they all *sing* in heaven. The brother who never sang on earth has found a voice there. The Quaker has broken his long silence, and the sound of their united voices is "as the sound of many waters and of mighty thunderings."

In the present life the compass of the human voice is but limited. It can be heard but a short distance. It has to be assisted and sustained, and the harmony perfected by harps and pianos and organs. It is easily exhausted, and finally fails the best of vocalists. Now suppose instead of this, when the body is raised "in sufficiency," the range shall be from the highest to the lowest conceivable note, say thirty octaves instead of eight. Suppose again it shall be capable of adapting itself to all the different *varieties* of sounds, like the flute and horn and cornet, etc., in the great organ in Boston, and shall have power to make itself heard distinctly at almost any distance. Then add to this ability to sing one part as well as another, or even several parts at once,[1] and to sing on without hoarseness or weariness for a day or a year or a century! Such, we conceive, would be the human voice "in power," or "sufficiency;" so that it could express all that the soul can then feel, could vie with the most powerful organ in compass and volume and variety, and dispense forever with all such artificial helps in the immortal praises of our God.

4. And why may not the same be true of the organs of TASTE and SMELL—the palate and the olfactories? Were not these organs made by a beneficent Creator, to minister to the delights of the soul in Paradise itself? Why, then, may they not serve the same purpose when man shall be fully redeemed from the power of sin and death, to shine in the image of God forever?

5. It is the opinion of some that in the bright and glorious hereafter, the saints will not only possess immortal bodies, with all their senses complete and perfect, but will also possess new and additional organs of sensation; which shall convey new and unknown

[1] There was a negro boy in the vicinity of New York in June, 1865, who was able to sing the alto and the soprano of a tune at the same time; and Prof. E. Arnold, of the Black River Conference, upon seeing this statement in the New York *Christian Advocate*, wrote the author that he had a son who had "a double voice," and could perform the same feat.

delights to the soul, and develope new powers in the immortal spirit.

"It seems to me not improbable," says Archbishop Whately, "that the change which shall take place in the body may be itself the appointed means for bringing about a change in the powers and tendencies of the mind. It is plain that the mind greatly depends on the body as its instrument; and on the several members of the body depend the exercise of several distinct powers of the mind: so that the loss or imperfection of one particular organ—of the eye, for instance—or the ear—will shut out one particular kind of knowledge and of thought from the mind;—that of colors, for instance,—or that of sounds.

"It is quite possible, therefore, that our minds may at this moment actually possess faculties which have never been exercised, and of which we have no notion whatever; which have lain inactive, unperceived, and undeveloped, for want of such a structure of bodily organs as is necessary to call them forth and give play to them. A familiar instance of this kind, is the case of a man born blind; whose *mind* or spiritual part is as perfect in itself as another man's; his mind is as capable even of receiving impressions of visible objects by the eyes, as if the eyes themselves (the bodily part) were perfect; for it is plainly, not the *eyes* that see, but the *mind* by means of the eyes; yet through this imperfection, one whole class of ideas,—all those of objects of sight,—are completely wanting in such a man. Nor could he ever even find out his imperfection, if he were not told of it; he learns from *others*, that there is such a thing as seeing, and as light and colors, though he cannot comprehend what they are. And if you could suppose such a case as blind persons brought up from childhood without ever being taught that others possessed a sense more than themselves, they would never suspect anything at all on the subject. Should they then obtain sight, they would be astonished at discovering that they had all along been in possession, so far as the mind is concerned, of a faculty which they had had no opportunity to exercise, and of whose very existence they had never dreamed, —the faculty of perceiving the visible objects presented to the mind by the eye."

"Now I think it is not unlikely—it certainly is not impossible—that the like may be our case;—that our minds may have, even now, faculties which lie dormant at present (as the power of sight does in a blind man;) and that these would be called into action by a mere change of our bodily frame, and a new system of organs. And if this should take place in a future state, we should at once be enabled to perceive, merely by means of a bodily change, whole classes of objects as new to our minds as colors are to a blind-born man; and as totally different from any we are now acquainted with, as colors are from sounds. And by some change of this kind in the *brain,* an equally great revolution may, for aught we can tell, be produced in our *thinking* faculties also,—those by which we are distinguished from brutes;—and an equal enlargement produced in our powers of reasoning and judging.

On all these points, however, the sacred writers have not thought fit to gratify our curiosity, but have been content to tell us generally, that we shall be greatly changed, without attempting to explain what that change shall be." [1]

And yet all that is here supposed may actually be included in the change that shall pass upon our vile bodies in the glorious resurrection; "for it doth not yet appear what we shall be."

VI. *The new body is to be raised* IN GLORY.

"It is sown in dishonor, it is raised *in glory*." It is "sown" or buried "in dishonor," in that it is conquered and under the curse of sin, and corruptible and loathsome; but it is raised in glory in that death is swallowed up of victory; the curse is gone, and the corruptible and mortal and loathsome becomes incorruptible, immortal, and glorious. Macknight thinks there is here an allusion to Daniel xii. 2, "They that be wise shall shine as the brightness of the firmament," etc.; and also to our Lord's word, Matthew xiii. 43: "Then shall the righteous shine forth as the sun in the kingdom of their Father," as descriptive of the resurrection bodies of the saints.

The apostle Paul tells us, that the bodies of the saints shall become like the glorious body of Christ, "who shall change our vile body, that it may be fashioned like unto his glorious body." [2] What his glorious body was, we may judge somewhat from its appearance on several occasions.

1. Upon the summit of Tabor, upon the occasion of his transfiguration, when "his face did shine as the sun, and his raiment was white as the light." St. Mark says his "raiment became shining, exceeding white as snow, so as no fuller on earth can white

[1] *Future State*, pp. 104–106. [2] Phil. iii. 21.

them;" and St. Luke, that "the fashion of his countenance was altered, and his raiment was white and glistering." No doubt this was designed to give the disciples some idea of the glory of the human body when it shall have put on incorruption. So glorious was Christ's body that its light flamed out through his raiment, and made it also "white as the light,"—"exceeding white as snow."

2. When he appeared to Saul on the way to Damascus the same supernatural light attended him, even "above the brightness of the sun."

"And as he journeyed, he came near Damascus: and suddenly there shined round about him a light from heaven.

"And he fell to the earth, and heard a voice saying unto him, Saul, Saul, why persecutest thou me?

"And he said, Who art thou, Lord? And the Lord said, I am Jesus whom thou persecutest."—Acts ix. 3–5.

3. In his manifestation of himself to St. John, Rev. i., this "immortal glory" is still more conspicuous.

"And I turned to see the voice that spake with me. And being turned, I saw seven golden candlesticks;

"And in the midst of the seven candlesticks one like unto the Son of Man, clothed with a garment down to the foot, and girt about the paps with a golden girdle

"His head and his hairs were white like wool, as white as snow: and his eyes were as a flame of fire:

"And his feet like unto fine brass, as if they burned in a furnace: and his voice as the sound of many waters.

"And he had in his right hand seven stars; and out of his mouth went a sharp two-edged sword; and his countenance was as the sun shineth in his strength.

"And when I saw him, I fell at his feet as dead. And he laid his right hand upon me, saying unto me, Fear not; I am the first and the last:

"I am he that liveth, and was dead; and, behold, I am alive for evermore, Amen; and have the keys of hell and death."—Rev. i. 12–18.

Here let it be noticed that Christ is careful to identify himself to St. John as one who "*was dead*," though then alive for evermore. Mark also the appearance of his *hair* and *eyes* and *feet*, and "his *countenance* as the sun shineth in his strength." His *voice* also was "in power," "as the sound of many waters."

Such is Christ's "glorious body" as it appeared on earth on several occasions. And inconceivable as such a change may be to us, we are distinctly assured that Christ "shall change our vile body, that it may be fashioned like unto his glorious body, according to the working whereby he is able even to subdue all things unto himself." Phil. iii. 21.

But it may be asked, *how can* such an incorruptible and glorious body be evolved from death and corruption?—the mouldering dust of our present mortal bodies? We can have no conception of the philosophy of a miracle, for the reason that it is above and beyond philosophy; that is, a supernatural event. And the resurrection in all its parts is miraculous.

And yet the same question may be asked in regard to a thousand things in nature, that we know actually do take place. How can God produce such an infinite variety of birds, and fish, and insects, and quadrupeds, and fruits, and flowers, and trees, and gems, from the few simple elements of nature? And yet he does it incessantly.

To one who was not aware of the fact, it seems hardly possible that common coal and the brilliant and imperishable diamond are the same substance—carbon in different states. So, too, a person who had never witnessed the phenomenon, or been assured of it, would find it hard to believe that a beautiful bird could be evolved from the colorless and inanimate egg; or the gorgeous butterfly from the loathsome caterpillar. Yet so it is. And if God can thus reconstruct the body of an insect and adorn it with peerless beauty of form and color, how easily may he also change our vile body, and make it like unto Christ's glorious body.

A gardener buries the carcase of a dog or a huge snake in his garden, and subsequently in setting several rose-bushes, plants one over the decaying body. He has forgotten the circumstance of the burial, but at the end of a year or two this plant has outstripped its fellows, is larger, and more fresh and thrifty, and its blossoms are larger, more numerous, more beautiful and more fragrant than theirs. Now what has taken place? Obviously this: the plant has derived special vigor and life from the corruption through which its roots have penetrated; or, in other words, a portion of that loathsome rottenness and corruption has been taken up by the roots of the rose-bush, conveyed upward, and transmuted into leaves and flowers and the ottar of roses! And yet we stagger at the promise of God to change our vile bodies, and make them glorious like that of our ascended Redeemer!

By employing a sufficient degree of heat, we can decompose the hard and brilliant diamond into carbonic acid gas; but it is beyond the power of man to recrystalize it, and restore it to its original form and beauty. But God can do it, and has done it in millions of instances. So of the human body: man can kill it, and consign it to corruption; but is unable to restore it, or even to conceive how such an achievement can be accomplished. But God can and will do it. Though sown in weakness and corruption, it shall be raised in glory.

And yet it is not strange that we "whose foundation is in the dust," who "have said to corruption, Thou art my father; to the worm, Thou art my mother and my sister," should deem it almost incredible that a change so glorious should await us in the bright hereafter. No wonder that even the pious Bishop South exclaimed, "Can filth and rottenness be the preparatives for glory, and dust and ashes the seed-plots of immortality? Is the sepulchre the place to dress ourselves in for heaven, the attiring-room for corruption to put on incorruption, and to fit us for the beatific vision?"

Yes. The "sure word of prophecy" answers, and dispels all doubt. "There shall be a resurrection of the dead, both of the just and unjust." Nor is this all. We shall be raised with incorruptible, immortal, powerful and glorious bodies, like unto Christ's glorious body. As we have borne the image of the earthy, we shall also bear the image of the heavenly.

VIII. But in view of the revealed characteristics of the resurrection body, what becomes of the objection to a corporeal resurrection founded upon prejudices against matter, or against the body in its present condition? Does it lie at all against the body "that *shall* be?" Look at these additional characteristics, which, if not specifically revealed, are legitimately deducible from what is revealed:—

1. All its organs and powers will be perfect, and indestructible as the pillars of heaven.

2. It will need no food or rest to keep up its ceaseless life, and will be unaffected by cold or heat or sickness or pain forever.

3. It will be capable of *endless exertion* without weariness or decay. Here the eyes of a hard student may fail him, or his whole nervous system may give way at once, and he become a paralytic or a maniac. The strongest man placed at a ship's pump or a fire engine for a given period, without food or water, will faint from exhaustion. But not so the marine engine that crosses the ocean without stopping, driving the huge ship through winds and waves. *There* is *power without weariness.* So with "the angels that excel in strength," the "mighty angels;" and so will it be with the bodies of men when "raised in power." They will be capable of endless exertion without weariness or decay.

4. It is probable, from the analogy of Christ's resurrection body, which was visible or invisible at pleasure; was in and out of the upper room at Jerusalem without the opening of doors; and finally ascended from Mount Olivet in utter contempt of the laws of nature; that our future bodies will be exempt from the operation of *all* the laws that govern material forms in this world, as they are from corruption, even gravitation included; and that they may be transported at will from point to point with the celerity of the imagination, or the speed of a sunbeam. To suppose

that we shall measure the celestial pathways step by step as we walk in this world, is to remand the butterfly back to his chrysalis, and the soaring eagle back to his shell again.

"Being 'fashioned like unto Christ's glorious body,' its beauty will be exquisite, its symmetry perfect, its aspect bright and refulgent, and its motions various and nimble. Its sensitive organs will be refined and improved, and the sphere of their operations extended. Its auditory organs will be tuned to receive the most delightful sensations from the harmonies of celestial music, and its visual powers rendered capable of perceiving the minutest objects, and penetrating into the most distant regions. New senses and faculties of perception, and new powers of motion, fitted to transport it with rapidity from one portion of space to another, will, in all probability, be superadded to the powers with which it is invested." [1]

Now with such a body, (and both Scripture and reason authorize us to expect such a one,) what can an objector mean by talking about our "dragging it after us to all eternity?" What ideas of utility could Prof. Bush have had in suggesting, as he does, that the materials of the old body are worth more to make up into mortal bodies here for other probationers to live in, than to erect into such a glorious body, to be our home and servant forever?

The answer to all such cavils and objections is furnished in the stirring words of inspiration—"This corruptible must put on incorruption, and this mortal must put on immortality." "We shall be changed."

[1] Dick's *Philosophy of a Future State.*

"For our conversation is in heaven; from whence also we look for the Saviour, the Lord Jesus Christ:

Who shall change our vile body, that it may be fashioned like unto his glorious body, according to the working whereby he is able even to subdue all things unto himself."—Phil. iii. 21.

Yes, these, now rising from the tomb,
With lustre brighter far shall shine,
Revive with ever-during bloom,
Safe from diseases and decline.

Such are the nature and characteristics of the future bodies of the saints, as described in the Scriptures—a material and mortal body, changed by the power of Christ, and made spiritual, incorruptible, and immortal; powerful, in eye and ear, and voice, and in every organ and capability; and glorious as the celestial body of the Son of God.

CHAPTER XVII

SPECULATIVE QUESTIONS CONSIDERED, PHYSICAL DEFECTS, INFANTS, NATIONALITIES, ETC.

ALTHOUGH it illy becomes us to seek to be wise above what is written, it is neither irreverent nor unprofitable to *reason* upon revealed truth; and to deduce from principles and from undoubted facts, their legitimate consequences. God treats us as reasoning beings throughout the Bible; and would no more reveal to us specifically what is clearly deducible from a well-known principle or fact; than he would work a miracle when the same result could be reached by the operations of natural laws.

Applying these principles to the subject before us, we find, as we have seen in the preceding chapter, that the bodies of the saints are to be raised incorruptible, immortal, and glorious, like unto Christ's glorious body. That is all that is plainly and directly revealed. But by reasoning upon what is revealed, we reached certain conclusions, touching a variety of questions that arise in the mind in regard to the future body—questions, it may be, of little practical account, and to be regarded as speculative; and yet questions that *will* arise in the mind in spite of ourselves, and which may even perplex and confuse a child of God. To a few of these questions we propose now to call attention.

I. *Will the bodies of the saints exhibit* ANY PHYSICAL DEFECTS *or disabilities in the resurrection?*

No doubt they will all have passed away forever; for,

1. This follows from the preceding general declarations, as the greater always includes the less. If the future body is to be incorruptible, immortal, and glorious, it cannot be blind or deaf, or maimed, or deformed, or in any respect defective. It is therefore a just inference from what is clearly revealed, that all defects in the senses or limbs, whether natural or accidental, will be made good in the resurrection. Every immortal body will be complete and perfect in all its parts, performing every function that can properly be demanded of it in a state of retribution and immortality.

"If the human body, even in its present state of degradation, excited the pious admiration of the Psalmist, much more will it appear worthy of our highest admiration, when it emerges from darkness and corruption, to participate in the glories of the *immortal* life. Its faculties will then be invigorated, its tendencies to dissolution destroyed, every principle of disease annihilated, and everything that is loathsome and deformed forever prevented."[1]

On the 18th of February, 1854, the writer visited the Siamese Twins, then at No. 337 Broadway, New York. While looking at them as they stood bound together by that singular cartilaginous ligament which

[1] *Philosophy of a Future State,* by Thomas Dick, LL. D.

unites their bodies, we thought of the time when one or the other would die, and of its probable effect upon the other; and finally of the subject of the resurrection. We asked, "Do you profess to be Christians?" to which they responded in the affirmative. "Do you believe in the resurrection of the dead?" "Certainly we do." "Do you expect to be united there as you have been in this life?" "No. We shall be separate, and each with a body like Christ's glorious body." And so it will no doubt be in respect to all similar anomalies and defects. They are effects of sin; and with the righteous at least, will have passed away forever.

2. It is no valid objection to this view that our Lord's body exhibited the marks of violence in his hands and side after he arose from the dead; for, first, it is not certain that the wounds in his hands and feet, and side, still remain, as they appeared the evening after his resurrection; and, secondly, if they do, there may be a special reason for it in his case, which does not exist in regard to any other human body. For ought we know to the contrary, it may be the purpose of Heaven that the wounds in the immaculate body of the Lamb of God, shall be the visible memorials of his love and sufferings for us to all eternity. It may not be argued, therefore, from this case, that marks of violence to the body may remain in the resurrection state.

Neither do the words of Christ, Luke ix. 43, 47, imply that any will or can "literally" enter into life 'maimed' or "halt," or with one hand or one eye. It is simply a strong figure by which he inculcates the sacrifice of any earthly pleasure or benefit that may endanger the welfare of the soul, in order that we may not fail of eternal life.

II. *Will there be variety in the* SIZE *and* APPEARANCE *of bodies in the resurrection? or will they all be precisely alike in stature and physiognomy?*

For ought we can see to the contrary, the same law of *variety* that pervades all the works of God, may appear in the resurrection, and the world to come. We can see no reason for supposing that the infant body will be raised as a full-grown young man or woman; or that the venerable and patriarchal in appearance, will have gone back to the aspects of youth or early manhood. Take from the patriarchal form all traces of the curse, and every indication of death or decay, and it may be a pride and an ornament even in the heavenly mansions. And so the body of the tender infant—why should it be expanded to manhood? Is it at all necessary to its adaptation to the wants and happiness of the spirit that is to dwell in it? Why, then, should it be expected that all will be graded up or leveled down to the same plane of stature or appearance, unlike what we have ever been or seen in the present world, and unlike all the analogies of Jehovah's universe? Make all incorruptible, immortal, and glorious, and perfect in every part and function, and we can see no reason why they may not be as various in stature and appearance, as are the bodies of those who depart hence in the Lord. How tame and monotonous a flower-garden would be, if all the flowers were precisely alike in form and size and color. And, leaving out of view the perpetuity of the race, what would this world be without children? And so of the life to come,—though in respect to marrying and giving in marriage we are as the angels of God, we can see no necessity for, nor advantage in the idea that there shall be no infant or child-like bodies in the resurrection.

The promise that we shall be "like unto Christ's glorious body" certainly does not imply that all our bodies shall be precisely like his in stature, physiognomy, etc., but merely that "we shall be like him" in incorruption, and glory, and immortality; all of which is perfectly consistent with the idea of *variety* of stature and physiognomy in the life to come.

We therefore look upon it as probable, and cherish it as an opinion, based upon these analogies and reasonings, that in the resurrection there will be variety of form and stature, answering, perhaps, in a greater or less degree, to the stature, and physiognomy, and age, of the body at the hour of death.

III. *Will the distinctions of* NATIONALITY, COLOR, *etc., survive the sleep of death, and reappear in the resurrection?*

Of course no man can answer such a question, except so far as he may reason from certain principles or analogies that are plainly revealed. And yet, as already stated, we see no impropriety in reasoning, even upon such a topic.

In the first place, there is no absolute standard of beauty or perfection which all nations recognize. Hence a human form, and eye, and color, and countenance, which are beautiful in one country, may be quite repulsive in another. In the next place, neither God nor holy beings have any prejudices against nationality or physiognomy or color, but will regard all alike, as did our blessed Redeemer, in loving all alike, and tasting death alike for every man. Even, therefore, if national characteristics should reappear in the resurrection, to a greater or less degree, we see nothing in it incompatible with either the holiness or the happiness of the future state. But finally, if it be true, as it no doubt is, that all differences of stature, color, and physiognomy, among the different races and tribes of men, are due to climate, food, and habits of life; is it not probable that they will all disappear in the grand restoration, as mere accidents of a state of probation and mortality, in a world resting under the curse of sin? No doubt Adam and Eve had perfect human bodies; and it is not unreasonable to suppose that in the resurrection the body will be conformed to its original model, like the bodies of the first pair in Eden; sinking forever all national characteristics and peculiarities, as accidents of our mortal sojourn, to be known and remembered no more when all the saints get home.

But upon these questions we can affirm nothing. All we positively know is, that, whether Jew or Gentile, black or white, bond or free, all who die in Christ shall arise to glory and immortality, with bodies like unto his glorious body. And there, for the present, our absolute knowledge ends.

IV. *Wherein, if in any respect, will the bodies of the wicked differ from those of the saints?*

The Scriptures are by no means explicit as to the

resurrection bodies of the lost. And yet they are by no means silent upon the subject.

1. That they are to have a resurrection is certain (as we shall show more fully in a subsequent chapter;) but in what respect their bodies will differ from the bodies of the saints, we are not fully informed. And yet several considerations go to show that their future bodies will be very different from those of the righteous.

2. In the latter part of the fifteenth chapter of first Corinthians, it is very evident that the apostle speaks of the righteous only. Nothing, therefore, which he there says of the characteristics of the resurrection body, (as considered in the preceding pages,) can be properly applied to the bodies of the wicked. And so of the declaration, Phil. iii. 21, "who shall change our vile bodies," etc., it is legitimately applicable to the bodies of the saints only. In the absence, then, of any declaration to that effect, we know not that we are authorized to believe that the bodies of the wicked will be either incorruptible or immortal, in any such sense as the righteous are, much less that they will be like unto Christ's glorious body.

3. Our Lord seems to teach a different doctrine, John v. 29, where he says men will arise, "they that have done good unto the resurrection of life; and they that have done evil unto the *resurrection of damnation.*" What difference there will be in the bodies of the righteous and the wicked we cannot, of course, fully understand, but it seems probable that it will be very great; perhaps as great as the difference in their moral characters. In the present life we know that the moral character often has much to do with the condi-

tion of the body; so much, indeed, that it has passed into a divine axiom that the wicked do not live out half their days. Look at the indolent and filthy, the intemperate and the licentious, and see how sadly the moral character leaves its blight and curse upon the physical system. Now if such be a law of the present life, why may it not still prevail in the life to come?

Again: there can be little doubt that the state or condition of the mind—the passions and affections especially—has much to do in the present world in moulding the human physiognomy. If a man is treacherous, vindictive, or tyrannical, his physiognomy is very apt to proclaim the fact; and so of the benevolent, sympathetic and affectionate. May not this law also prevail in the future state, so that the bodies of the righteous shall answer to the moral purity of their blood-washed spirits, while the bodies of the wicked shall answer to their fiend-like spiritual natures, and shall exhibit in every lineament and aspect the vileness and the wretchedness of the lost soul within.[1]

The ancient Jews believed that the wicked would arise, subject to corruption and disease, and pain, through the body, the same as it is before death.

[1] "The *moral character* of the individual," says Prof. Bush, "may exert a controlling and moulding influence upon the constitution of that future body, through which it shall manifest itself. . . . Even in our present state—in our gross corporeal fabric—we see the most marked effects produced by the acting of the inward spirit upon the outward organization. Do we not often in the countenance of one admire the sweetness of the seraph, and in another shudder at the rage of a fiend? What an eloquent impress is stamped upon the features by the moods of the soul! And were the moods, which are often transient, but permanent,—could they continue in unabated intensity,—what a fixed and speaking character would it impart to the whole outer man!"—*Anastasis*, pp. 393, 394.

Hence Josephus says, "But as for the unjust, they will receive their bodies not changed, not freed from diseases or distempers, nor made glorious, but with the same diseases wherein they died; and such as they were in unbelief, the same shall they be when they shall be faithfully judged."[1]

4. If it be true that the bodies of the righteous are to be the medium of knowledge and enjoyment to the soul in a future state, is it not probable that the bodies of the wicked will be sources of woe and wretchedness beyond the resurrection? And yet few of us doubt the former. Why, then, may it not be true that the resurrection of the sinner, which comes through Christ despite his sin and unbelief, and which might have been to him an infinite blessing, will, in consequence of his sin and unbelief, be to him an endless curse? And may not all this be implied in the words of Christ—"the *resurrection* of *damnation*?"[2]

But upon these points also we "see through a glass darkly," and can only "prophesy in part." But when the dead are raised, and that which is perfect is come, then that which is in part shall give place to the more perfect knowledge of the heavenly state.

V. *The* MORAL DISTINCTIONS *of this life are to reappear and be distinctly recognized in the resurrection.*

[1] Discourse to the Greeks concerning Hades.

[2] Prof. Bush, writing as if he believed the wicked hereafter were to have corporeal bodies, says "*Their* bodies may become a perpetual source of corroding pain, of an anguish that knows no mitigation. . . . The spiritual tenements of wicked men will probably be moulded by their inward character, and the soul rent and torn by the actings of evil, will convert into a ministry of woe, and an object of horror, the corporeal vehicle in which it lives, and through which it acts."—*Anastasis*, p. 395.

The righteous and the wicked are everywhere recognized as distinct and widely different characters throughout the Scriptures. "Say ye to the righteous, that it shall be well with him: for they shall eat the fruit of their doings. Woe unto the wicked! it shall be ill with him: for the reward of his hands shall be given him."[1] So at death: "Let me die the death of the righteous, and let my last end be like his."[2] "The wicked is driven away in his wickedness: but the righteous hath hope in his death."[3] The same moral distinctions will reappear in the morning of the resurrection. The just and the unjust will both arise. "They that have done good, unto the resurrection of life; and they that have done evil, unto the resurrection of damnation."[4] The man who has died a sinner, must arise from the dead as a sinner, and in that character must face the Judge of quick and dead, and the realities of the eternal world. "If the tree falleth toward the south, or toward the north, in the place where the tree falleth, there it shall be,"[5] that is, as a man is, morally, when he dies, so shall he be forever. Once beyond the grave, the fiat of the Almighty has gone forth, "He that is unjust, let him be unjust still: and he which is filthy, let him be filthy, still: and he that is righteous, let him be righteous still: and he that is holy, let him be holy still."[6]

Consequently in the resurrection, whether unjust and filthy, or righteous and holy, as they have been before and at the hour of death, so shall they arise from the dead; and while God sits upon the throne

[1] Isa. iii. 11. [2] Num. xxiii. 10. [3] Prov. xiv. 32.
[4] John v. 29. [5] Eccl. xi. 3. [6] Rev. xxii. 11.

the righteous shall never descend to the abodes of sin and death, nor the ungodly ascend to the regions of holiness and eternal life.

VI. *All other distinctions of this life will have passed away forever.*

There will be no rich, or poor, high or low, noble or ignoble, bond or free, beyond the exaltation and glory that result from moral character, and the consequent favor of God.

See that poor old African, who has toiled as a slave for half a century, unrequited and despised. But amid injustice and oppression he has loved his God. At length sickness and death overtake him, and his old body is laid away in the negro burying-ground, as if wrong and outrage could not be satisfied, unless they pursued him even to the very abode of the dead. No funeral cortege follows his sable body to the slaves' burying-ground. No prayer is said over his despised remains, and no stone marks the spot where his ashes slumber. Nevertheless, he was a Christian, a child of God, an heir of glory, a brother of the angels; and they have conveyed his spirit to the land of endless freedom and immortal rest.

At length Christ appears in the clouds of heaven, the trumpet sounds, and every grave-yard begins to teem with life. Its resurrection peals are not confined to the Greenwoods, and Mount Auburns, and Cypress Hills of earth, but, rolling over land and sea, stir the dust of every potter's-field, and of every negro burying-ground. The old saint of God hears the summons, and arises to put on his immortal vestments, and wear his crown of life!

A poor negro woman had two children in the Colored Orphans' Asylum, in New York,[1] one of whom was very sick. Living far down town, she went out amid the sleet and rain to take a car to go up to 43d street, and see her dying child. But she was a negress, and could take no car but such as were specially appropriated to negroes—perhaps one in twenty; and there she was obliged to stand and watch by the gas-light nearly an hour, till she saw upon a car the welcome inscription, "COLORED PEOPLE ADMITTED TO THIS CAR." Thus delayed, she reached the Asylum, only in time to find her child dead!

But it shall not be so in the resurrection. When the chariots of God are wheeling around the grave-yards of earth, to convey the saints upward to the New Jerusalem, they will not jostle about the highest monument, as if to secure the noble and exalted of earth as passengers; but will be seen waiting in splendor where the halo of righteousness is seen resting over the graves of the saints, like the cloven tongues of fire on the day of Pentecost. In that day the old Christian negro will not be seen watching and waiting as chariot after chariot sweeps by, to see one labeled "COLORED PEOPLE TAKEN IN THIS CHARIOT;" but standing in his robes of righteousness, he shall be recognized by the angels as an heir of glory, and as such greeted, and made welcome to their endless fellowship. Despised negro slave as he was here, he shall mount the heavens with songs of everlasting joy, to wear his robes of light, and his crown of life forever.

[1] The institution that was burned by the Irish Catholic and pro-slavery mob in July, 1863.

To our own mind it seems clear that all these consequences follow from what is clearly revealed in the Scriptures; but it may not so appear to others. Hence they are submitted, not as revealed truth, or as matters of faith, but rather as speculations upon the characteristics of the body in a future life. "Neither has any one a right to insist on the reception, as an article of faith, of any doctrines which he may conceive deducible indeed from Scripture, but deducible only by some process of reasoning, which ordinary Christians cannot follow."[1]

[1] Archbishop Whately, Preface to Future State, p. 9.

CHAPTER XVIII.

USES OF THE RESURRECTION-BODY IN ANOTHER LIFE.

ALTHOUGH we have in some measure anticipated this topic in the preceding chapters, we return to it again because we deem it worthy of a distinct and more extended consideration.

One of the objections to the doctrine of a corporeal resurrection is the alleged non-utility of such a body in the future world. "Reason," says Kant, "can see no advantage in the supposition that a body which, however it may be purified, is still to be formed substantially of the same materials; a body to which we have never been rightly attached in this life, should be dragged after us to all eternity." Prof. Bush reproduces the same objection when he says, "We may justly propose the question of the *cui bono* in relation to the resurrection of our former bodies. . . . What desirable accessions will they bring to the conditions of that being upon which we enter when mortality is swallowed up of life?"[1] To this we answer,

1. It would be no valid objection to a physical resurrection, even if we were unable to see in the present life of what advantage material bodies can be in the world to come. So different may that world be from this, that if our bodies *as now constituted* were of no

[1] *Anastasis*, p. 80.

utility to the indwelling spirit in this life, they might, under the altered circumstances of the unknown hereafter, be of inconceivable utility and importance.

The caterpillar, if told that he should at some time fly through the air, and sip his food from the flowers of spring, might say, "Of what use can my body be then? A worm flying? How ridiculous to talk of 'dragging such a body after me in the next state!'" But despite his reasonings, the substance of his body is absorbed and changed into a butterfly! And instead of being a clog, to retard his progress, or restrict his enjoyments, it bears him at will whithersoever he desires, challenges the admiration of thousands who would never have noticed him but with loathing in his former state, enlarges the sphere of his activities, and ministers inconceivably to his knowledge and happiness.

2. But little as we know of the details of the life to come, there are a variety of considerations that many be premised, as stepping-stones, leading toward the conclusion that we shall not only be able to use our resurrected bodies to advantage, but that we may absolutely need them; or, in other words, that they may be a necessity of our future well-being and happiness.[1]

To a few of these reasons we shall now call attention.

I. Disordered as our world is by sin, and corruptible

[1] A Congregational minister of some note, has recently preached a sermon, in which he suggests that from death to the resurrection, the soul may make no progress in knowledge, for lack of the body and its organs of sensation and perception. But we doubt the correctness of such a position. God, who is a pure spirit, without bodily form or organs, can certainly perceive without sensation; and we see no reason why a human spirit, made in his image, may not do the same thing when disrobed of its vestments of flesh and corruption.

and mortal as are our present bodies, pleasure and advantage from them are the *rule*, and pain and disadvantage the exception. How much, after all, of knowledge and enjoyment do we owe to these mortal bodies, with all their liabilities to pain and death. What harmonies the ear bears home to the soul! what scenes of beauty and grandeur are conveyed to her through the eye! What delicious flavors are perceived through the palate! what fragrant odors through the olfactories! How thrilling the emotions of love and of gratitude, which, despite all effort at abstraction from the physical, seem to gush and sweep around our poor throbbing and corruptible hearts of flesh.

And so of the world of matter outside ourselves. Has it not ministered incessantly to our knowledge and enjoyment all our lives? The beautiful landscape, the lofty mountain, the boundless ocean, the glorious sun, the gorgeous sunset and starry firmament, the flowers and trees, and birds and fish and shells and gems—what have they done but to minister to our knowledge and happiness, and lead us upward in our contemplations to *Him* whose workmanship they are, and whose skill and goodness and infinite resources they forever proclaim. "All thy works shall praise thee, O Lord." "The heavens declare the glory of God, and the firmament showeth his handywork."

Taking the body, therefore, *as it now is*, and even admitting, for the sake of the argument, that it shall still be flesh and blood in the life to come, its vast utility in this life, in ten thousand ways, and even as the medium of divine truth, and of our present spiritual joys, would seem rather to *demand* than to forbid its perpetuity in the world to come. What a calamity it is here to have the ear or the eye or the palate fail us! How precious their offices from the cradle to the grave!

Why, then, this prejudice against matter? and especially against our own bodies? Why this ignoring of their inestimable services for the soul in this life, and the implication of their worthlessness in the long hereafter?

II. But it may be replied, "Are not our bodies the medium also of weariness and pain?" Certainly they are. But, we repeat, pleasure is the *rule*, suffering the *exception*. And even the exceptional suffering is not because the body is matter; if it were, the suffering would be incessant, since the body is always material. Suffering, therefore, is not a necessary result of the *materiality* of the human body, else we should never be free from pain; and Adam would have been in agony the moment his spirit entered the body formed of the dust. We are free from pain and happy most of the time, even in this world, and in our bodies of flesh and blood; and we suffer through the body, not because it is *material*, but because it is *under a curse*, and is, therefore, *corruptible* and *mortal*. But material and gross as it is, if it could be kept in health and strength and youthfulness, and with all the senses perfect and acute, who of us could reasonably object to wearing it forever?

III. With all our theoretical denunciations of the body, we love it still, despite all its disabilities in the present life.

Stoutly as some may object to the body in a future

state, even with all the improvements it is to undergo in the resurrection, they usually think quite as much as they ought of their own bodies, despite all their defects and pains and liabilities to death and corruption. Well has the apostle said, "No man ever yet hated his own flesh." They may do it in theory, but not in fact. And we doubt if the man could be found, tall or short, uncouth or comely, who would be willing to *exchange* the body in which he dwells for that of any other man living.

Instead, therefore, of depreciating the body, and objecting to its resurrection on the ground that it will be useless in a future state, we should endeavor more justly to estimate its services under its present disabilities, to anticipate its increased importance and utility in another world, and to draw therefrom the more legitimate conclusion that it will be raised again and be the abode and the servant of the soul to all eternity.

From these preliminary considerations in regard to the body as it now is, and in the present world, let us now pass to consider some of the conditions of our existence in a future state.

IV. The material universe is to continue to exist after the conflagration of the last day. The sun, moon, and stars will shine on beyond the resurrection morning; and even the earth, restored like the body of man, its mundane proprietor, shall, so far as we have either revelation or analogy to the contrary, roll on its pathway forever. Neither is matter to be remanded back to its primeval and organized state of gas or granite. The shadow never goes back on the dial of Jehovah's progress. Not only is it rational to expect matter to maintain its present status of organization, utility, and beauty, in its ten thousand forms; but that each successive cycle or epoch in the ongoing ages of eternity shall develop new glories and new displays of Jehovah's skill in the realm of material existence, as it has been in the history of our own globe, and will be in the unfolding glories of the spiritual world. Who imagines that matter, made for mind, and after mind had being, will cease to exist when human probation terminates?

"According to the New Testament," says Knapp, "man will possess a *body*, even in the future life, and continue to be, as he now is, a being composed of both *sense* and *reason;* and so there, as well as here, he will have the want of something *cognizable by the senses.*"

And what reason have we for supposing that botany, and geology, and natural history, and chemistry, and astronomy, will not remain hereafter as objects of research, and sources of knowledge and delight, as well as intellectual and moral science and theology? In our contemplations of the world to come are we not liable to eliminate matter quite too much from the problem of our coming existence?

V. It should be borne in mind that heaven and hell are *places* as well as *states.* This, too, is a necessity of our finite social natures. The tabernacle in the wilderness was a "figure" or type of the "true tabernacle on high," "which the Lord pitched, and not man." It was a *place,* with its holy of holies and its mercy-seat. And so of those other types, the gorgeous temple on Mount Zion, and Jerusalem the holy city.

The angels descend from heaven.—Christ and Enoch and Elijah ascended to heaven. Christ shall descend from heaven at the end of time, with his mighty angels and the souls of the righteous dead, to raise their bodies, burn the world, judge all men and angels, and distribute the awards of eternity. Then the wicked will be consigned to hell, the "place of torment," and the righteous, with their new and incorruptible bodies, —the whole man now practically and fully redeemed, —will ascend again to heaven, to be forever with the Lord. Heaven, then, must be a *place* as well as a *state*.

Though God is everywhere present, his throne is in the heavens, where he reveals his glory and receives the unceasing homage of the heavenly hosts.

> For though past all his essence is diffused,
> Yet local is his throne; to fix a point,
> A central point, collective of his sons,
> As standards call the 'listed from afar,
> Since finite every nature but his own.

"The scenery of heaven presented to us in Scripture, is similar to what we see on earth, and its representations are perhaps not entirely metaphorical and figurative. That we shall find these trees, streams, mountains, etc., I will not affirm, but much less will I deny. . . . That a material world, even with similar scenery to that of earth, is a fit abode for holy spirits, is evident from the fact that Adam and Eve lived in such a world in their holy state. . . . If such was Eden, created by God himself as a fit abode for holy beings, and adapted by his own hands to their purest and highest joys, why should we consider it as gross to think of similar scenery in heaven? Similar—yes, for Paradise on earth is a type of Paradise above; and it must needs be that the pattern of heavenly things on earth, should have some similarity to their substance in heaven." [1]

And so of the final abode of lost souls. Hell is a *place* of punishment, to which the unrighteous shall "depart" from Jehovah's judgment-seat. Whatever may be thought of the intermediate state or place of souls, from death to the resurrection,[2] one thing is certain, and that is, that after the dead are raised and judged, the unforgiven will "go away into everlasting punishment." Hell, therefore, is a *place*, and not a mere state of mental wretchedness.

VI. Aside from the translations of Enoch and Elijah, the ascension of the material body of Christ to heaven, the coming resurrection of the bodies of all the saints, and their translation to heaven; we have other reasons for supposing that even heaven itself—the heaven of heavens, where the special presence of God and the Lamb are revealed, and where saints and angels forever rejoice—has a material basis. Granted though it be that "the holy city, New Jerusalem," the harps and streets of gold, the trees, the crowns, the river of life, and the sea of glass mingled with fire, are figures employed by inspiration to represent the beauty and purity and glory of that "better

[1] Harbaugh.

[2] For the author's views upon the subject of the Intermediate State, see his work on the *Immortality of the Soul,* p. 95, and onward.

country," it does not by any means follow that heaven has not a material basis; and as the dwelling-place of God may not be the most gorgeous temple of material forms and grandeur in all the universe.

There is no moral impurity in matter—in gold or ivory or quartz or diamonds; and with myriads of worlds rolling and shining through immensity, we can conceive of no reason why heaven—the metropolis of the universe, and the "city of the Great King"—should not also have its material foundations, and be itself the most perfect specimen of the material workmanship of the all-wise and the infinite Creator.

VII. It is reasonable to suppose, as matter is to continue in its unnumbered forms of beauty and utility, that we shall have more or less *knowledge* of and *connection with* it, in some way, beyond the resurrection. It seems hardly possible that it should be otherwise. Such knowledge and such connection seem to be a necessity of our existence, in the midst of a material world. We must either be kept in close confinement there, or in some way come in contact with the outside material universe. We can conceive of no alternative.

VIII. It being conceded that matter is to continue, and that in some way we are to be in communion with it, the next question is, How shall this intercourse be kept up? Shall it be through a material medium, or without a medium?

That the holy angels can conceive of material things without the organs of sensation, may be granted. Admit, also, that disembodied human spirits can see without eyes, hear without ears, feel without nerves, and think without a brain, during the intermediate period from death to the resurrection; still, it does not follow that they will do so forever. For, 1. The angels are *angels*, and not men, and never dwelt in houses of clay. 2. The disembodied souls of men are in an abnormal condition, and their present mode of perceiving should therefore be regarded as an abnormal and not the normal method. God made man in Eden to perceive through eyes and ears and palate and nerves. Such was his normal method in a state of holiness and immortality. And even when "death passed upon" him in consequence of sin, the same mode of intercourse with the material universe is continued. If, then, we are to be made alive in Christ as we die in Adam, what can we expect but that we shall be restored to our original and normal state, as before death came? Redemption does not propose to reconstruct man after the model of the unbodied angels, but to restore him to his primeval state of holiness and immortality, as a spirit in a body; and thus, by his resurrection and translation, to carry out the original purposes of the Creator, in his final removal from earth to the everlasting mansions?

The only rational conclusion, therefore, from all these considerations is, that the resurrection body will be the medium of communion with the material universe in the world to come.[1]

[1] Isaac Taylor has shown, (we think quite conclusively,) in one of his chapters, that the future body is necessary to "the occupation of place, or a relationship to space and extension—the consciousness of equable motion, or a knowledge of time—the consciousness of the properties of matter, or sensation—an active power over matter, to originate motion—the susceptibility to imaginative emotions, and to mixed

Whether sights, or sounds, or tastes, or odors, or touch; whether mineral, or flower, or bird, or insect; whether microscopic atoms, or telescopic systems of worlds, all may be brought under the immediate scrutiny of the soul through the medium of the resurrection body. Thus may we be learning more and more of God, through his works, forever and ever; and thus may the notes of praise to him swell louder and louder through all the cycles of eternity.

IX. The resurrection body may be one of the means of personal recognition in a future state.

The flowers that die in Autumn, and reappear in the Spring, are recognized as the same flowers, though they have passed through a process of decay and reproduction. Why, then, may not human bodies be recognized, when the winter of death shall give place to the spring-time of the resurrection?

It is a strange fact that probably no two countenances were ever so exactly alike in this world that persons familiar with them could not distinguish the one from the other.

"A social system demands the means of immediate recognition individually; and this, in the present state, is provided for by the endless, yet distinct peculiarities of bodily conformations, and by that law of the animal organization which gives to each peculiarity of the mind, and temper, and temperament, a characteristic exterior expression."[1]

moral sentiments—and a defined, recognizable individuality." But we have not space to quote his arguments at length. See *Physical Theory*, chapters ii. and iii.

[1] *Physical Theory*, p. 39.

Now are we to suppose this arrangement ordained merely to serve the purposes of the present life? Would it not have been substantially the same if man had never died? And in his translation, in such an event, would not the body have been a means of personal recognition, as it was in Eden, and has been ever since? Why, then, should it not serve the same purpose when restored again as the undying home of the immortal spirit?

"Our present organization will not exist there; but this does not imply that there will be no organization. Nay, the more perfect and exalted character of that state would rather teach us that the future organization will be far more exquisite and wonderful than the present; and hence it would be strange if there should not also be still more marked peculiarities by which each individual should be clearly known from all others."[1]

"That the body will be the same in such a sense as to be known, appears sufficiently evident from the Scriptures; mankind will know each other in the future world, and their bodies will so far be the same as to become the instruments of such knowledge."[2]

"When the apostle says, that *God giveth to every seed his own body*, and that so it will be with the resurrection of the dead, every naturalist feels sure that there will exist also such marks of identity between the natural and the spiritual body, as will enable those familiar with the one, to recognize the other."[3]

[1] *Hitchcock's Religious Lectures*, p. 19.

[2] *Dwight's System of Theology*, Glasgow, pp. 868, 869.

[3] *Hitchcock*, p. 19.

X. Our resurrection bodies may serve as so many changeless, indestructible, and glorious monuments of the final victory of Christ over hell and the grave. They will be so many trophies wrested from the power of death; so many inscribed tablets to chronicle the Redeemer's triumphs. To all eternity will they proclaim his wisdom, and his love, and his power to "save to the uttermost," of soul and body, all who come unto God by him.

Such are a few of the considerations that lie within the comprehension of every reader, showing *why* God should raise the dead, and also that the clothing of the spirit of man in such a body as the Scriptures promise the righteous, may be an inconceivable blessing, and source of knowledge and of happiness to them forever.

Reader! Do not despise or undervalue the body, which God has so fearfully and so wonderfully made. It was a part of man in Paradise, and will be a part of yourself forever. Use it well, then, while here, under the blight and burden of corruption. Take the best care of it you can. Honor it as the temple of the Holy Ghost, and the future and endless dwelling-place of the soul. Even love it, if you will; for this almost universal instinct of our nature, is but one of many auguries of its future and everlasting reunion with the spirit. Though it will decay, and finally die and be dissolved, look hopefully toward the grave! "There shall be a resurrection of the dead, both of the just and unjust." And when it shall be thine to part company with the body, that has served thee so faithfully and so well here, dismiss it to corruption and the tomb with triumphant hope and joy.[1]

Companion dear! the hour draws nigh,
The sentence speeds,—*to die, to die.*
So long in mystic union held,
So close with strong embrace compelled,
How canst thou bear the dread decree,
That strikes thy clasping nerves from me?

* * * * * * * *

Well hast thou in my service wrought,
Thy brow hath mirrored forth my thought,
To wear my smile thy lips hath glow'd,
Thy tear, to speak my sorrows, flowed,
Thine ear hath borne me rich supplies,
Of richly varied melodies,
Thy hands my prompted deeds have done,
Thy feet upon my errands run,—
Yes, thou hast marked my bidding well,
Faithful and true! Farewell, farewell.

* * * * * * * *

Yet we shall meet. To soothe thy pain,
Remember—we shall meet again.
Quell with this hope the victor's sting.
And keep it as a signet-ring.
When the dire worm shall pierce thy breast,
And naught but ashes mark thy rest,
When stars shall fall, and skies grow dark,
And proud suns quench their glow-worm spark,
Keep then this hope, to light thy gloom,
Till the last trumpet rends the tomb.

Then shalt thou glorious rise, and fair,
Nor spot, nor stain, nor wrinkle bear,
And, I with hovering wing elate,
The bursting of thy bonds shall wait,
And breathe the welcome of the sky,
"No more to part, no more to die,
Co-heir of Imortality."[2]

[1] For a variety of curious theories and speculations upon the utility of the human body in a future state, see *Physical Theory of Another Life*, by Isaac Taylor.

[2] Mrs. Sigourney.

CHAPTER XIX.

TIME AND EXTENT OF THE RESURRECTION.

LET us now inquire more specifically as to the *extent* of the resurrection, and the *time* when that event is to take place.

I. *The resurrection is to be* UNIVERSAL. So explicit are the Scriptures upon this point, that no other idea has ever been entertained upon the subject among those who believed in the resurrection of the body, till within a few years. Recently a portion of the "second adventists," as they are called, who have formerly held to the annihilation of the wicked at the Day of Judgment, have made the discovery that the wicked dead are already annihilated; and consequently that they are not to be included in the resurrection.

A few years ago George Storrs found the Bible full of proofs of the annihilation of the wicked at the last day; but now he finds that the wicked will not even *exist* at that time, much less suffer annihilation. These facts render it proper to devote a few pages to the proofs that the resurrection is to be universal.

1. This doctrine is taught by the prophet Daniel, in the following passage:

> "And many of them that sleep in the dust of the earth shall awake, some to everlasting life, and some to shame and everlasting contempt."—Dan. xii. 2.

There can be no doubt as to the fact that the prophet is here speaking of the resurrection of the dead; and unless some of the righteous are to arise to "shame and everlasting contempt," it is quite as certain that the wicked are to arise, as well as the righteous, in the last day.

2. The following is still more explicit:

> "Marvel not at this: for the hour is coming, in the which all that are in the graves shall hear his voice,
>
> "And shall come forth; they that have done good, unto the resurrection of life; and they that have done evil unto the resurrection of damnation."—John v. 28, 29.

These words of Christ are so very clear and explicit, as to defy all attempts at perversion. We have first the broad declaration that "all that are in the graves" "shall come forth;" and then the difference in the resurrection of the righteous and the wicked,—"they that have done good, unto the resurrection of life, and they that have done evil unto the resurrection of damnation." How could language more clearly affirm the resurrection of all men, both the righteous and the wicked?

3. In his defence before Felix, at Cæsarea, St. Paul plainly teaches the same doctrine:

> "But this I confess unto thee, that after the way which they call heresy, so worship I the God of my fathers, believing all things, which are written in the law and in the prophets,
>
> "And have hope toward God, which they themselves also allow, that there shall be a resurrection of the dead, both of the just and the unjust."—Acts xxiv. 14, 15.

Three things are clear from this passage,—that the Jews held to or "allowed" a universal resurrection; that St. Paul held to the same doctrine; and that both so understood "the law and the prophets." "There shall be a resurrection of the dead, both of the *just* and the *unjust*."

4. The same doctrine is explicitly taught by the same apostle, in his first epistle to the Corinthians:

> "But now is Christ risen from the dead, and become the first-fruits of them that slept.
>
> "For since by man came death, by man came also the resurrection of the dead.
>
> "For as in Adam all die, even so in Christ shall all be made alive."—1 Cor. xv. 20–22.

In the second of these verses it is implied that the resurrection that comes by the redemption of Christ, shall be coextensive with the *death* that comes by the sin of Adam; and in the last verse it is explicitly asserted. As in Adam all die, so in Christ all shall arise from the dead. The subject of the chapter is the resurrection of the body, and as certain as it is that the wicked die in consequence of Adam's sin, so certain is it that they shall arise from the dead, as an unconditional result of our Lord's victory over death.

5. The same doctrine is implied wherever we are taught that the wicked are to be judged and punished.

> "For we must all appear before the judgment seat of Christ; that every one may receive the things done in his body, according to that he hath done, whether it be good or bad."—2 Cor. v. 10.

Mark the expression, "*all*" and "*every one*;" and also the closing statement,—"according to that he hath done," etc. How plain that the wicked are to be judged as well as the righteous!

6. Take also our Lord's description of the judgment, and the punishment of the wicked, Matt. xxv., with the following from the Apocalypse:

"And I saw the dead, small and great, stand before God; and the books were opened; and another book was opened, which is the book of life; and the dead were judged out of those things which were written in the books, according to their works.

"And the sea gave up the dead which were in it; and death and hell delivered up the dead which were in them; and they were judged every man according to their works.

"And death and hell were cast into the lake of fire. This is the second death.

"And whosoever was not found written in the book of life was cast into the lake of fire."—Rev. xx. 12–15.

In the passage, Matt. xxv. the wicked are represented as standing before the Judge of all, who reminds them of their former lives, and finally says to them, "Depart, ye cursed, into everlasting fire." If, then, they will be there to be judged, they must arise from the dead.

In the texts above cited the phrase "small and great" imports universality—that he saw *all* the dead stand before God. The same is implied in the language, "And the sea gave up the dead which were in it;" for it will not be claimed that none but Christians are buried in the sea. In the third place the twice-repeated declaration that they were judged "according to their works," implies that the wicked will be there to be judged as well as the righteous; and finally the fact that some were "cast into the lake of fire," shows that the wicked will be raised and judged, as well as the righteous, though sent from the judgment seat to everlasting punishment, prepared for the devil and his angels!

Many other passages teach the same doctrine, as, for instance, those which speak of the rising up of the Sodomites and others in the judgment, etc.; but it is not necessary to multiply proofs. The texts cited are unequivocal, and directly to the point; and if *they* do not prove that the resurrection shall be universal, no human language could prove it.

II. *The resurrection of the righteous and the wicked is to be* SIMULTANEOUS; *that is, they will all arise* AT THE SAME TIME.

At first view some will regard this proposition as erroneous. They have read and heard of "the first resurrection," and have imbibed the idea of two resurrections, viz., that of the righteous first, and subsequently that of the wicked. Nevertheless, we believe the proposition to be strictly true, and that "the first resurrection" is not a literal resurrection of the bodies of men, either saints or sinners. But let us look first at the proofs that all will arise together:

1. The passage already cited from Daniel, ignores the idea of two distinct resurrections, one of the righteous and another of the wicked, either a thousand years or a single day apart.

2. Our Lord plainly teaches, John v. 28, that all the dead shall hear the same "voice," and "come forth," the saint and the sinner at the same "hour."

3. We are not aware of an intimation in the Psalms, or Prophets, the gospels, or the Acts of the Apostles, nor in any of the Epistles, that there are to be two distinct resurrections of the dead, separated by any appreciable interval of time.[1] On the contrary the

[1] There is indeed an order in the resurrection, 1 Cor. xv. 24; but we nowhere observe mention made of a first and second resurrection at the distance of a thousand years from each other: yet, were the millennium hypothesis well founded, the words should rather have run thus:

teaching of the apostle Paul is, that "the trumpet shall sound, and the dead [*all* the dead] shall be raised!" And the passage in the same connection often cited to prove a different doctrine, has no reference (as we shall show hereafter) to any distinction of time between the righteous and the wicked.

4. The appearing of the righteous and the wicked before the same judgment-seat of Christ, implies a simultaneous resurrection.[1]

5. St. Paul expressly teaches that Christ is to punish the wicked when he is revealed from heaven; which could not be possible if the wicked were not to be raised at the same time with the righteous.

> "And to you who are troubled rest with us, when the Lord Jesus shall be revealed from heaven with his mighty angels,
>
> "In flaming fire taking vengeance on them that know not God, and that obey not the gospel of our Lord Jesus Christ:
>
> "Who shall be punished with everlasting destruction from the presence of the Lord, and from the glory of his power;
>
> "When he shall come to be glorified in his saints, and to be admired in all them that believe (because our testimony among you was believed) in that day."—1 Thess. i. 7–10.

No comment of ours is necessary to elucidate this passage. It is conclusive as it stands, beyond the possibility of being misunderstood or invalidated.

6. The scene of the resurrection, Rev. xx. 12 and onward, already cited, is also conclusive upon this point. The Judge is seen upon his great white throne, and the dead, small and great, are summoned before

"Christ, the first-fruits, then the martyrs at his coming, and a thousand years afterward the residue of mankind,—then cometh the end," etc.—*Watson's Theo. Dic., art., Millennium.*

[1] See Matt. xxv.; 2 Cor. v. 10, and Rev. xx. 12.

him; not a part at one time and a part at another, but *all at once.* Nothing is here said of "the first resurrection;" nor of any interval whatever between the resurrection of the righteous, and that of the wicked.

For these reasons, and many others that might be given, we believe the dead will all arise at the same time, and in obedience to the same "voice" or "trump of God."

III. *The* TIME *of the resurrection is that of the second coming of Christ.*

This is generally admitted, so far as the righteous are concerned. But there are those who believe that the righteous only will then arise, and the wicked a thousand years afterward. But we have already shown that there is no such difference in the time of the resurrection—that all are to hear the same "voice," and arise in the same hour. The following passage tells us when that "hour" will arrive:

> "When the Son of man shall come in his glory, and all the holy angels with him, then shall he sit upon the throne of his glory:
>
> "And before him shall be gathered all nations: and he shall separate them one from another, as a shepherd divideth his sheep from the goats."—Matt. xxv. 32.

When Christ comes, all nations shall be gathered before him, the judgment proceed at once, the righteous and the wicked be separated forever, and each assigned to his everlasting abode and portion.

The same doctrine is taught in Rev. xx. 12, already twice referred to. Christ is seen upon the great white throne, and the dead are at once summoned before him, judged, and assigned to their eternal allotment.

IV. *The second coming of Christ and the resurrection of the dead will not occur* TILL THE END OF TIME.

This is plainly taught in the passage already cited. The resurrection and judgment are always represented as immediately following the "glorious appearing" of the Son of God. And so in the parables of Christ—the unfaithful steward, foolish virgins, etc., are always punished when the Householder or Bridegroom come. But of this point more in a subsequent chapter.

CHAPTER XX.

THE FIRST RESURRECTION.

We have shown in the preceding chapter, that the resurrection is to be *universal*—that all the dead are to be raised *at the same time*, and that this stupendous miracle is to take place at the second coming of Christ and the end of the world. What, then, it may be asked, is "the first resurrection?" and when is *that* to take place?

We purposely ignored this question in the main, in the last chapter, not only that we might have space for the direct proofs of the true theory, as therein presented, but that we might give the greater prominence to the subject, by treating it somewhat at length in a distinct chapter. Setting aside, then, all preconceived opinions, let us inquire what authority, if any, we have for believing, as many do, in a "first resurrection," what that resurrection is, and when it shall take place.

I. In his first epistle to the Thessalonians, St. Paul tells us that "the dead in Christ shall rise first." From this expression many have imbibed the idea that the dead in Christ are to arise before the wicked; but certainly nothing of the kind is taught in the passage. Let us look at it in its connections:

"But I would not have you to be ignorant, brethren, concerning them which are asleep, that ye sorrow not, even as others which have no hope.

"For if we believe that Jesus died and rose again, even so them also which sleep in Jesus will God bring with him.

"For this we say unto you by the word of the Lord, that we which are alive and remain unto the coming of the Lord, shall not prevent them which are asleep.

"For the Lord himself shall descend from heaven with a shout, with the voice of the archangel, and with the trump of God: and the dead in Christ shall rise first:

"Then we which are alive and remain shall be caught up together with them in the clouds, to meet the Lord in the air: and so shall we ever be with the Lord."—1 Thess. iv. 13–17.

Now let the reader notice,

1. That the apostle is not speaking of the resurrection of the wicked, but only "of them which sleep in Jesus," or of the righteous dead only.

2. The comparison is between the saints who are alive when Christ comes, and those who are dead; and not between the righteous and the wicked.

3. It is affirmed that "we which are alive and remain unto his coming, shall not prevent,"[1] that is, shall not go before or outstrip "them which are asleep." The plain meaning then is, that those who still live, and whose bodies are not dissolved by death, shall have no advantage over their brethren who have been long dead, and whose bodies have gone back to dust. They shall not start at once to meet the Lord in the air, because they are alive, while their brethren of other ages are still under the dominion of death.[1]

[1] The use of this word here, in its old English sense, has caused great obscurity in the passage. It used to signify *assist*. From that it came to signify *anticipate*, or *go before;* and now, in common parlance, it signifies to *hinder effectually*—the very opposite of its original meaning. Hence the obscurity.

4. Having thus declared what shall *not* be, the apostle proceeds to set forth the order in which events *shall* transpire. "For the Lord himself shall descend from heaven with a shout, with the voice of the archangel, and with the trump of God: and the dead in Christ shall rise first." But "first" of whom? or before what? Certainly not before the *wicked* arise, for nothing is being said of them, or of their resurrection. "The dead in Christ shall rise first;" that is, *before the living saints ascend.*

The "dead in Christ" having been raised to stand beside the saints who have not seen death, they will then be caught up together with the risen dead, to meet the Lord in the air: and so shall we ever be with the Lord. The dead will be raised, the living changed and made incorruptible,[2] and both together ascend to heaven.

There is nothing, then, in this passage to favor the idea of a "first resurrection" of the righteous before the wicked. It is "first" only in reference to the ascension of the living, and not in reference to another resurrection to follow.

II. Let us now pass to the only remaining passage in the Bible that speaks of a "first resurrection:"

> "And I saw thrones, and they sat upon them, and judgment was given unto them: and I saw the souls of them that were beheaded for the witness of Jesus, and for the word of God, and which had not worshipped the beast, neither his image, neither had received his mark upon their foreheads, or in their hands: and they lived and reigned with Christ a thousand years.

[1] See Macknight, who renders the passage "shall not *anticipate* them who are asleep," and the *Comprehensive Diaglot,* which renders it "will by no means precede," etc.

[2] See 1 Cor. xv. 50-52.

"But the rest of the dead lived not again until the thousand years were finished. This is the first resurrection,

"Blessed and holy is he that hath part in the first resurrection: on such the second death hath no power, but they shall be priests of God and of Christ, and shall reign with him a thousand years." —Rev. xx. 4–6.

Now keeping distinctly in view the question before us, namely, whether the Scriptures teach that the saints shall arise before the wicked, let us carefully examine this passage.

1. Whatever the nature, extent or order of the resurrection spoken of, it is a resurrection of "*souls*," and not of the bodies of men. "*And I saw the ψυχας—*—*psuchas*—SOULS, etc."

2. They were not the souls of all the saints, but of "them that were beheaded for the witness of Jesus." —the martyrs who had proved faithful amid the most violent persecutions, and had finally sealed their testimony with their blood. Even then, if the passage related to a resurrection of the *bodies* of men, (which it does not) it would only teach a "first resurrection," for the *martyrs;* leaving the great body of the saints to arise with "the rest of the dead," when the "thousand years are finished."

These two points, then, are clear—the "first resurrection" is not a resurrection of the *bodies* of men; nor a resurrection of *all* the righteous dead. On the contrary, whatever its *nature* may be, it is simply a resurrection of the *souls of the martyrs.* Nothing further is asserted; and to make the passage mean anything more, is to do violence to the obvious meaning of the Holy Spirit.

3. Understood as a figurative resurrection of the

spirits of the martyrs, (as upon its face the text purports,) it harmonizes with all those Scriptures that teach a simultaneous resurrection of all the dead, and an immediate judgment; and affords us a bright and cheering view of the true millennium.

In the last chapter of Malachi we have this prophecy: "Behold, I will send you Elijah the prophet, before the coming of the great and dreadful day of the Lord." This "day" the Jews very properly understood to be the time of the Messiah; and hence, when Christ came they rejected him, among other reasons, because Elijah the prophet had not yet come.

Understanding the prophecy literally, they expected Elijah to appear bodily, as the harbinger of the Messiah. And yet the prophecy meant nothing of the kind; but simply that one having the *spirit* and *power* of the old prophet, should arise, as the forerunner of the divine Redeemer. Hence, when Gabriel appeared to Elizabeth, the mother of John the Baptist, before his birth, he said:—

> "And many of the children of Israel shall he turn to the Lord their God.
>
> "And he shall go before him in the spirit and power of Elias, to turn the hearts of the fathers to the children, and the disobedient to the wisdom of the just; to make ready a people prepared for the Lord."—Luke i. 16, 17.

And so our Lord himself, in the seventeenth chapter of Matthew.

> "And his disciples asked him, saying, Why then say the scribes that Elias must first come?
>
> "And Jesus answered and said unto them, Elias truly shall first come, and restore all things.
>
> "But I say unto you, That Elias is come already, and they knew him not, but have done unto him whatsoever they listed."—Matt. xvii. 10–12.

The resurrection or reappearing of Elijah the prophet, then, meant simply that a man having his "*spirit* and *power*" should arise, and nothing more. As in metaphorical language, we call one man by the name of another,—a Washington, or a Napoleon,—because of their resemblance to each other; so John is called "Elijah the prophet," by Malachi, because he was to be *like* him—a bold, earnest and true prophet.

Now upon precisely the same principles we interpret the Scripture under consideration. The Revelator looks forward and sees a bright and glorious era for the church, down near the close of time—call it a millennium if you prefer, and let its duration be a literal "thousand years."[1]

At the commencement of this period he sees the "souls" or spirits of the martyrs rising, to live on through the millennium; not literally, but to be reproduced in men of like spirit, and zeal, and devotion, who shall be raised up in the last days. As John represented Elias, and was called Elias, because he possessed the same zeal and power. so the morally courageous, and zealous and sacrificing, who shall help to usher in the millennial day, are represented as the souls of the martyrs rising from the dead, and living again on the earth a thousand years.[2]

Such we believe is "the first resurrection;" and *all* the first resurrection the Bible teaches— a resurrection

[1] We think a long indefinite period is intended, but in the present inquiry it makes no difference which view is adopted.

[2] It has been asked why, if this exposition be a correct one, this figurative reappearing of Elijah was not also called a resurrection? We answer, Elijah *never died*, and could therefore have no resurrection, literal or figurative. He simply reappeared.

of *zeal* and *courage*, and *devotion*, and *moral power*, which shall usher in and continue through the millennium, and thus precede the general resurrection. And "blessed and holy is he that hath part in this first resurrection,"—every true evangelist and reformer who goes forth in the spirit and power of the early apostles and martyrs—"on such the second death shall have no power, but they shall be priests of God, and of Christ, and shall reign with him a thousand years." [1]

From these considerations, and many others that might be stated, we conclude that "the first resurrection" is both *spiritual* and *figurative*—that the *bodies* of men are all to be raised at the same time, as the Scriptures so plainly teach; and that there is no such thing as a first resurrection of the bodies of the saints, a thousand years before the end of the world, and the resurrection of the wicked.

Of the order of events, and other circumstances connected with the resurrection of the dead, we shall speak somewhat at length in the next chapter.

Speaking of the passage under consideration, Archbishop Whately says: "It may signify not the literal raising of dead men, but the raising up of an increased Christian zeal and holiness: the revival in the Christian church, or in some considerable portion of it, of the *spirit* and *energy* of the noble martyrs of old (even as John the Baptist came in the spirit and power of Elias;) so that Christian principles shall be displayed in action throughout the world in an infinitely greater degree than ever before." So D'Aubigne, in his *History of the Reformation*, speaks of John Huss as having said, "I am no dreamer, but I maintain this for certain that the image of Christ will never be effaced. They [his enemies] have wished to destroy it, but it shall be painted afresh in all hearts by much better preachers than myself. The nation that loves Christ will rejoice in this. *And I, awaking from among the dead, and rising, so to speak, from my grave,* shall leap with great joy." So also Pope Adrian, in his address to the Diet at Nuremburg, said, "The heretics Huss and Jerome are now alive again in the person of Martin Luther."

CHAPTER XXI.

THE MILLENNIUM.

ALTHOUGH this topic cannot be discussed at length in the present treatise, it deserves at least a passing notice, as it is more or less involved by, and included in, the subject of the resurrection.

The term *millennium* is from two Latin words, *mille*, a thousand, and *annus*, a year, and signifies a thousand years. It is used especially to designate the supposed personal reign of Christ for a thousand years before the end of time. At the commencement of this period some suppose that Christ will descend from heaven in person, as he ascended from Mount Olivet, establish his seat of government at Jerusalem; gather the Jews together there as his willing and loving subjects; raise the righteous dead; and literally reign over the nations as their only ruler and king for a thousand years. And then comes the resurrection of the wicked and the final judgment.

But we have shown in a previous chapter that the resurrection of the dead will be universal and simultaneous; that no lapse of a thousand years is to intervene between the resurrection of the saints and of the ungodly; and that Christ is not to come till the end of time, when the judgment will immediately take place. Having taken this position, it seems highly proper that we give the reader our theory of the reign of Christ, and of the Scriptural millennium. This we will now do, therefore, in the least possible space, and with but little attempt at argument.

I. *It is very clear from the prophecies that in some sense Christ was to be a* KING; *and to reign over the house of Jacob forever.*

Take the following passages as proofs of this proposition:

> "Yet have I set my king upon my holy hill of Zion.
>
> "I will declare the decree: The LORD hath said unto me, Thou art my Son; this day have I begotten thee.
>
> "Ask of me, and I shall give thee the heathen for thine inheritance, and the uttermost parts of the earth for thy possession."—Ps. ii. 6–8.

The prophet Isaiah inculcates the same idea:

> "For unto us a child is born, unto us a son is given: and the government shall be upon his shoulder; and his name shall be called Wonderful, Counsellor, The Mighty God, The Everlasting Father, The Prince of Peace.
>
> "Of the increase of his government and peace there shall be no end, upon the throne of David, and upon his kingdom, to order it, and to establish it with judgment and with justice, from henceforth even for ever. The zeal of the LORD of hosts will perform this."—Isa. ix. 6, 7.

Jeremiah is equally explicit:

> "Behold, the days come, saith the LORD, that I will raise unto David a righteous Branch, and a King shall reign and prosper, and shall execute judgment and justice in the earth.
>
> "In his days Judah shall be saved, and Israel shall dwell safely; and this is his name whereby he shall be called, THE LORD OUR RIGHTEOUSNESS."—Jer. xxiii. 5, 6.

When Gabriel announced to Mary that Christ should be born of her, he said:

"And behold, thou shalt conceive in thy womb, and bring forth a son, and shalt call his name JESUS.

"He shall be great, and shall be called the Son of the Highest; and the Lord God shall give unto him the throne of his father David.

"And he shall reign over the house of Jacob forever; and of his kingdom there shall be no end."—Luke i. 31–33.

When Zechariah predicted the triumphant entrance of the Messiah into Jerusalem, he said:

"Rejoice greatly, O daughter of Zion; shout, O daughter of Jerusalem; behold, thy King cometh unto thee; he is just, and having salvation; lowly, and riding upon an ass, and upon a colt the foal of an ass.

"And I will cut off the chariot from Ephraim, and the horse from Jerusalem, and the battle-bow shall be cut off: and he shall speak peace unto the heathen; and his dominion shall be from sea even to sea, and from the river even to the ends of the earth."—Zech. ix. 9, 10.

These passages need no comment to make apparent either their pertinency or their conclusiveness. In some sense Christ was to be a *king*, and to reign in the earth.

II. *The kingdom of Christ was to be set up* AT THE TIME OF HIS ADVENT, *and not thousands of years afterward.*

This is plainly implied in all the passages cited in the last section. Still more plainly is it declared in the following:

"And in the days of these kings shall the God of heaven set up a kingdom, which shall never be destroyed: and the kingdom shall not be left to other people, but it shall break in pieces and consume all these kingdoms, and it shall stand forever."—Dan. ii. 44.

This kingdom was further represented under the figure of a stone, "cut out of the mountain without hands," that "became a great mountain and filled the whole earth."[1] The prophet Amos inculcated the same idea.

> "In that day will I raise up the tabernacle of David that is fallen, and close up the breaches thereof; and I will raise up his ruins, and I will build it as in the days of old."—Amos ix. 11.

Here the kingdom of God is represented by a tabernacle or house; which was to be raised from its ruins "in that day;" that is, when Christ should come. And the blessings to follow are thus represented:

> "Behold, the days come, saith the LORD, that the ploughman shall overtake the reaper, and the treader of grapes him that soweth seed: and the mountains shall drop sweet wine, and all the hills shall melt.
>
> "And I will bring again the captivity of my people of Israel, and they shall build the waste cities, and inhabit them; and they shall plant vineyards, and drink the wine thereof; they shall also make gardens, and eat the fruit of them.
>
> "And I will plant them upon their land, and they shall no more be pulled up out of their land which I have given them, saith the LORD thy God."—Dan. xi. 13–15.

A Millenarian or a literalist will, of course, see in this a restoration of the Jews, and great temporal prosperity; but the apostles understood it as referring to the kingdom of God set up by our Lord, and as having its fulfilment in part on the day of Pentecost. Hence James said:

> "And to this agree the words of the prophets; as it is written,
>
> "After this I will return, and will build again the tabernacle of David which is fallen down; and I will build again the ruins thereof, and I will set it up."—Acts xv. 15, 16.

So when Christ came, though they were in error as to the *nature* of his kingdom, they expected it to be set up at once. Hence it is said:

[1] Dan. ii. 34, 35.

"And as they heard these things, he added and spake a parable, because he was nigh to Jerusalem, and because they thought that the kingdom of God should immediately appear."—Luke xix. 11.

Such were the expectations of the Jews, founded upon the prophecies which they misunderstood. Hence we read again:

"And when he was demanded of the Pharisees, when the kingdom of God should come, he answered them and said, The kingdom of God cometh not with observation:

"Neither shall they say, Lo here! or, Lo there! for behold, the kingdom of God is within you."—Luke xvii. 20, 21.

"Within you," that is, in your midst, already here. It will not come with observation—be set up by a visible and public coronation.

In harmony with all this is the constant teaching of Christ, that the kingdom of God had come, and was already among them; "The kingdom of God is come nigh unto you"[1]—"No doubt the kingdom of God is come upon you"[2]—"The time is fulfilled, and the kingdom of God is at hand."[3] The gospel was "the glad tidings of the kingdom;"[4] Joseph of Arimathea "waited for the kingdom of God;"[5] even harlots entered the kingdom before the Jews;[6] and alluding to the day of Pentecost, our Lord said: "Verily I say unto you, That there be some of them that stand here which shall not taste of death, till they have seen the kingdom of God come with power."[7] And so all through the gospels and the Acts of the Apostles especially; under the phrases "kingdom of God," or "kingdom of heaven," the idea is constantly

[1] Luke x. 9, 11. [2] Luke xi. 20. [3] Mark i. 15. [4] Luke viii. 1.
[5] Mark xv. 43. [6] Matt. xxi. 31. [7] Mark ix. 1, and Luke ix. 27.

conveyed that the prophecies were fulfilled, the kingdom of Christ set up, and his reign in the earth already begun.

III. *The Jews expected the Messiah to be a* TEMPORAL PRINCE; *and that, when he came, he would break the Roman yoke, and restore again the kingdom of Israel.*

Nathaniel recognized his regal character when he said, "Thou art the King of Israel;"[1] and the mother of James and John betrayed the same idea of his temporal reign when she said, "Grant that these my two sons may sit the one on thy right hand, and the other on thy left, in thy kingdom."[2] On one occasion they were about to take him by force and make him king;[3] and when he was questioned by Pilate, he virtually declared himself a king.[4] The accusation placed over his head upon the cross was, "*This is Jesus of Nazareth, the King of the Jews;*" and though the Jews wished it altered so as to read, "who *said* I am King of the Jews," Pilate answered, "What I have written I have written."[5]

The Jews were disappointed and exasperated by the fact that Christ did not assume the throne in *their* temporal sense. Hence they not only put on the mock crown and robes, and in derision cried, "Hail King of the Jews,"[6] but while he hung upon the cross they said, "If he be King of Israel, let him now come down from the cross, and we will believe him."[7]

And notwithstanding all that Christ had said to the contrary, the apostles themselves still clung to this idea, even after the resurrection. Hence, in the conversation with him, while on the way to Emmaus, they

[1] Jno. i. 49. [2] Matt. xxii. 20. [3] Jno. vi. 15. [4] Matt. xxvii. 11. [5] Jno. xix. 19-22. [6] Jno. xix. 2, 3. [7] Matt. xxvii. 42.

said, "But we trusted that it had been he which should have redeemed Israel;"[1] that is, from the power of the Romans. And when our Lord spoke to them of the day of Pentecost, they said, "Lord, wilt thou at this time restore again the kingdom to Israel?"[2] showing that they still looked for his literal reign at Jerusalem.

While, therefore, the Jews united with the Romans in crucifying the Messiah as an impostor, they evidently rejected and slew him more because he did not assume the throne, in their literal and worldly sense, than for any other reason.

IV. *Our Lord never was a king in any secular sense, and expressly disclaimed all such dominion.*

While he claimed to be a king, at the bar of Pilate, who asked him, "Art thou the King of the Jews," he explained the nature of his kingdom by saying:

> "My kingdom is not of this world: if my kingdom were of this world, then would my servants fight, that I should not be delivered to the Jews: but now is my kingdom not from hence.
>
> "Pilate therefore said unto him, Art thou a king then? Jesus answered, Thou sayest that I am a king. To this end was I born, and for this cause came I into the world, that I should bear witness unto the truth."—Jno. xviii. 36, 37.

This is equivalent to saying, "Thou sayest the truth in speaking of me as a King; and I bear witness to that truth; but my kingdom is not a secular one; it is spiritual and heavenly."

So careful was our Lord not to countenance the idea of his temporal reign, that when one of his disciples said to him, "Master, speak to my brother, that he divide the inheritance with me," though a word from

[1] Luke xxiv. 21. [2] Acts i. 6.

him would have settled the controversy, he replied, "Man, who made me a judge, or a divider over you?"[1]

Now if Christ was to be a king, and in some sense to set up his kingdom at his first appearing; and if he did not set up a secular kingdom, it follows either that he was not the promised Messiah (as the Jews allege,) or that they and others who can see no "kingdom of God" set up in the apostles' days, have misunderstood the nature of his reign; and are looking for the earthly and secular, where they should discern the spiritual and the heavenly.

V. *Our Lord and his apostles explain the kingdom of Christ as altogether* SPIRITUAL AND HEAVENLY.

We have seen what Christ himself said of it at Pilate's bar—"My kingdom is not of this world, etc." And so St. Paul, "For the kingdom of God is not meat and drink, but righteousness, and peace, and joy in the Holy Ghost."[2] "For the kingdom of God *is* not in word, but in power."[3]

From all these testimonies the conclusion is irresistible, that Christ was to reign over a spiritual and not over a temporal kingdom; that this spiritual reign was emphatically inaugurated on the day of Pentecost; that as Christianity has been extending from age to age, and from land to land, the reign of Christ has been extending; and that when it becomes the acknowledged religion of all lands; his dominion will be from sea even unto sea, and from the river to the ends of the earth. Thus,

Jesus shall reign where'er the sun
Does his successive journeys run;

[1] Luke xii. 13, 14. [2] Rom. xiv. 17. [3] 1 Cor. iv. 20.

His kingdom spread from shore to shore,
Till moons shall wax and wane no more.

But it will be asked, what about the conversion of the Jews, and their return to their ancient heritage. We answer:

VI. *The various promises of the restoration of Israel to their own land, etc., are but figurative representations of the gathering of the true Israel of God, to the church of Christ in this world, and to the heavenly Jerusalem hereafter.*

1. We are repeatedly assured that in the true sense no man was a Jew or an Israelite, merely because he was a descendant of Abraham, and had been circumcised.

"Neither, because they are the seed of Abraham, *are they* all children: but, In Isaac shall thy seed be called.

"That is, They which are the children of the flesh, these *are* not the children of God; but the children of the promise are counted for the seed."—Rom. ix. 7, 8.

"For he is not a Jew, which is one outwardly; neither *is that* circumcision, which is outward in the flesh:

"But he *is* a Jew which is one inwardly; and circumcision *is that* of the heart, in the spirit, *and* not in the letter; whose praise *is* not of men, but of God."—Rom. ii. 28, 29.

2. The true believer in Christ, is the Jew, in the spiritual sense—the real Israelite; and the true heir according to the promise.

"Know ye therefore, that they which are of faith, the same are the children of Abraham.

"And the Scripture, foreseeing that God would justify the heathen through faith, preached before the gospel unto Abraham, *saying*, In thee shall all nations be blessed.

"So then they which be of faith are blessed with faithful Abraham."—Gal. iii. 7-9.

"And if *ye be* Christ's, then are ye Abraham's seed, and heirs according to the promise."—Ver. 29.

3. All such,—the true Israel of God,—will finally be gathered to Mount Zion above, where Christ shall reign over the house of Jacob forever. Hence it is said,

"And so all Israel shall be saved; as it is written, There shall come out of Sion the Deliverer, and shall turn away ungodliness from Jacob."—Rom. xi. 26.

"And the ransomed of the LORD shall return, and come to Zion with songs and everlasting joy upon their heads: they shall obtain joy and gladness, and sorrow and sighing shall flee away."—Isa. xxxv. 10.

As the poet has well expressed it,

By death and hell pursued in vain,
  To thee the ransomed seed shall come;
Shouting, their heavenly Zion gain,
  And pass through death triumphant home.

VII. *That there is to be a millennium—a long period near the close of time, when the reign of Christ will be universal, that is, over all lands, we fully believe.*

1. It is promised beyond all question in the sacred writings. The heathen are to be his inheritance, and the uttermost parts of the earth his possession.[1] His dominion shall be from sea to sea, and from the river even to the ends of the earth.[2] The stone cut out of the mountain without hands, is to become a great mountain, and to fill the whole earth.[3] In the prophet's vision of one like the son of man, there was given him dominion, and glory, and a kingdom, that all people nations and languages should serve him.[4] The kingdom of heaven is to be like the growth of the mustard, from a small seed to a tree; and like the

[1] Psalm ii. 8.
[2] Zech. ix. 10, and Psalm lxxii. 8.
[3] Dan. ii. 35.
[4] Dan. vii. 14.

leaven, which does not cease its working till the whole lump is leavened.[1]

But the *nature* of the kingdom is to be the same that it now is—a *spiritual reign*. The man whose heart is right in the sight of God, and who is happy in his love, and at peace with God and man, has the *essence* of the millennium within him. Christ reigns over all his powers, and, if he is faithful to God, will thus reign in him, and over him, forever. If the same blessings be extended to a *family*, there is a *family* millennium. If a whole village or city fear God, and walk in his ways, and under his smile, there is a *village* or a *city* millennium; and when Christianity shall permeate states and nations, modify their laws and institutions, and breathe its blessed spirit and influence like the breath of spring over all the earth, then the world will have realized its long promised, and long hoped for period of holiness, and peace, and rest.

2. Of this millennial reign the prophets furnish us with the most glowing and enchanting description:

"In his days shall the righteous flourish: and abundance of peace so long as the moon endureth.

"He shall have dominion also from sea to sea, and from the river unto the ends of the earth.

"They that dwell in the wilderness shall bow before him; and his enemies shall lick the dust.

"The kings of Tarshish and the Isles shall bring presents; the king of Sheba and Seba shall offer gifts.

"Yea, all kings shall fall down before him: all nations shall serve him.

"For he shall deliver the needy when he crieth; the poor also, and him that hath no helper.

"He shall spare the poor and needy, and shall save the souls of the needy.

[1] Matthew xiii. 31, 32.

"He shall redeem their souls from deceit and violence: and precious shall their blood be in his sight.

"And he shall live, and to him shall be given of the gold of Sheba: prayer also shall be made for him continually; and daily shall he be praised."—Ps. lxxii. 7–15.

The prophet Isaiah had a similar vision of this glorious era of peace and love:

"And he shall judge among the nations, and shall rebuke many people; and they shall beat their swords into plough-shares, and their spears into pruning-hooks: nation shall not lift up sword against nation, neither shall they learn war any more."—Isa. xi. 4.

Still more striking, if possible, are the figures employed in the following passage:

"The wolf also shall dwell with the lamb, and the leopard shall lie down with the kid; and the calf and the lion and the fatling together; and a little child shall lead them.

"And the cow and the bear shall feed; their young ones shall lie down together: and the lion shall eat straw like the ox.

"And the sucking child shall play on the hole of the asp, and the weaned child shall put his hand on the cockatrice's den.

"They shall not hurt nor destroy in all my holy mountain: for the earth shall be full of the knowledge of the LORD, as the waters cover the sea."—Isa. xi. 6–9.

To the same effect are the numerous exceeding great and precious promises in regard to the Church; which, in reality, is no other than the kingdom of Christ:

"Behold, I will lay thy stones with fair colors, and lay thy foundations with sapphires.

"And I will make thy windows of agates, and thy gates of carbuncles, and all thy borders of pleasant stones.

"And all thy children shall be taught of the LORD; and great shall be the peace of thy children."—Isa. liv. 11–13.

"Thou shalt also suck the milk of the Gentiles, and shalt suck the breasts of kings; and thou shalt know that I the LORD am thy Saviour and thy Redeemer, the Mighty One of Jacob.

> "For brass I will bring gold, and for iron I will bring silver, and for wood brass, and for stones iron: I will also make thy officers peace, and thine exactors righteousness.
>
> "Violence shall no more be heard in thy land, wasting nor destruction within thy borders; but thou shalt call thy walls Salvation, and thy gates Praise.
>
> "The sun shall be no more thy light by day; neither for brightness shall the moon give light unto thee: but the LORD shall be unto thee an everlasting light, and thy God thy glory.
>
> "Thy sun shall no more go down; neither shall thy moon withdraw itself: for the Lord shall be thine everlasting light, and the days of thy mourning shall be ended."—Isa. lx. 16–20.

That these descriptions are to be *literally* fulfilled, that is, when taken literally, we do not suppose; but that the peace and righteousness and prosperity represented by these glowing figures will be realized in the last days, we fully believe. The first resurrection will give the world a race of evangelists who will go forth to all peoples, and tongues, and nations, in the spirit and power of the early martyrs; and the world will be filled with the knowledge of the true God, and of Jesus Christ the true Messiah and Saviour.

Such, then, are our views of the millennium.—It is to be the universal triumph of the same reign of Christ which began eighteen centuries ago, for a long but indefinite period before the second coming of Christ; to be followed by the general resurrection, the final judgment, and the end of time.

VIII. *The opposite theory is liable to many and serious objections, both Scriptural and rational.*

We have space to enumerate but a few of them.

1. In our view it has no proper and legitimate support in the word of God. Of course, some suppose

they find ample proofs of the millenarian theory, but we cannot.

2. It virtually affirms that Christ did not set up his kingdom in the earth, before he ascended to glory; thus not only contradicting all the prophecies upon that point, but his own express teachings, and those of his apostles.

3. It is an endorsement of the old Jewish error, that Christ was to be a temporal prince, and by so much not only, as we think, degrades both him and his kingdom, but justifies the Jews in rejecting him, and crucifying him as an impostor. For certainly he was to be a king, and was to set up his kingdom *at that time;* and as he did not set up a temporal kingdom, and it is denied that he then set up a spiritual reign; it follows that he did not fulfil the prophecies, was an impostor, and was justly rejected!

4. The idea that Christ's kingdom is not yet established, and cannot be till he comes and raises the righteous dead, is well calculated to paralyze all effort for the enlightenment and conversion of the world. If none can enter his kingdom till he appears in the clouds of heaven, why labor to multiply converts? And why use *moral* means,—preaching, prayer, Bibles, etc.,—when Christ is to use regal power and authority in the millennium? But we have not space to elaborate these objections.

5. The history of the Church shows that this error has been productive of evil, and evil only, in all ages and lands, wherever it has been promulgated.

The following, from Dr. Clarke's Notes on Rev. xx. is a mild and charitable statement of the case:

"How many visions have been seen on this subject both in ancient and modern times! This, and what is said in vs. 3, 4, and 5, no doubt refers to a time in which the influence of Satan will be greatly restrained, and the true Church of God enjoy great prosperity, which shall endure for a long time. But it is not likely that the number, a thousand years, is to be taken literally here, and *year* symbolically and figuratively in all the book beside. The doctrine of the *millennium*, or of the saints reigning on the earth a thousand years, with Christ for their head, has been illustrated and defended by many Christian writers, both among the ancients and moderns. Were I to give a collection of the conceits of the primitive fathers upon this subject, my readers would have little reason to applaud my pains. It has long been the idle expectation of many persons that the millennium, in *their* sense, was at hand; and its commencement has been expected in every century since the Christian era. It has been fixed for several different years during the short period of my own life! I believed those predictions to be vain, and I have lived to see them such. Yet there is no doubt that the earth is in a state of progressive moral improvement; and that the light of true religion is shining more copiously everywhere, and will shine more and more to the perfect day. But *when* the religion of Christ will be at its meridian of light and heat, we know not. In each believer this may speedily take place; but probably no such time will ever appear, in which evil shall be wholly banished from the earth, till after the day of judgment, when, the earth having been burnt up, a new heaven and a new earth shall be produced out of the ruins of the old, by the mighty power of God: righteousness alone shall dwell in them."

To this may be added the history of the Miller excitement in 1841–3, and the still more deplorable wanderings of Geo. Storrs and his followers; first denying the immortality of the soul, then teaching the resurrection and annihilation of the wicked at the day of judgment, and now (1866) in the face of the most explicit statements to the contrary, denying the resurrection and future punishment of the wicked altogether! Where they will next land in their self-styled "progress," Heaven only can tell.

And all this from the one original error of the Jews, that Christ's reign is to be personal and literal.

But we can give no more space to this topic, as it is legitimate to our pages only so far as it stands connected with the subject of the resurrection, and especially with its order, or relations to other events with which it is to be connected, or which are to precede or to follow that event.

"Hasten, Lord, the glorious time,
When, beneath Messiah's sway,
Every nation, every clime,
Shall the gospel call obey.
Mightiest kings his power shall own;
Heathen tribes his Name adore;
Satan and his host, o'erthrown,
Bound in chains, shall hurt no more."

CHAPTER XXII.

ORDER AND ACCOMPANIMENTS OF THE RESURRECTION.

THE true nature of the first resurrection and of the millennium having been ascertained, we are now prepared to consider the *order of events* at and near the close of time, and also the *circumstances* and *accompaniments* of the general resurrection.

I. *The truth of God will continue more and more to leaven the nations, till all the ends of the earth have seen the salvation of God.*

We speak not now of the special reign of peace that shall follow the first resurrection, but of that general and less influential knowledge of the true God, which will pervade all lands, before the more perfect and universal reign of the Prince of Peace.

So numerous and so well known are the prophetic and the New Testament promises of such an era in the future of the Church of God, that we need waste no space in citing them.

II. *A great and effectual restraint will be put upon Satan, the ruler of the darkness of this world.*

This idea is conveyed under the figure of an angel binding him, shutting him up, etc.

"And I saw an angel come down from heaven, having the key of the bottomless pit and a great chain in his hand.

"And he laid hold on the dragon, that old serpent, which is the Devil, and Satan, and bound him a thousand years,

"And cast him into the bottomless pit, and shut him up, and set a seal upon him, that he should deceive the nations no more, till the thousand years should be fulfilled: and after that he must be loosed a little season."—Rev. xx. 1–3.

Of course no sane expositor would contend that Satan is to be literally bound with a chain, or shut up. The figure is employed, therefore, to represent a *restriction* put upon the devil and his angels, and a limitation of their power to do evil. *How* or *by what means* this restraint is to be imposed, we are not informed. In chapter fourteen of this same revelation, the spread of truth is represented by the flight of an angel through the heavens, "having the everlasting gospel to preach unto them that dwell on the earth, and to every nation, and kindred, and tongue, and people;" and here in the twentieth chapter the *effect* of this wide diffusion of the gospel of Christ, may be represented under the figure of the binding of Satan by another angel. Let Christianity so permeate all lands as to give form and character to their laws and institutions—to suppress all rum shops, and lotteries, and duelling, and slavery, and gambling, and profanity, and horse racing, and Sabbath breaking, and theatres, and brothels, and we shall have reached the period when Satan will be bound and shut up, that he shall deceive the nations no more.

III. *Next in order will come the "First Resurrection."*

Not only will the powers of darkness be restricted, but there will arise a class of evangelists, missionaries, pastors, and holy laymen in the Church, who, consecrating heart and life and possessions to the extension of Christ's kingdom, will go forth in the spirit and power of the early martyrs—blessed, faithful, holy men, on whom the second death shall have no power—who shall live and reign with Christ, they and their successors, to the end of time.

IV. *Following this resurrection of the spirit and power of the holy martyrs will come the long reign of Christ, and the happy era of peace and love.*

So completely will the stone cut out of the mountains without hands fill the whole earth, and the leaven of Christianity leaven the whole lump, that Christ's dominions will be from sea even to sea, and from the river to the ends of the earth.

The characteristics of this golden age of the world are thus happily specified by Dr. Albert Barnes:

1. There will be a great increase in the population of the globe. Let wars cease, and intemperance cease, and slavery cease, and the numberless passions that now shorten life be stayed, and it is easy to see that there must be a vast augmentation in the number of the human species.

2. There will be a general diffusion of intelligence on the earth. Every circumstance would be favorable to it, and the world would be in a condition to make rapid advances in knowledge. Dan. xii. 4.

3. That period will be characterized by the universal diffusion of revealed truth. Isa. xi. 9, xxv. 7.

4. It will be marked by unlimited subjection to the sceptre of Christ. Ps. ii. 7; Zech. ix. 10; Ps. xxii. 27–29; Isa. ii. 2, 3, lxvi. 23; Zech. xiv. 9; Matt. xiii. 31, 32; Rev. xi. 15.

5. There will be great progress in all that tends to promote the welfare of man. We are not to suppose that the resources of nature are exhausted. Nature gives no signs of exhaustion or decay. In the future, there is no reason to doubt that there will yet be discoveries and inventions more surprising and wonderful than the art of printing, or the uses of steam, or the magnetic telegraph. There are profounder secrets of nature that may be delivered up than any of these, and the world is tending to their development.

6. It will be a period of the universal reign of peace. The attention of mankind will be turned to the things which tend to promote the welfare of the race, and advance the best interests of society. The single fact that wars will cease, will make an inconceivable difference in the aspect of the world; for if universal peace shall prevail through the long period of the Millennium, and the wealth, the talent, and the science now employed in human butchery shall be devoted to the interests of agriculture, the mechanic arts, learning, and religion, it is impossible now to estimate the progress which the race will make, and the changes which will be produced on the earth. For Scripture *proofs* that it will be a time of universal peace, see Isa. ii. 4, Mic. iv. 3, Isa. xi. 6–9.

7. There will be a *general* prevalence of evangelical religion. This is apparent in the entire description in this passage, for the two most formidable opposing powers that religion has ever known—the beast and the false prophet—will be destroyed, and Satan will be bound. In this long period, therefore, we are to suppose that the gospel will exert its fair influence on

governments, on families, on individuals; in the intercourse of neighbors, and in the intercourse of nations. God will be worshiped in spirit and in truth, and not in the mere *forms* of devotion; and temperance, truth, liberty, social order, honesty, and love, will prevail over the world.

8. It will be a time when the Hebrew people—the Jews—will be brought to the knowledge of the truth, and will embrace the Messiah whom their fathers crucified. Rom. xi. 26–29; Zech. xii. 10, xiii. 1.

9. Yet, we are not necessarily to suppose that *all* the world will be absolutely and entirely brought under the power of the gospel. There will be still on the earth the remains of wickedness in the corrupted human heart, and there will be so much *tendency* to sin in the human soul, that Satan, when released for a time, (vs. 7, 8,) will be able once more to deceive mankind, and to array a formidable force, represented by Gog and Magog, against the cause of truth and righteousness.[1]

During this long and happy age of righteousness and peace, the poet's bright vision may be well nigh, if not fully, realized:

All crimes shall cease, and ancient frauds shall fail,
Returning Justice lifts aloft her scale;
Peace o'er the world her olive wand extend,
And white-robed innocence from heaven descend.

No sigh, no murmur, the wide world shall hear:
From every face he wipes off every tear;
In adamantine chains shall Death be bound,
And hell's grim tyrant feel th' eternal wound

[1] Barnes' Notes on Rev. xx. 1–4.

V. *Satan will be loosed for a season, and the Powers of Darkness will make one more desperate onset upon the kingdom of Christ.*

"And when the thousand years are expired, Satan shall be loosed out of his prison,

"And shall go out to deceive the nations which are in the four quarters of the earth, Gog and Magog, to gather them together to battle: the number of whom is as the sand of the sea."--Rev. xx. 7, 8.

Gog was a hostile prince, who had invaded the land of Israel, Ezek. xxxviii. 2–18 and xxix. 11, and *Magog* is mentioned Ezek. xxxiii. 2, "the land of Magog," and in Ezek. xxxix. 6, "I will send a fire on Magog." Under the figure of these ancient foes of God's people, the enemies of the cross of Christ—infidelity, spurious Christianity, etc.—are represented as combining and marshaling their hosts against the church of the living God.

"And they went up on the breadth of the earth, and compassed the camp of the saints about, and the beloved city: and fire came down from God out of heaven, and devoured them.

"And the devil that deceived them was cast into the lake of fire and brimstone, where the beast and the false prophet are, and shall be tormented day and night for ever and ever."—Rev. xx. 9, 10.

"We are not to suppose that the nature of mankind as fallen will be essentially changed, or that there may not be sin enough in the human heart to make it capable of the same opposition to the gospel of God which has thus far been evinced in all ages. From causes which are not fully stated, (vs. 8, 9,) Satan will be enabled once more to rouse up their enmity, and to make one more desperate effort to destroy the kingdom of the Redeemer by rallying his forces for the conflict."[1]

[1] Barnes.

But his defeat will be signal and final; and "the kingdom and dominion, and the greatness of the kingdom under the whole heaven, shall be given to the people of the saints of the Most High, whose kingdom is an everlasting kingdom, and all dominions shall serve and obey him."[1]

VI. *An angel from heaven shall proclaim the end of time.*

How impressive the description of this announcement!

> "And I saw another mighty angel come down from heaven, clothed with a cloud; and a rainbow was upon his head, and his face was as it were the sun, and his feet as pillars of fire:
>
> "And he had in his hand a little book open: and he set his right foot upon the sea, and his left foot on the earth,
>
> "And cried with a loud voice, as when a lion roareth: and when he cried, seven thunders uttered their voices.
>
> "And when the seven thunders had uttered their voices, I was about to write: and I heard a voice from heaven saying unto me, Seal up those things which the seven thunders uttered, and write them not.
>
> "And the angel which I saw stand upon the sea and upon the earth lifted up his hand to heaven,
>
> "And sware by him that liveth forever and ever, who created heaven, and the things that therein are, and the earth, and the things that therein are, and the sea, and the things which are therein, that there should be time no longer."—Rev. x. 1–6.

What an announcement to fall upon a slumbering world! For there will be those even then who will be squandering their precious time, as many do now,

> Who, counting on long years of pleasure here,
> Are quite unfurnished for the world to come.

But the days, and weeks, and months, and years of time will have an end.

[1] Dan. vii. 27.

"Take a view of that morning. The sun rises strong and clear, and rejoiceth as a strong man to run a race; all nature is swarming with life; the songsters of the grove are chanting their morning anthems; the breeezes àre sporting with the leaves of the forest; the milk-maid sings merrily to the fields; the farmer whistles by the side of his team; the lawyer weaves his sophistries; the mechanic is in his shop; the merchant counts his gains; the pious contemplates new plans of usefulness; and the sceptic proves there is no God, *no coming judgment.* But suddenly there is a change. An awful stillness pervades all nature, like that which presages the tremendous earthquake—a stillness so deep that it can almost be heard, yea, felt. Nothing moves; no zephyr shakes the ivy bower. *All,* ALL, *wondering and amazed,* STAND STILL. But hark! from the adjunct of sea and land, a superhuman voice is heard, so loud that all the world can hear: 'THERE SHALL BE TIME NO LONGER!' The wheels of time stop in a moment! Eternal things are now begun!" [1]

VII. *Christ will then appear in the clouds of heaven.*

As he ascended from Mount Olivet, the angel said, "This same Jesus, which is taken up from you into heaven, shall so come in like manner as ye have seen him go into heaven." [2] He is to come in power and great glory; [3] to be revealed in flaming fire, [4] and attended by all the holy angels. [5]

[1] Sermon on the Resurrection of the Human Body, preached at Wapping, Conn., in 1841, by Rev. A. Latham.

[2] Acts i. 11. [3] Matt. xix. 30. [4] 2 Thess. i. 7, 8. [5] Matt. xvi. 27.

The souls of the righteous dead will also accompany him from Paradise.

"And the Lord my God shall come, and all the saints with thee." —Zech. xiv. 5.

"Behold, the Lord cometh with ten thousand of his saints."—Jude 14.

"At the coming of our Lord Jesus Christ with all the saints."—1 Thess. iii. 13.

Though there will be scoffers in those last days who will be saying: "Where is the promise of his coming? for since the fathers fell asleep, all things continue as they were from the beginning of the creation;"[1] a cry will be heard, "Behold, the bridegroom cometh, go ye out to meet him," and the summons will be obeyed.

Soon shall ocean's hoary deep,
  Tossed with stronger tempests rise;
Darker storms the mountains sweep,
  Redder lightnings rend the skies.
Evil thoughts shall shake the proud,
  Racking doubt and restless fear,
And amid the thunder-cloud,
  Shall the Judge of men appear.

The souls of the wicked dead will be summoned from Hades, or the place of departed spirits. This is taught where it is said that "death and hell [the place of departed souls] shall deliver up the dead that are in them."[2]

This revelation of the Son of God is to be upon a throne of universal dominion and of final judgment.

"When the Son of man shall come in his glory, and all the holy angels with him, then shall he sit upon the throne of his glory."—Matt. xxv. 31.

[1] 2 Pet. iii. 4.

[2] Rev. xx. 13. For the author's views of the intermediate state of souls, see volume on the Immortality of the Soul, Part I., chap. viii.

"And I saw a great white throne, and him that sat on it, from whose face the earth and the heaven fled away; and there was found no place for them."—Rev. xx. 11.

VIII. *The trumpet of the Resurrection will then be blown.*

God told Moses to make two silver trumpets for the purpose of assembling the people together, and of issuing marching orders.

"Make thee two trumpets of silver; of a whole piece shalt thou make them: that thou mayest use them for the calling of the assembly, and for the journeying of the camps.

"And when they shall blow with them, all the assembly shall assemble themselves to thee at the door of the tabernacle of the congregation."—Num. x. 2, 3.

And so at the end of time when all men shall be assembled for judgment. "The Lord himself shall descend from heaven with a shout, and with the voice of the archangel and the trump of God.[1]

What is called the voice of Christ, John v. 28, is elsewhere called, "the voice of the archangel and the trump of God." And as the silver trumpets of Moses were blown to assemble all to the door of the tabernacle, so the blast of a trumpet is used to represent the final summons to appear before the judgment seat of Christ. The time will come

When shriv'ling like a parched scroll,
The flaming heavens together roll;
And, louder yet, and yet more dread,
Swells the high trump that wakes the dead!

IX. *In obedience to this "trump of God," the dead will all arise.*

[1] 1 Thes. iv. 16.

"For the hour is coming, in the which all that are in the graves shall hear his voice,

"And shall come forth; they that have done good, unto the resurrection of life; and they that have done evil, unto the resurrection of damnation."—John v. 28, 29.

"The trumpet shall sound, and the dead shall be raised incorruptible."—1 Cor. xv. 52.

And now the Trump of wondrous melody,
By man or angel never heard before,
Sounded with thunder, and the march began.

This final trumpet "pours its amazing thunders into all the caverns of the dead," and the dead small and great will arise and stand before God.

"Green turfy grave-yards and tombs of marble
Give up their dead, both small and great;
See! the whole world, both saint and sinner,
Are hastening to the judgment seat."

X. *The same "voice of the archangel and trump of God" that raises the dead, will change all the living.*

This is distinctly taught by the apostle in the following passage.

"Behold, I show you a mystery; We shall not all sleep, but we shall all be changed,

"In a moment, in the twinkling of an eye, at the last trump; for the trumpet shall sound, and the dead shall be raised incorruptible, and we shall be changed.

"For this corruptible must put on incorruption, and this mortal must put on immortality."—1 Cor. xv. 51. 52.

XI. *The souls of all the dead will then re-enter their resurrected bodies.*

This is no where expressly stated, but it is implied in the return of the souls of the righteous dead with Christ, the summoning of all souls from Hades, the resurrection of the bodies of all, and the judgment that follows. For no one can believe that mere souls or bodies separately considered, will be the subjects of the final judgment. Still further: as souls could not re-enter their bodies *before* the resurrection, and none will be judged till restored to their original and normal condition of soul and body in union, it follows that the re-union must take place at this point in the order of events; that is, between the resurrection and the judgment scene.

XII. *Then will all men and angels be gathered before the Judgment Seat of Christ.*

For to raise the dead, and judge all men, and to gather his redeemed and faithful children to the everlasting mansions, are the great ends for which Christ shall descend from heaven, and blow the final trumpet.

'Tis done; again the conquering chief appears,
In the dread vision of dissolving years;
His vesture dipped in blood, his eyes of flame,
The Word of God, his everlasting name,
Throned in mid-heaven, with clouds of glory spread,
He sits in judgment on the quick and dead.

Of this scene of grandeur we have predictions and descriptions, both in the Old and New Testaments.

"I beheld till the thrones were cast down, and the Ancient of days did sit, whose garment *was* white as snow, and the hair of his head like the pure wool: his throne *was like* the fiery flame, *and* his wheels *as* burning fire.

"A fiery stream issued and came forth from before him: thousand thousands ministered unto him, and ten thousand times ten thousand stood before him: the judgment was set, and the books were opened."—Dan. vii. 9, 10.

It is appointed unto men once to die, and after this

the judgment;[1] and St. Paul declares, that we must all appear before the judgment seat of Christ; that every one may receive the things *done* in *his* body, according to that he hath done, whether *it be* good or bad."[2]

The Father has committed all judgment to the Son, who will judge the secrets of all hearts, and distribute to each a just and eternal reward.

> "When the Son of man shall come in his glory, and all the holy angels with him, then shall he sit upon the throne of his glory:
>
> "And before him shall be gathered all nations: and he shall separate them one from another, as a shepherd divideth *his* sheep from the goats."—Matt. xxv. 31, 32.

And the description proceeds to the final sentence. And so again the Revelator:

> "And I saw the dead, small and great, stand before God; and the books were opened; and another book was opened, which is *the book* of life: and the dead were judged out of those things which were written in the books, according to their works.
>
> "And the sea gave up the dead which were in it; and death and hell delivered up the dead which were in them: and they were judged every man according to their works."—Rev. xx. 12, 13.

Then will be realized the scene, "Behold he cometh with clouds; and every eye shall see him, and they *also* which pierced him: and all kindreds of the earth shall wail because of him."[3] Then will be heard the cry to the mountains and rocks, "Fall on us, and hide us from the face of him that sitteth on the throne, and from the wrath of the Lamb: for the great day of his wrath is come; and who shall be able to stand?"[4]

[1] Heb. ix. 27.
[2] 2 Cor. v. 10.
[3] Rev. i. 7.
[4] Rev. vi. 16, 17.

"Horror all hearts appals;
They groan, they shriek, they cry,
Bid rocks and mountains on them fall—
But rocks and mountains *fly*."

There stand the countless generations of the dead! All races and tongues and ages are there. There are Adam and Eve, and Noah and the Antediluvians, and Lot and the Sodomites, and Moses and Pharaoh and all their hosts. Jonah and the Ninevites are there, with all of Israel's judges, kings, and prophets. David, and Solomon, and Zedekiah, and Ahab, and Jezebel, and Elijah, and Jeremiah—all are there.

From Assyria and Egypt, and Palestine and Babylon, and Damascus, and Tyre, and Sidon, and every zone and island and continent and sea—all are there.

Nimrod, and Xerxes, and Alexander, and Pompey, and Hannibal, and Wellington, and Napoleon, and Washington, and Burgoyne, and all their hosts, will then stand before the bar of God.

From Austerlitz, and Marengo, and Waterloo, and Buena Vista, and Bull Run, and Petersburg, and Antietam,—every battle-field of earth will have poured forth its unnumbered hosts, to meet the Judge of quick and dead!

And all relations will be there,—rulers and subjects, husbands and wives, parents and children, masters and slaves, ministers and people. Abel and Cain will be there, and Jezebel and Naboth, and Herod and John the Baptist, and Pilate, before whose bar Jesus of Nazareth once stood, will now stand before Christ, to receive at His mouth his everlasting doom. Then Queen Mary and John Rogers will meet again. Then

Prof. Webster and Dr. Parkman will stand face to face, and Abraham Lincoln and J. Wilkes Booth, his murderer, will confront each other. Then shall we hear from all who have perished at sea—on the Lexington or the Erie, or the London, from whatever ship, or in whatever waters. Then shall we hear from the beloved Cookman, who went down or was consumed, (God knoweth,) with the steamship President. The fate of Sir John Franklin will then be known, for he will be there from the icy North to unveil the mystery of his tragic end.

It is *the judgment of the Great Day!* It was a great day when Napoleon was defeated at Waterloo, and another when his remains were brought from St. Helena to Paris, and they sang,

> Sound the trumpet, roll the drum,
> Come, in long procession, come.

It was a great day when the monument at Bunker Hill was dedicated, and another when Queen Victoria was coronated. It was a great day when General Lee surrendered to the Federal army, and when the victorious hosts of the army retired through Washington to their homes in the North. It was a still greater day—one of the greatest of earth—when the remains of the good and the patriotic ABRAHAM LINCOLN were borne from the seat of government, where he had perished by the hand of slavery, to their final resting-place in Springfield. But what are these, or all combined, to the gathering of the final judgment!

That the fallen angels will be judged at the same time, is also plainly revealed in the Scriptures:

"The angels which kept not their first estate, but left their own habitation, he hath reserved in everlasting chains under darkness unto the judgment of the great day."—Jude 6.

"God spared not the angels that sinned, but cast them down to hell, and delivered them into chains of darkness, to be reserved unto judgment."—2 Pet. ii. 4.

And reasoning from analogy, as righteous men are to be judged as well as the wicked, it is probable that the holy angels will also be judged, as well as the Devil and his angels.

XIII. *Meanwhile the world will be wrapped in the flames of the final conflagration.*

Christ is to be revealed from heaven "in flaming fire,"[1] and St. Peter expressly predicts the burning of the world:

"But the heavens and the earth, which are now, by the same word are kept in store, reserved unto fire against the day of judgment and perdition of ungodly men.

* * * * * * * *

"But the day of the Lord will come as a thief in the night; in the which the heavens shall pass away with a great noise, and the elements shall melt with fervent heat, the earth also and the works that are therein shall be burned up.

"Seeing then that all these things shall be dissolved, what manner of persons ought ye to be in all holy conversation and godliness,

"Looking for and hasting unto the coming of the day of God, wherein the heavens being on fire shall be dissolved, and the elements shall melt with fervent heat?"—2 Pet. iii. 7–12.

This will not be an annihilation of the globe by any means, but its purification by fire.

Man, starting from his couch, shall sleep no more!
The day is broke which never more shall close!
Above, around, beneath, amazement all!
Terror and glory join in their extremes!
Our God in grandeur, and our world on fire!
All nature struggling in the pangs of death!

[1] 2 Thess. i. 8.

Whether this universal conflagration will occur just as the dead arise, or immediately after that event, we may not be able definitely to determine. But it will occur. Then will

> Fierce meteors with the lightning's blaze conspire,
> And darting downward, set the world on fire.

Of the visible heavens it is said, "They shall perish, but thou remainest: and they all shall wax old as doth a garment: and as a vesture shalt thou fold them up, and they shall be changed: but thou art the same, and thy years shall not fail."[1]

> The seas shall waste, the skies in smoke decay,
> Rocks fall to dust, and mountains melt away;
> But fixed His word, his saving power remains,
> Thy realm for ever lasts, thy own Messiah reigns!

XIV. *Finally the Judge will pronounce the irrevocable sentence; the righteous and the wicked separate, and depart, each to their respective abodes; and the scene of human redemption and probation will close forever!*

Then will the King say to his faithful servants, "Come, ye blessed of my Father, inherit the kingdom prepared for you from the foundation of the world;"[2] but to the wicked he will say, "Depart from me, ye cursed, into everlasting fire, prepared for the devil and his angels." "And these shall go away into everlasting punishment: but the righteous into life eternal."[3] The wise virgins, whose lamps are trimmed and burning, will be admitted to heaven, while the foolish are excluded forever. The servant who has improved his talent will then hear the Judge say to him, "Well

[1] Heb. i. 11, 12. [2] Matt. xxv. 34. [3] Ibid. vs. 41, 46.

done, thou good and faithful servant: thou hast been faithful over a few things, I will make thee ruler over many things: enter thou into the joy of thy Lord;"[1] while the neglecter of salvation through Christ shall hear it said, "Thou wicked and slothful servant—cast ye the unprofitable servant into outer darkness; there shall be weeping and gnashing of teeth."[2] Then the wheat will be gathered into the heavenly garner, and the chaff consigned to unquenchable fire. When Christ shall next appear it shall not only be without a sin-offering, as he came at the first, but "taking vengeance on them that know not God, and that obey not the gospel of our Lord Jesus Christ: who shall be punished with everlasting destruction from the presence of the Lord, and from the glory of his power; when he shall come to be glorified in his saints, and to be admired in all them that believe."[3]

Such we conceive to be the revealed order of events, and the relations of the resurrection to the second advent, the millennium, etc. We cannot, of course, discuss the several points included in this chapter to any great length, but we have said enough to give the reader an idea of our views, and of a few of the proofs and arguments upon which they rest. More than this could not be expected in a work upon the resurrection of the dead.[4]

[1] Matt. xxv. 23. [2] Ibid. v. 26, 29. [3] 2 Thess. i. 8–10.

[4] It may be a matter of interest to the student to be told that the stereotypers being waiting for "copy," this chapter was written entire, without assistance, and notwithstanding several interruptions, in one day (Feb. 6, 1866,) between the hours of 8.30 A. M. and 5 P. M.; that is, in about eight hours. Should it therefore appear less finished than it should, no one need be surprised.

CHAPTER XXIII.

NATURAL EMBLEMS OF THE RESURRECTION.

THAT there are any phenomena in nature that *fully* answer to or illustrate the resurrection of the body, after it has been dead for ages and has crumbled back to dust, we do not by any means affirm; for if this were the case, the resurrection of the dead would be a natural event, (as some erroneously suppose,) and not a stupendous miracle wrought by the power of God as the Scriptures plainly teach. Nature furnishes no instance in which a plant or a seed or a chrysalis that is really *dead* and disorganized, and its component particles scattered, ever lives again. And yet there are various phenomena in nature that *partially* illustrate the glorious truth that the dead shall live again. As George Horne, dean of Canterbury, has well said, "If Nature teach any religion, it is the Christian; if she preach any doctrine, it is this resurrection and change."[1] Let us then devote a brief chapter to the natural emblems (such as they are) of the resurrection of the dead, and of the future life of the smitten and decayed body.

Upon this subject no writer with whom we are acquainted has written so fully or so well as did the late Dr. Hitchcock, whose views upon other points we have

[1] Works, Oxford, 1782, p. 143.

felt it our duty to controvert, but whose lecture upon "*The Resurrections of Spring*," is in our view both orthodox and beautiful. We cannot do better, therefore, either by the subject or the reader, than to quote freely from this original and pertinent discourse.

I. *Spring presents us with numerous examples of life emerging from apparent death.*

Had we no experience of the effects of spring, we could not imagine, during the winter months of such a climate as ours, that leaves, and flowers, and fruit, would ever clothe the barren trees, or a green carpet again cover the earth, or the air, the earth and the waters swarm with animal life.[1] And when we should witness the ten thousand forms of vegetable and animal existence, which the genial influences of spring develop, it would seem almost as if a new creation had taken place. Experience, indeed, and the aid of the microscope, enable us to discover evidences of vitality, where to common observation, nature seems bound only in icy fetters. Yet without such aids, all the developments of spring would seem to be made on the bosom of death.

Just so it is with the resurrection of the dead. Go to their burial place, and see if among the great congregation that lie side by side beneath the soil, you can

[1] And yet, as we have said, this is only a very imperfect emblem of the resurrection. We have somewhere read of an incident like this, in the life of Richard Watson. He was walking in a garden in autumn, as the leaves were falling. Picking up a withered leaf, and moralizing upon it, a lady present spoke of the future spring as a resurrection. True, said he, these leafless trees will bud and bloom again, but no dead and fallen leaf will ever know a resurrection. Such was the general idea, as we recollect it.

discover any signs of life. You call, but there is no answer: you remove three feet of earth; but you shrink back horrified at the corruption that riots there upon all ages and all classes. Yet when the last trumpet shall sound, that whole surface shall become instinct with life, and corruption shall put on incorruption. Go if you will and traverse the ten thousand battle-fields, that have been the very slaughtering-places of man, from Nimrod to Bonaparte; and all is silence and solitude over the graves of these millions. But how changed the scene on the resurrection morning! Then not less than one thousand millions of human beings shall start up from these battle-fields, and crowd upwards to the judgment-seat. What vast multitudes too, shall ascend from the site of such ancient cities as Nineveh, and Babylon, and Thebes, and Palmyra, and a hundred other great centers of population, now the seat of solitude and desolation. Think of Jerusalem, which for more than two thousand years has been the great central slaughter-house of the world; where human relics and comminuted dwellings have accumulated on the surface to the depth of forty or fifty feet, and the whole has been soaked a thousand times with blood. Oh, think of the scene, when the millions that lie buried there shall start into life at the shout of the descending Judge and the archangel's voice! From the sea's broad surface, too, what multitudes shall be seen ascending to be judged according to the deeds done in the body. Indeed, when we remember that probably as many as ten billions of human beings have already dwelt upon this globe, reasonably may we inquire, from what portion of its surface will not myriads start into life at the final summons?

II. *Spring presents us with marvelous developments of structure and changes of condition in the organic world.*

As we look abroad over the unfolding landscape of spring, how should we be struck with the contrast, could all the seeds producing the vegetation of that landscape be laid before us! Who, by looking at the seed, could once in a thousand times predict the character of the plant that would spring from it; or trace out any analogy between them? That such an analogy exists, I admit; but vernal developments can alone show us what it is; and we are often amazed and delighted by these developments. And the wonder rises higher as our instruments of examination are more perfect. There is, indeed, more simplicity of structure in the vegetable than the animal frame. But the organs are minute and complicated enough in the former, to set at defiance the powers of the microscope; or rather, there are wonders in the vegetable structure, which lie beyond the reach of that instrument. And yet, how easily are they all unfolded when spring applies to the vegetable world her transmuting touch.

But the changes among animals which spring developes are still more striking, and analogous to those of the future resurrection. At that time, many of the animals that have lain during the winter months in a state of torpidity, hardly to be distinguished from death, begin to show signs of returning vitality, and soon assume the whole activity of their natures, and enter upon a new scene of enjoyment. Many too, not entirely torpid, pass through transformations which bring them into states of existence so different from all former ones, that it must seem to them almost a new creation. Indeed, almost up to the present time, they have been regarded by the ablest naturalists as different species of animals, and even as belonging to different classes in their different states. In fact, could they answer the question themselves, they would probably testify that their experience in one state is totally diverse from their experience in every other state. I refer to those cases which the naturalists denominate alternate reproduction: in some of these cases the whole series of transformations is not completed till the eighth or ninth generation: that is, it is only in the eighth or ninth generation that the perfect animal is produced. It is in the spring, also, for the most part, that we witness what has long been thought an illustration of this subject; I mean the metamorphosis of insects. Enveloped in his silken shroud, the chrysalis has passed the winter months in some obscure spot. But in the vernal season it bursts from its prison, endowed with new life and beauty. It entered its narrow tomb an unsightly worm; but it comes forth a perfect insect, with splendid colors and strong wings, to pass through a season of great activity and apparently of high enjoyment.

Now, so striking is the analogy between these metamorphoses and the reanimation of man, that many able writers on natural theology, have considered them as direct proof of his future resurrection. But unfortunately there is one defect in the analogy that seems to have been overlooked. When man is laid in the grave, we know that no vestige of life remains. We may inflict whatever injury we please upon the dead body, but it will exhibit no signs of sensibility. Not so with the chrysalis. In its most torpid state, you can always find marks of vitality, or rather, if you cannot discover signs of life, it will never come forth as a perfect insect. The conclusion, therefore, is, that the curious facts respecting insect metamorphosis, although a beautiful emblem of man's resurrection, are but a poor argument in direct proof of the doctrine. They do, however, show us in what widely different states the same animals may exist, and what curious means nature has provided, by which they may pass from one of those states into another, not only unharmed, but with higher developments of beauty and richer means of enjoyment; all this, I say, does afford a strong presumption that the change of death may pass upon man with no other effect upon his interior nature, than to fit it to unfold in higher perfection in eternity.

And everything in religion and philosophy indicates that man will come forth from the grave with a body vastly better adapted for the exercise of his mental and moral powers than his present organization. Indeed, wonderful as that organization is, both Scripture and experience testify, that in this world, because it is a state of sin and death, the whole creation groaneth and traveleth in pain together. In this tabernacle man's spirit groans, being burdened, and God meant it to be in a fettered, and, in many respects, an uncongenial state, in order that it might wait with earnest expectation for the manifestation of the sons of God,

—in other words, for the adoption, which the apostle declares to be, the redemption of the body. Here, it is a natural body; there, it will be spiritual: sown in dishonor in the grave, but raised in glory. We have shown how wide the difference may be between the natural and the spiritual body, consistently with the Scriptural representations: and doubtless the changes that will be undergone will far transcend our present conceptions. Here, it is mortal; there, immortal: here, gross, and the seat of gross appetites; there, etherial and free from every taint of sense or sin: here, the seat of pain: there, invulnerable to violence, disorganization, and disease. Oh, what wonders will such a body contain; and how will its study force from us, with far deeper emphasis than it was ever uttered in this world, the exclamation, *I am fearfully and wonderfully made!*

III. *In the spring hope changes into fruition.*

During the long winter months of high latitudes, how often do men sigh after the return of spring! Having had so long experience of the certain revolutions of the seasons, their expectation of spring's return, to scatter the snows, unlock the streams, mantle the earth with a green carpet, and cover the vegetable world with flowers of every form and hue, and make the air, earth, and waters again to teem with life and motion; this expectation, I say, is almost too strong to be called hope. And yet it may fail. We know not when the last vernal season may come: for of that *day knoweth no man, but the Father only.* But when we are actually rioting in the midst of vernal glories, we feel that all is a rejoicing reality. Every doubt and fear have departed, and the fruition is richer than the anticipation.

As the Christian turns his thought and his eyes to the place of the dead, he also hopes and longs for the day when all that sleeping dust shall be reanimated, and the grave shall give up its charge. And yet, when faith is weak, how often do desponding doubts and fears come over his mind! Oh, could he hear that voice which once said, *Lazarus, come forth*, in like manner summon all the countless millions of earth from their long sleep, what a glorious realization of fond hope would he experience! And ere long he shall hear it, and his hopes be changed into vision.

Oh, what a change, and what a vision! And to know, too, that his own body, on earth so frail, and, it may be, so full of pain and infirmity, shall then come forth purified, etherial, incorruptible, and adapted to be the residence of the sinless and immortal spirit, how delightful the anticipation!

* * * * * * * *

IV. *Spring opens upon us brighter displays of Divine Power, Wisdom, and Goodness.*

Every season has, indeed, its peculiar exhibitions of these attributes. But in the winter months, they are chiefly manifestations of inorganic laws. Chemistry is at work, with its curious transmutations and molecular forces, to convert water into splendid and most useful forms of crystalization; mantling the earth with snow and ice, and thus guarding organic beings from the loss of vital heat. But after all, it is when organic nature is most fully developed, that we are most impressed by the Divine wisdom and power. Indeed, the germination and growth of an animal or plant, such as we witness in the spring, are most wonderful processes; and were they not so common, they would be as impressive as miracles. And really, what is it but the direct power of God that produces these astonishing effects? True, we speak of the laws by which vegetables and animals are made to grow and flourish. But this is only saying that God works according to fixed rules: for what is a law without the efficient agency of the lawgiver? Why not at once ascribe to Divine Power the developments of organic life, which that Power can alone produce, and thus follow the example of the sacred writers, who seem as much impressed by the ordinary as by the extraordinary movements of nature, and see the hand of God in the one as distinctly as in the other. In like manner, when spring opens upon us unnumbered examples of expanding organisms, we should look upon them all as the direct proofs of Divine Power and Wisdom, and rejoice in them as indications of Divine Goodness.

And just so when the winter of the grave is past, and spring shall visit the mouldering urn, and the spiritual shall replace the natural body, how astonishing, have we reason to suppose, will be the manifestations of these Divine attributes which that new condition will present! If in this world, so marred by sin, the organism is full of wonders, what shall be its marvelousness when an organization exists adapted to a sinless and immortal state, to the free exercise of the intellectual and moral powers, and to ever-advancing holiness and happiness! The Scriptures allow us to give our imagination free scope, in attempting to conceive of the splendors of that state: for they seize upon the most brilliant scenes of time to set forth its external glories.

V. *The animating scenes of spring inspire the expectation of yet richer developments of organic nature.*

To see the expanding bud, the opening flower, and the green fields, and to drink in the balmy breezes loaded with refreshing odors, is indeed most animating and delightful. But a part of the pleasure arises from the confident expectation that the fresh beauties of spring shall ripen into the more enduring glories of summer, and the mellow fruits of autumn. The latter, indeed, we confidently expect as a consequence of the former, and therefore, as they come on, we are less impressed by their novelty. But let them cease to follow at the expected time, and we should find that beautiful as were the blossoms of spring, they could not compare in intrinsic importance with the more substantial developments of summer and autumn.

When the spring time of the resurrection shall arrive, and man finds himself united to his spiritual body, he will no doubt be amazed and delighted by the novelty and splendor of *his house not made with hands eternal in the heavens.* I know not what will be the anatomy and physiology of the spiritual body. But since it is adapted to a far higher state of existence, can we doubt that in structure and function it will equally transcend the natural body? It may not possess such senses as we now employ; but there must be means of receiving knowledge, far more delicate, certain, and rapid, than we now enjoy. Then, too, the spiritual body must be possessed of an activity incapable of fatigue, and eminently fitted for abstraction. The memory may be expected to retain, without effort, every impression made upon it. The organization must likewise be so exquisite as never to mislead or allure from duty. All the powers, indeed, of body and mind, must be in perfect harmony, and never know any of those conflicts which in this world so cloud the intellect, pervert the will, and estrange the affections from holiness and God.

But though the soul, when it first enters such a body, will experience intense delight, yet it will doubtless soon discover that still richer developments are in reserve for it: for we have every reason to suppose, both from the nature of the soul, and the whole analogy of the world, that everlasting progress and develment are the destiny of the glorified spirit; and that the grand means of such progress will be the exercise of all the powers, corporeal, mental, and moral. Nay, where is the objection to the supposition that the glorified spirit may pass successively into higher and higher conditions of being, by means of changes as great, it may be, as those that conduct it from this world into another: yet not of such a nature as implies the least amount of suffering. For even what we call death might be made a transition delightful in prospect and in experience.

It is reasonable then to suppose that the enchanting scenes of the spring time of future existence will be only an earnest of richer glories, which can be seen in bright perspective along the pathway of the whole immortal existence, and that, as the soul advances on that path, the vision will become wider and more magnificent forever and ever.

VI. *Finally, spring restores to us many well-remembered forms of vegetable and animal life.*

When the frosts of autumn came on, it was saddening to see how many familiar forms of the vegetable world, to which we had become attached, were yielding up their foliage; and though they descended to the grave in a gaudy dress, we could not but feel that we were losing the society of friends. Then too, the song of birds ceased in the fields and the woods, or they uttered only a few solitary and farewell notes, as they withdrew to their southern retreats. In like manner, nearly all other voices of the animal world soon ceased, and during the long months of winter, it was the analogy of nature only that inspired the expectation of ever again beholding forms that seemed to have disappeared forever. Yet with the opening spring they have come back: in a new dress indeed, but still identically the same, and awakening delightful reminiscences and anticipations. Some of them have been concealed among us and subjected to the stern power of winter: and others have fled far away to escape his withering blasts. But they have reappeared as fresh and lovely as ever: yea more so: nor can we perceive that one feature is gone, or changed, save that the fresher charms of youth are upon them. Every spire of grass is developed with the same form and color and position as its progenitors, so that the Festuca is at once known from the Poa and Agrostis, and the Dactylis from the Phleum. The Anemones and the Violets, the Gnaphalium, the Trifolium, the

Leontodon, the Hepatica, and the Trillium, have been restored without the loss of a single tint of coloring, or change in the form of their leaves, their stems, or their flowers. The oak also, and the maple, the elm and the poplar, the willow and the birch, the Cornus and the Pyrus, the pine and the spruce, and a thousand other species of trees and shrubs, put forth the same peculiar leaves and flowers, and take the same specific shapes and colors, which they have had since first they rose out of the earth at the Divine Command. The same familiar voices meet us too, from the fields and the groves. At the earliest dawn, the robin's cheerful song is heard, with the clear rich note of the lark, the soft tone of the bluebird, the twitter of the swallow, the cooing of the dove, the clear and cheerful voice of the blackbird, and the hoarse yet welcome garrulity of the crow. In short, wherever we turn our eyes, or whenever we open our ears, forms and sounds of vegetable and animal life meet us in almost endless profusion, yet familiar to us from our earliest days; and most of them dear to us, not only because of their inherent beauty and loveliness, but because they are associated with the most cherished recollections of our lives. When we look back upon life, we see much that is painful because marred by sin. But natural objects are always remembered with pleasure, because they wear the freshness and the innocence of Paradise. During the stern reign of winter we often sighed for the return of the foliage and the flowers, and the countless voices of gladness which burst forth from all nature in the vernal season. And now the desire is gratified, and while the soft and healthful breezes fan us, the smile and the song of nature make us almost forget for a time that we are in a world of sin and suffering.

How delightful now to be able to say, thus shall it be with the resurrection of the dead! Then, indeed, shall the grave deliver up a multitude of well-remembered and endeared forms, which in sadness we committed to its charge. In another part of this discourse I have endeavored to show, that the spiritual body will possess a specific and individual identity. Now what is it that enables us in the spring to recognize the plants and animals emerging from the grave of winter, as the same in kind with those that flourished in the previous year? It is simply by their specific identity, which has been preserved through all the changes and rigors of winter. Just so does the Bible describe the specific character of man, and by parity of reason that of individuals, as being unharmed by the mechanical and chemical changes consequent upon death. We may expect, therefore, to be able at the resurrection to distinguish those whom we have known on earth as readily as we do the plants and animals of spring. It is strange, indeed, apart from this doctrine of the preservation of specific identity, how theologians could ever have doubted whether men would be able to recognize one another in the eternal world: for they all admit that memory will remain, and some means of intercommunication be possessed, at least as certain as on earth. How, then, could individuals be prevented from learning to recognize one another, even though every evidence of corporeal identity be lost? But when the apostle says, that *God giveth to every seed his own body*, and that so it will be with the resurrection of the dead, every naturalist feels sure that there will exist also such marks of identity between the natural and the spiritual body, as will enable those familiar with the one to recognize the other. I pretend not, indeed, to describe *how* that specific identity can be preserved amid the decompositions of the grave; especially when I know that *flesh and blood cannot inherit the kingdom of God*. But I do know, that the specific characteristics of plants and animals are maintained in this world under changes perhaps equally great: and when Jehovah declares, that so shall it be in the resurrection of the dead, I joyfully acquiesce in the doctrine, because I know that infinite power can accomplish that which infinite wisdom determines."[1]

In addition to the foregoing, the following from another source will not be out of place:

The seed is to the plant what the egg is to the insect or the bud which proceeds from it. In each egg there is a germ, containing the lineaments of a little animal, which needs only the heat to develop it. In each seed, also, is a germ from which the plant issues. And, as no vegetable is produced without a seed, to which it owes its first existence, no animal can come to the light which has not been prepared in the egg.

But science has already numbered, upon the globe, ten thousand species of insects, and eighty thousand different species of plants, each of which proceeds from a germ peculiar to itself. And yet, it is surpris-

[1] *Religious Lectures*, pp. 33–50, delivered to the students at Amherst College, in 1845, 1847, 1848, and 1849, and then published, with others, in 1850.

ing that all these seeds of plants, and eggs of insects, scattered every where, by millions upon millions, are never mistaken by the spring in its innumerable resurrections; the cochineal never arising when we expect the ant, or the tamarind in the place of the sycamore, or the mint and the cummin in the place of the hyssop or the mustard. But it is especially surprising how all these germs can, previous to their renewal, brave the power of the elements, the moisture of the night, the rigor of the winter, frequently long years, and sometimes also ages, without losing anything of their germinating virtue, or of the mysterious life which lies concealed in their interior.

A few years ago a number of Celtic tombs were discovered near Bergerac, in France. Under the head of each skeleton, buried, it is said, two thousand years ago, the Druid priests had placed a block, and under each of these blocks, in a little circular cavity covered with cement, a small quantity of seeds. Well, these seeds, of two thousand years' duration, being collected and sown with particular care, have rapidly germinated; and the heliotrope,[1] the trefoil, and the bluebell have been seen springing, in the resurrection of life, after twenty centuries of burial: so that last year you might have beheld, with your own eyes, those marvellous plants blossoming in beauty, under the light of our own spring, after their germs had slept

[1] The name *heliotrope* is from the Greek ἥλιος, *helios*, the sun, and τρεπω, *trepo*, to turn. What a beautiful emblem of the Christian rising from the dead, after the lapse of ages, and turning to his Redeemer shining amid the clouds of heaven, is this flower, springing to life and beauty after centuries of silence and inertness, and turning its fresh and beautiful face towards the natural sun.

two thousand years under the heads of the dead, and in the dust of the tombs."[1]

In these copious extracts we have the substance of all that can be said upon the subject. There are indeed many phenomena in the natural world that somewhat resemble a life from the dead, and may therefore be denominated emblems of the resurrection; and yet, as we said at the outset, and as Dr. Hitchcock also has well observed, nature furnishes no instance of life from a state of actual death; and consequently affords no really appropriate or complete illustration of the resurrection of the body. Though both require omnipotence, one is a natural phenomenon, while the other is supernatural and miraculous, and is represented as the result of the special exercise of almighty power.

Had we no *better* light upon the subject than that which is furnished by these "emblems," we should be constrained to exclaim in the language of Beattie's Hermit.

> But when shall spring visit the mouldering urn,
> O when shall day dawn on the night of the grave!

There is nothing in *nature alone* to assure us of a future life for the body of man. The chrysalis and the seed, the egg and the bulb of the flower, still have *life*, despite the blasts of autumn and the snows of winter; but let *that* once be extinguished, and no butterfly or bird will ever spread their bright wings therefrom; no plant or tree will ever spring forth. But

[1] We are in doubt as to the author of this extract. We find it among the gatherings of years, and think it is from Gaussen, but are not able to verify this supposition.

man *dies*. There is no living ovum or germ in the dead body that retains its vitality through the long and cold winter of the tomb. *Our* dust is never warmed into life by the showers and sunshine of spring. We are *dead;* and therefore never vegetate or live again, as lives the plant or seed, which, in fact, has never ceased to live.

While, therefore, nature may faintly illustrate the glorious resurrection, her more legitimate lesson, aside from the blessed light of the Bible and of the cross, would be, that man, once dead, will live no more forever. Her brightest beams are but faint reflections of that stronger and steadier light with which Christ, the Conqueror of Death, has cheered our vision. We place no value, therefore, upon these "natural emblems," so far as the *argument* is concerned. They prove nothing, and but faintly shadow forth the resurrection of the dead.

We still need a divine revelation to assure us of a life to come, either for the soul or the body; but with this and the resurrection of Christ, all is clear. Life and immortality are fully brought to light, and the doubter may exchange his sad forebodings for the jubilant song of the true believer,—

And darkness and doubt are now fleeing away,
No longer I roam in conjecture forlorn.
So breaks on the traveler, faint and astray,
The bright and the balmy effulgence of morn.
See Truth, Love, and Mercy in triumph descending;
And nature all glowing in Eden's first bloom!
On the cold cheek of death smiles and roses are blending,
And Beauty immortal awakes from the tomb.

CHAPTER XXIV.

PRACTICAL OBSERVATIONS AND REFLECTIONS.

WE are now done with the argument, and with the consideration of the various side issues and speculative questions that stand connected with the subject. Following the general plan indicated in the first chapter, we have shown—

1. That whether right or wrong, the doctrine of a corporeal resurrection has been the faith of the Jews from the exodus out of Egypt to the present time. Thus did *they* understand the writings of Moses and the prophets.

2. That such was the faith of the early Christians and martyrs, and such has been the faith of the Church of Christ in all ages, and in all its various branches and denominations, (with a few inconsiderable exceptions,) from the day of Pentecost to the present hour.

3. That the Old Testament fully warrants the belief of the Jews, that there will be a resurrection of the bodies of men to life and immortality.

4. That the Son of God—the prophet like unto Moses who was to be raised up, and whom God has commanded us all to hear,[1] distinctly taught the doctrine of a corporeal resurrection.

[1] Deut. xviii. 15; Mark ix. 7; Acts iii. 22.

5. That he demonstrated his own teachings and those of Moses and the prophets, so far as the *possibility* and the *nature* of the phenomenon is concerned, by actually arising from death, to die no more forever. "Christ, being raised from the dead, dieth no more; death hath no more dominion over him."[1]

6. That the apostles believed and taught, not only that Christ actually arose from the dead, in the identical body laid in the grave, but that his resurrection is a specimen and proof of the resurrection of all others; and that there will be a similar resurrection of all the dead, both of the just and unjust.

7. That the various theories of the resurrection designed to obviate the supposed difficulties of a corporeal resurrection, relieve few or none of these supposed difficulties, and are themselves in many respects both unscriptural and absurd.

8. That the alleged difficulties in the way of, and the objections to a literal resurrection, are either founded upon an erroneous conception of the orthodox view, or are, for other reasons, of no force as against the true theory; and

9. Finally, that taking the resurrection body as described in the Scriptures, its restoration is not only demanded by the honor of Christ, the great Restorer, but is a *necessity* of our future perfection and happiness; and that the future body will be the medium of knowledge and of immortal felicity to the soul forever.

All these points we claim to have established beyond successful contradiction in the preceding pages; or in other words, that having defined the true doctrine, we

[1] Rom. vi. 9.

have fully *proved* it; and have vindicated it against all opposing theories, objections and reasonings.

The remaining chapters respecting the extent, time, order, and circumstances of the resurrection, and the nature of the first resurrection and the Millennium, though upon topics somewhat involved in the discussion, are only incidental to the main question. Whatever opinion, therefore, the reader may entertain upon these points, the main argument remains unaffected; and the moral demonstration equally complete.

Here, then, we stand upon the ancient foundation—the foundation of the apostles and prophets—Jesus Christ himself being the chief corner-stone. As the faithful Jews from Moses to Christ understood their Scriptures, so *we* understand them. As Jesus taught and demonstrated in his own person, so *we* believe. As the apostles believed and preached, so *we* trust and preach that there shall be a resurrection of the bodies of all men from the dead, to live immortal in heaven or hell forever. In this faith the martyrs bled and died, and in this faith the saints of eighteen centuries have toiled, and suffered, and conquered, and passed onward to a bright and glorious future. And for any one to attempt now, with all the evidences of the truth before him, to impeach the wisdom of prophets and apostles, and Christ and his Church in all ages, and under the guise of "philosophy," falsely so called, to fritter away and abandon the ancient doctrine of the resurrection of the dead, is, in our view, the height of folly and presumption, if not also of impiety and moral insanity. And it by no means relieves the case that the caviller and the opposer of the truth belongs to a church, so-called; perhaps occupies a pulpit and uses a Bible,—that he professes not to *deny* the resurrection, but merely to *explain* it, as he claims, "philosophically." The truth is, that defeated oft and again in open combat, upon its own avowed ramparts, infidelity has sought baptism, and has joined the Church (so-called;) and is now with pen and tongue, in pulpits and over open Bibles, preaching down the faith of Christ! Such is the strategy of the enemies of Christ to-day, in this and in other lands. How few avowed infidels can be found! No. They are all "Christians"—certainly! But they are "philosophical Christians." They have all "sheep's clothing," though their mission is to slaughter every essential truth of God.

But to return to the main subject of this chapter—the practical bearings and utility of the Scriptural truth that the body shall rise again, etc., we ask attention to the following closing observations.

I. *Does not this doctrine vindicate the Lord Jesus Christ as a true Prophet and Redeemer?*

"If there be no resurrection of the dead," says the apostle, "then is not Christ risen: and if Christ be not risen, then is our preaching vain, and your faith is also vain. Yea, and we are found false witnesses of God; because we have testified of God that he raised up Christ; whom he raised not up, if so be that the dead rise not. For if the dead rise not, then is not Christ raised; and if Christ be not raised, your faith is vain; ye are yet in your sins."[1]

The *prophets* said Christ should arise. He pro-

[1] 1 Cor. xv. 13–17.

mised that he would rise; and if there is no resurrection of the bodies of men, and Christ never arose, then he is an impostor, the gospel a cunningly devised fable, and, as the apostle has well said, "our faith is vain, and we are yet in our sins."

According to St. Paul, therefore, to deny the doctrine of the resurrection of the body, is to deny the resurrection of Christ; and to deny the resurrection of Christ is to overthrow the whole Christian system.[1] And who does not see that such is the necessary sequence? The doctrine of a physical resurrection is consequently the only doctrine that can vindicate the veracity or the character of Christ as the true Messiah, or afford us the slightest ground to hope for salvation through him. It is therefore such a resurrection or no salvation through our Lord Jesus Christ.

II. *This is the only doctrine that exalts the redeeming plan, as adapted to man's necessities, and competent to restore him to his primeval condition and glory.*

1. In his state of innocency in Eden his soul and body were united. Such was his normal condition, for he was not *man* till the immortal spirit was breathed into the body by its Maker. But man sinned, and natural death followed. "By one man sin entered into the world, and death by sin, and so death passed upon all men, for that all have sinned."[2] Thus "by one man's offence death reigned by one."[3] But "since by man came death, by man came also the resurrection of the dead. For as in Adam all die,

[1] Prof. Bush thinks that St. Paul reasons very *loosely* in this entire passage.

[2] Rom. v. 12.

[3] Rom. v. 17.

even so in Christ shall all be made alive."[1] So far, then, as a simple resurrection is concerned, as men die involuntarily in consequence of the first transgression, so shall they rise involuntarily, in virtue of the atonement of Christ, the second Adam, whether they be Christians or infidels. And beyond this, all who believe in Christ and follow him, shall be *like* him in that day. They shall arise "to the resurrection of life," and shall shine like him in incorruption and glory and immortality.

2. But suppose it be true that the *body* of man shall never rise again? Sin has stripped it off from the immortal spirit, and sent it back to dust; and despite the atonement of Christ, and the believer's faith in him, redemption is but partial, and is in no respect co-extensive with the effects of the fall, inasmuch as it leaves the body of man under the dominion of death; and thus dooms him to an everlasting disability and reproach, in spite of all that Christ has done or can do for him! How, then, is death swallowed up in victory?[2] How, then, does Christ restore even his saints from all the bitter fruits of sin and death?

To deny the resurrection of the body is, therefore, to disparage the atonement, and to make sin and death triumphant forever; while the true doctrine exalts Christ as the victorious conqueror, holding the keys of hades and of the grave, and exclaiming in triumph at last, "O death, where is thy sting? O grave, where is thy victory?"

III. *This doctrine alone explains that mysterious love for our own bodies, which is felt by every soul of man.*

[1] 1 Cor. xv. 21, 22. [2] Isa. xxv. 8.

"No man," says the apostle, "ever yet hated his own flesh;"[1] and such is the universal consciousness. The touching address of the soul to the body, by Mrs. Sigourney, reprinted in part in these pages, finds a response in every reader's heart. We all love our bodies. They are a part of ourselves—of our essential being. Instead of hating and blaming them, we excuse their disabilities and defects, and regard them with tenderness and affection. And when called to part company with them at death, instead of separating without a sigh, we *feel* if we do not *express* the sentiments of the poetess—

If I have ever caused thee pain,
The throbbing heart, the burning brain,
With cares and vigils turn'd thee pale,
And scorned thee when thy strength did fail—
Forgive! Forgive!—thy task doth cease:
Friend! Lover!—let us part in peace.

And do we not with equal tenderness and affection excuse the defects and imperfect services of the body, in a manner that we never should but for that innate love for it which the Creator has implanted in every bosom? Are we not ever ready to say—

If thou didst sometimes check my force,
Or, trifling, stay mine upward course,
Or lure from heaven my wavering trust,
Or bow my drooping wing to dust,—
I blame thee not, the strife is done,
I know thou wert the weaker one,
The vase of earth, the trembling clod,
Constrained to hold the breath of God.

A young cavalry officer lay upon the surgeon's table,

[1] Eph. v. 29.

after the battle of Fair Oaks, with his right arm shattered to pieces at the elbow. The chloroform was administered, and the arm taken off and thrown upon the pile of amputated limbs. As consciousness returned, he saw that the arm was gone; and turning his languid eye upon the surgeon, he said, "Doctor, won't you hand me my arm? I want to see it." The surgeon looked it out from among the rest, and passed it to him on the couch where he had been laid. Taking the cold fingers in his left hand, and gazing upon them for a moment, he broke forth in a low and plaintive voice—"Farewell, my good right hand. You have been a good hand to me. You have served me and my country well. But you will never swing another sabre, or fire another carbine. You will write no more letters to mother or sister. Good-bye! my good right hand!" And kissing it affectionately, as the tears streamed down his pale cheeks, he handed it to the surgeon, who threw it back upon the pile.

Such is our love for our own bodies. How sacred to many a maimed soldier is the spot, if he knows where it is, where his lost arm or foot or leg is buried. But why this love for our bodies, if they are really no part of our proper selves, and are soon to be left behind forever? But with the doctrine of the resurrection, all is clear and natural. We love the body because it is a part of ourselves, and shall be redeemed from death, and live on forever!

This very love, therefore, which we cherish for our own bodies, is nature's testimony in the soul of every man to the truth of the glorious doctrine that there shall be a resurrection of the dead, both of the just and unjust.

IV. *This doctrine alone explains our deep-seated love for the bodies of deceased friends and relatives, even after the spirit has departed, and the dust is hasting back to dust again.*

In vain does the minister remind the stricken mother at the funeral that the little form there in the coffin is not her Emma—that the deathless spirit that alone could know, or love, or remember her, has spread its wings for a fairer clime, and is not there. All that she believes, knows, feels; but yet she bends over the marble-cold body. "O Emma! my *dear*, DEAR Emma!" and she kisses the cold clay with an affection as pure and holy as that which binds the angels together in the heavenly sisterhood. And no measure of faith, or superior love to Christ, can extinguish this deep-seated and ardent love for the bodies of sisters, brothers, parents, or children, though we know that the *soul* is not there, and that the deserted body is rapidly tending to corruption.

2. It is this instinctive love for the bodies of the dead we love, that robes them in costly shrouds, places them in rich and expensive coffins, and then watches over and garnishes their sepulchres for long years to come. It is this love that adorns our Greenwoods, and Cypress Hills, and Mount Auburns, and Laurel Hills, and Evergreens, and makes it even a pleasure to wander in these cities of the dead. We feel ourselves to be among those we love.

On one occasion the writer was going to a burial in Greenwood, in the winter of 1861. The ground was covered with snow, and the cold wind was whistling among the branches of the leafless trees. As the procession passed near the potter's field, where the children of the poor are buried, we saw a poor woman, in scanty raiment, away up on the hill-side, and bending over a little grave, with her face covered with a handkerchief. Why was she there amid the cold winds and snows? What powerful magnet had drawn her to that spot and kept her there? There lay the precious dust of her little boy; and like the Marys at the tomb of their brother Lazarus, she had gone to weep there!

Now, upon the hypothesis that the body is really no part of the man, any more than the abandoned shell of the chrysalis is a part of the departed butterfly, what means this continued love for the bodies of the dead, when the soul has flown away? Is it not really God's witness in the soul of every man—the echo which nature herself gives back in response to the glorious revealed truth, that the body we love so well is bound to the spirit by ties that death can never dissolve; and that it will rise and live again when mortality is swallowed up of life. Thus every sigh that is heaved over the coffin and the tomb, every tear that is shed, and every kiss imprinted upon the marble brow of the dead, are but so many witnesses to the truth that the dead shall live again, though now they crumble back to dust.

3. It is a somewhat remarkable fact, that even those who in *theory* discard the body as in no proper sense a part of ourselves, and therefore of little consequence; and who talk and write very "philosophically" of its grossness and non-utility, weep just as sincerely over

the dead, and kiss them just as fondly at the funeral, and build just as high monuments over their graves, as do those who believe in a corporeal resurrection. This undeniable fact is strangely inconsistent with their creed; for,

> Why do they wish for the hollowed-out rocks?
> Or wherefore the beautiful monuments crave?
> Unless 'tis believed that the body but slumbers,
> And is not abandoned to death in the grave.

We answer, Because, though the intellect is beclouded, and darkness has taken the place of light, the *heart* is yet true to its heaven-implanted instincts; and clings fondly to the very body which a false philosophy pronounces of no importance. Thus every feeling of the soul of man rises in rebelling against the doctrine of the non-resurrection of the dead; and despite all creeds and theories, records its testimony in favor of a corporeal resurrection.

V. *The doctrine of the resurrection enthrones the Lord of Life as a Prince and Conqueror in the hearts of all true believers.*

1. It exalts his *goodness.* Though we have deserved death, both of soul and body, and that forever, yet has he ordained that with those who accept his proffered salvation, neither soul nor body shall die eternally. It is his good pleasure that every trace of sin and of its curse shall be wiped away forever.

2. It exalts his *power.* As it was not possible that he should be holden of death,[1] so it is not possible for death to hold the bodies of any of his followers under his power forever, since Jesus has abolished death, and

[1] Acts ii. 24.

brought life and immortality to light.[1] Oh, what majesty and triumph in the words, "I will swallow up death in victory!"[2] "I am he that liveth, and was dead; and behold, I am alive for evermore, Amen; and have the keys of hell and of death."[3] If it is asked, "Who is this that cometh from Edom, with dyed garments from Bozrah? this that is glorious in his apparel, traveling in the greatness of his strength?" the appropriate answer of Christ is, "I that speak in righteousness, MIGHTY TO SAVE!"[4] But he would not be "mighty to save" if the bodies of his saints were to remain forever under the power of death.

3. It is only in the light of this doctrine that we can fully understand and appreciate the redeeming acts of the Son of God. If the dead rise not, why did Christ come under death's dominion at all? And what is the value or even the significance of his resurrection? But looking upon him as our Forerunner, who was crucified, dead and buried, and rose and ascended to heaven as a proof and pledge of our resurrection, all is clear. Then,

——In his blessed life
I see the path, and in his death the price,
And in his great ascent the proof supreme
Of immortality.

It is then no marvel that the apostles constantly pointed to his resurrection, and preached through him the resurrection of all men. *His* triumph is *our* triumph, and his ascent to glory thus becomes our passport to glory and immortality.

[1] 2 Tim. i. 10. [2] Isa. xxv. 8. [3] Rev. i. 18. [4] Isa. lxiii. 1.

Lift your glad voices in triumph on high,
For Jesus hath risen, and man shall not die;
Vain were the terrors that gather'd around him,
  And short the dominion of death and the grave;
He burst from the fetters of darkness that bound him,
  Resplendent in glory to live and to save:
Loud was the chorus of angels on high,—
The Saviour hath risen, and man shall not die.

VI. *This doctrine alone assures the believer of final and complete salvation through Christ.*

It is not a salvation of a *part* of our being which it promises, but of *the whole man*, soul and body. It is not a mysterious metempsichosis, or transmigration, nor yet a new creation; but *salvation*—the washing of the soul from all its stains, and the restoration of the body laid low in the dust by sin and death, to immortality and eternal life. And this covenant is well-ordered and sure. I must die, but *I shall live again* to die no more!

An angel's arm can't snatch me from the grave;
Legions of angels can't confine me there.

Blessed be the God and Father of our Lord Jesus Christ, which, according to his abundant mercy, hath begotten us again unto a lively hope by the resurrection of Jesus Christ from the dead, to an inheritance incorruptible, and undefiled, and that fadeth not away.[1]

There, at the Father's right hand, is our Elder Brother—the God-man—who was dead, but is alive. There, too, are doubtless the bodies of Enoch and Elijah, who were translated without seeing death; and also the bodies of the saints who arose after Christ's resurrection, and came into Jerusalem, and appeared unto many.[2]

[1] 1 Pet. i. 3, 4. [2] Matt. xxvii. 52.

Some have supposed that Moses, also, was raised from the dead, (and we once held this opinion,) but we are convinced that it is erroneous. It is true that he appeared on Mount Tabor with Elias talking with Jesus,[1] but he could not have been there in his resurrected body.

Unlike Enoch and Elias, Moses *died* near fifteen centuries before Christ. "So Moses the servant of the LORD died there in the land of Moab, according to the word of the LORD. And he buried him in a valley in the land of Moab, over against Beth-peor: but no man knoweth of his sepulchre unto this day."[2]

It appears from Jude 9th, that there was some contention between Michael the archangel and Satan about the body of Moses, but to what this remark relates we cannot fully understand. Of one thing, however, we are certain, and that is, that there is nothing in this obscure allusion to warrant the belief that God raised Moses' body from the dead, lest Satan should use it as a means of leading the Jews into idolatry.

That the body was dead and buried is clear. It is also clear that in some sense Moses appeared with Elias on Mount Tabor, and talked with Jesus. But that his *body* was not there, is in our opinion certain from the following considerations: (1.) The Scriptures repeatedly declare that Christ should be "the first that should rise from the dead;"[3] the "first-fruits of them that slept;"[4] and the "first-born from the dead, that in all things he might have the pre-eminence."[5] Not that he was to be or was the first who should arise at

[1] Matt. xvii. 1–3. [2] Deut. xxxiv. 5, 6. [3] Acts xxvi. 23.
[4] 1 Cor. xv. 20. [5] Col. i. 18.

all, but the first who should arise *immortal,* that is, *to die no more.* For, all others who arose before, died again. But (2,) the transfiguration was before the crucifixion of Christ, and consequently before he had risen from the dead. If, then, he was to be the first, is it not certain that at that time Moses had not risen, and was not there in his immortal body? For if he had risen at that time, then *he* was the first, and not Christ, and the Redeemer has *not* "the pre-eminence" as to the order of his resurrection.

Moses was there as a specimen of disembodied spirits, and a representative of the souls of the righteous dead in Paradise; and Elias as a specimen of humanity fully redeemed, soul and body, from the power of sin and death. But the *body* of Moses still slept in the land of Moab, over against Beth-peor, where it still awaits the trump of God and the general resurrection.

But though Moses still waits, like the prophets and martyrs, and all the saints of God, who sleep in death, for the redemption of his body,[1] there are others, and we have reason to suppose "a goodly company," who have attained through Christ's victory to the full salvation of the gospel; and stand with him on Mount Zion above, soul and body united, immortal, and forever glorified—earnests and guaranties of our own resurrection to glory. The first-fruits are already there—human beings, fully recovered from all the power of death and hell—and the harvest is sure to follow.

[1] Rom. viii. 23.

VII. *How consoling this doctrine to the bereft and sorrowing.*

How many Marys and Marthas of earth, who mourn the loss of those they love, have been cheered and comforted by the assurance, "*Thy brother shall rise again!*" —thy husband, father, or tender infant, shall one day triumph over death and the grave, through the might of the Crucified, and shall soar aloft to die no more.

"I come, then, my hearers, with my heart full of this consoling doctrine, to pour it into the bosoms of the afflicted. And who of us have not sometimes been afflicted in the removal of those whose forms and features have been ever since remembered with the deepest interest? We have called in the aid, it may be, of painting and photography to embalm their features and the expression which the workings of the soul within gave to the countenance. And how deep was our anguish, when we last looked upon them, although death had marred their countenances, as we saw the grave closing over their remains. But if the doctrine of this discourse be true, and if they were the true disciples of Christ, they shall be restored to us in the resurrection morning, and we shall recognize them amid the millions who will then awake from the grave, as we now recognize the plants and animals of spring. There shall be a characteristic something in their spiritual bodies, that will lead us at once, and with exulting joy, to fly to their embrace. Fathers and mothers who have been called to yield to the demands of death a darling and pious child, while yet the dew and the beauty of youth were fresh upon him, go forth at the shout of the archangel, and you shall find that child, glowing indeed with celestial beauty and glory, yet retaining something of that same expression which has stamped his image so deeply on your heart. And thou disconsolate man, from whom death has taken the wife of your youth, go thou forth at the same signal, and you shall at once distinguish her too, amid ascending millions, and become her everlasting companion, in that world where they *neither marry nor are given in marriage, but are as the angels of God.* The lonely widow, let her come, and she shall recognize that countenance, which a noble soul and generous affection have made indelible on her heart, as once her husband and protector, nor shall any power be able again to tear him from her side; but the holy joys of eternity shall be doubly sweet, because enjoyed together. Children of beloved Christian parents, come ye, also, and rush again into the embrace of those who gave you being, and trained you up for heaven, and they shall take you by the hand and still be your guides and companions amid the wonders of the New Jerusalem. There likewise shall the brother, from whom death has torn an affectionate brother or sister, and the sister, who has often wept over a departed brother or sister, find them again radiant with heavenly glory, yet retaining the traces of their earthly character. And whatever Christian weeps over the memory of a Christian friend, let him wipe away his tears, and prepare to meet that friend, when the graves have given up their dead, with a body like unto Christ's, yet fashioned so as to make it only a transmuted and glorified natural body, recognized by one of those golden links that bind the natural to the spiritual, the mortal to the immortal. Oh, blessed season of recognition and joy begun! How will it wipe away in a moment every Christian mourner's tears, and restore to him his departed friends, and bring them all together in the presence of their common Lord, to enjoy his smiles, and the delightful intercourse of one another, with no fear of disastrous change or separation, forever and ever. Surrounded as we are, my Christian friends, by the resurrections of spring, let us look upon the thousand forms of life and beauty that meet us from day to day, as symbolizations of that nobler resurrection, when forms a thousand times dearer shall start into life from a deeper winter and put on a verdure that will never decay, and a glory that will never fade. Oh, that this bright hope might stimulate us so to live and to labor, that not only ourselves, but all whom we love on earth, shall come forth at the resurrection of the just, purified from the stains and sins of earth, and ripe for the perfect holiness and happiness of heaven."[1]

Glory to God in full anthems of joy;
The being he gave us death cannot destroy;
Sad were the life we may part with to-morrow,
  If tears were our birthright and death were our end;
But Jesus hath cheer'd the dark valley of sorrow,
  And bade us immortal to heaven ascend:
Lift then your voices in triumph on high,
For Jesus hath risen, and man shall not die.

VIII. *Equally cheering is the hope of the resurrection, as we see our own bodies slowly tending to death and the tomb.*

The eye grows dim, the locks grow thin and gray. The keepers of the house tremble, and the strong men

[1] Hitchcock's *Religious Lectures*, pp. 33–50.

bow themselves. The doors are shut in the streets, and the grinders cease because they are few. Fears are in the way, and the daughters of music fail. All these omens one by one admonish us that we are going to our long home, and that the dust is tending to its kindred dust. The grave will soon cover us, and death will feed upon us. But what of all this if from the depth of our souls we can exclaim with the pious German,—

> Thou shalt rise! my dust, thou shalt rise!
> Not always closed thine eyes;
> Thy life's first Giver
> Will give thee life forever.
> Ah! praise his name!

"Take for an example the long-tried and desponding invalid. Year after year, and decade after decade, it may be, his frail system has battled manfully with the insidious workings of disease. Those in vigorous health regard the most of his complaints perhaps as imaginary, and suppose they might easily be thrown off by vigorous effort; or at the most, they look upon him with silent pity. But the feverish pulse, the aching head, the failing strength, the desponding spirits, and the enfeebled mind, too surely teach him that disease is gaining strength, and must ere long be conqueror. He tries all that the strictest rules of hygiene can do, to restore the wasting energies; and sometimes hope cheers him for a little while with the sweet vision of renovated health; but a deeper darkness succeeds, and each successive alternation of hope and despondency gives to the latter more and more of a predominance. At length, if his heart has felt the transforming power of the Gospel, his thoughts turn with a deepening interest to that world where the inhabitant will not say, I am sick; and the hope of a resurrection of his now diseased and suffering body to immortal health and vigor, sends a thrill of delightful anticipation through his sinking heart. Much as he has suffered in his present body, he still feels for it a strong attachment; especially when he reflects how wonderfully it has held out under the assaults of disease; and it is a delightful thought that it shall one day be restored to him, transformed indeed gloriously, but retaining its identity, and having become invulnerable to all created power, shall be his eternal and happy dwelling-place. Oh, animating hope! And it is eminently the invalid's hope; for how little do they know of its mighty power, whose pulse of health always beats strong, and whose spirits are always buoyant and happy."[1]

No matter *when* or *how* or by what disease this earthly tabernacle is taken down. If it shall be rebuilt like the ruined temple at Jerusalem, and especially if the glory of the latter house shall exceed the glory of the former house, all is well.

Let sickness blast, let death devour,
  If heaven must recompense our pains;
Perish the grass, and fade the flower,
  If firm the word of God remains.

IX. *Such being the practical value of this glorious doctrine, ought not every believer to see to it that he understands it well, and that he is not "shaken in mind," or his feet removed from the sure foundation?*

Even in the days of the apostles there were those

[1] Hitchcock's *Lectures*, pp. 41, 42.

who troubled the disciples, and toiled to pervert the gospel of Christ.[1] Some, like the Gnostics and the modern "New Church" theologians, declared that the resurrection was past, and thus overthrew the faith of some.[2] There were then as now abundant reasons for the apostolic warning, "Beware lest any man spoil you through philosophy and vain deceit, after the tradition of men, after the rudiments of the world, and not after Christ."[3]

In the primitive church the doctrine of the resurrection was everywhere prominent and magnified. Upon no point were the ministry more tenacious than upon "*the resurrection of the* FLESH," or, as they sometimes expressed it, "*the resurrection of* THIS *flesh.*" In this faith every convert was baptized; and to doubt the resurrection of the body was regarded as a pernicious heresy. These facts no well-informed person will deny. And such being the case, is it not well, nay, indispensable to the stability and hope and religious comfort of every Christian, that they be well grounded in this ancient gospel of Christ? Is it wise or prudent, or even safe for us, to practically neglect this glorious central truth of Christianity? or above all, to give ourselves up to the idle dreams and vagaries of a false philosophy? "Stand ye in the ways, and see, and ask for the old paths, where is the good way, and walk therein, and ye shall find rest for your souls."[4]

X. *In view of the importance and practical value of the doctrine of the resurrection, and especially of the present efforts to pervert or discard it, we appeal to the*

[1] Gal. i. 7. [2] 2 Tim. ii. 18. [3] Col. ii. 8. [4] Jer. vi. 16.

ministry of this country to meet the issue thus tendered like true watchmen and successors of the apostles.

Next to the doctrine of the Divinity of Christ, perhaps no one doctrine of the Bible is at this day assailed with greater earnestness, open or covert, than is the doctrine of the resurrection. True, as we have elsewhere said, most of this opposition is made in the name of Christianity, and by men who profess to revere Jesus of Nazareth and his teachings; but their hostility is all the more to be feared for that very reason. For we have long since seen that "art thou in health my brother," may be the precursor of the fatal stab;[1] and a kiss may be the very means of an infamous betrayal of the Son of God into the hands of his enemies.[2]

If this outpost of truth be carried, all is lost. If there be no resurrection of the dead, then is Christ not risen; and if Christ is not risen, Christianity is a fable, and our faith and hope are vain. Then, indeed, the dead have perished forever!

In view of all these facts, we respectfully submit to our brethren in the ministry, of every name, the question, Have we done, and are we doing, our full duty upon this subject?

1. Have we given it that *attention* which its relative importance demands? As the key, so to speak, to the theological situation, have we bestowed upon it that *thought* and *reading* which so vital a subject deserves? Many no doubt have; but we fear many others have not. And some, perhaps, have given the adversary occasion to triumph, for lack of that attention

[1] 2 Sam. xx. 9. [2] Matt. xxvi. 42.

to, and understanding of, the subject which are essential to its proper presentation and defence. Ought not every orthodox minister in the land to be "thoroughly furnished" upon this subject as well as upon any other, to meet the insidious scepticism of the times under all its disguises, and at whatever point the assault may be made? So it seems to us; and to this we urge all our brethren of the Christian ministry.

2. Ought we not to *preach* more upon the subject?

"One remark," says Dr. Adam Clarke, "I cannot help making; the doctrine of the *resurrection* appears to have been thought of much more consequence among the primitive Christians than it is *now*. How is this? The apostles were continually insisting on it, and exciting the followers of God to diligence, obedience, and cheerfulness through it. And their successors in the present day seldom mention it! So apostles preached, and so primitive Christians believed; so we preach, and so our hearers believe. There is not a doctrine in the gospel on which more stress is laid; and there is not a doctrine in the present system of preaching which is treated with more neglect."[1]

And if such neglect was to be deplored in the days of Dr. Clarke, is it not still more to be deprecated now, when the enemies of the cross of Christ are combining and employing every art and agency to impair the faith of the people in the truth of God? Let any one read over the discourses of Peter and Paul, as recorded in the Acts of the Apostles, and he will see that this doctrine entered largely into almost every sermon and defence. Wherever they went, and be-

[1] Notes on 1 Cor. xv., in fine.

fore whomsoever they spoke, they preached through Jesus the resurrection from the dead. Why, then, should we, who profess to minister the same glorious gospel of Christ, content ourselves with preaching a single sermon upon the subject, perhaps once in two or three years? Would it be too much to give Easter Sunday—the reputed anniversary of the resurrection of Christ—to that particular and glorious theme *every year*, with prayers and hymns and thanksgivings to correspond; and then, on suitable occasions, and from time to time, to treat the general subject, in all its bearings and relations, and with all the ability and grace that God has given us? Is not the theme *worthy* of such consideration and labor? and would it not be promotive of stability, and faith, and hope, and religious comfort among those to whom we minister?

The writer has now (1866) been in the ministry over thirty years, during which time he has preached in various places, in city and country, and to a great variety of character, as to culture, occupation, and moral status. And though utterly opposed to all theological specialties or religious hobbies, he has felt it to be a duty and a pleasure to present the evidences of man's immortality, both of soul and body, to every congregation to whom he has ministered. And so far as our observation is concerned, we here record it as our deliberate judgment, that no portion of the gospel of Christ which we have at any time preached, has been listened to with so great attention, or been more profitable to the people under our care, or the means of leading more sinners to repentance and faith in Christ.

While, then, we say to all our brethren in the ministry, now living, and to all who may read these lines when we are dead, preach the tri-unity of the Godhead, and the Deity of Christ—preach the atonement and remission of sins through faith in his blood—preach holiness of heart and life, a day of judgment, a heaven for the righteous, and a hell for the wicked—do not neglect to preach distinctly and strongly, and we will add, *elaborately and fully*, the immortality of the soul, and the resurrection of the body. They are a vital part of the gospel—are themes in which all feel an interest, and to which all will listen with attention; and the effect can only be healthful and salutary.

3. There is yet another point upon which a word may be permitted, and that is this: Ought not the ministry of our times to *defend* the truth of God against the assaults of its enemies more directly and fully than it is now generally done? There is a theory abroad, and which is even adopted by some ministers, that the best way to refute error, and prevent the spread of false doctrines, is to let them entirely alone—to ignore them as if they had never existed! This certainly is an *easy* way of discharging duty, but it is not the strategy of the prophets and apostles. When the older watchmen saw the sword coming, they blew the trumpet and warned the people; and so did the Great Teacher and the inspired apostles. "Beware of false prophets," said the Saviour, "who come to you in sheep's clothing, but inwardly they are ravening wolves."[1] Writing to Titus respecting certain "vain talkers and deceivers," the apostle says, "whose mouths

[1] Matt. vii. 15.

must be stopped."[1] But how "stopped" by saying nothing about them or their errors?

We are no advocate for personal controversies upon theological questions, except in extreme cases; much less for religious wrangling and strife among evangelical Christians. But at the same time, we are utterly opposed to the policy of letting error and false teachers alone. It is worldly wisdom, and not the wisdom from above.

"St. Paul," we are told by some of our modern "philosophers," "was a rough, primitive sort of man, very sectarian and illiberal, and a very poor pattern for a modern minister." No doubt such "preachers" would prefer a tolerant, "let alone" minister to the stern old apostle. See how he wrote to the Galatians: "I marvel that ye are so soon removed from him that called you into the grace of Christ, unto another gospel: which is not another; but there be some that trouble you, and would pervert the gospel of Christ. But though we, or an angel from heaven, preach any other gospel unto you than that which we have preached unto you, let him be accursed. As we said before, so say I now again, If any man preach any other gospel unto you than that ye have received, let him be accursed. For do I now persuade men, or God? or do I seek to please men? for if I yet pleased men, I should not be the servant of Christ. But I certify you, brethren, that the gospel which was preached of me is not after man: for I neither received it of man, neither was I taught it, but by the revelation of Jesus Christ."[2]

[1] Titus i. 11. [2] Gal. i. 6–12.

Here is none of that false charity and prudence which some so much admire. He has a message from God, and whoever opposes or attempts to pervert it, is an enemy to the gospel, and to be regarded and treated as such.

And even John, the sweet-spirited and "beloved disciple," inculcates the same etiquette as to the treatment of false teachers:

"If there come any unto you, and bring not this doctrine, receive him not into your house, neither bid him God speed: for he that biddeth him God speed, is partaker of his evil deeds." [1]

Thus the holy apostles believed and acted, and thus it appears to us that we should act, as Christ's ambassadors and watchmen. If we do not discriminate between truth and error, preach the former and combat the latter, and warn the people old and young against the errors that are coming in like a flood, we shall awake, perhaps too late, to find the foundations gone, and the land filled with scoffers and contemners of everything sacred.

"The time has come," says Bishop Kingsly, "when in regard to the doctrine of the resurrection, it is necessary to contend earnestly for the faith once delivered to the saints;" [2] and we fully endorse the sentiment. And does not God expect every minister especially to do his duty? May he plenteously endue us all with wisdom and grace—with fidelity, courage, and fortitude—that when the Chief Shepherd shall appear, we may be found to have done our duty, and may each receive a crown of life that fadeth not away!

[1] 2 John 10, 11. [2] Preface to Treatise, p. 9.

Our task is done. And now, grateful to God that we have been spared to complete this second volume of our promised series, and commending what we have written to the gracious favor of heaven, we consecrate it to Christ and to his glory forever.

PRAYER.

O God of infinite mercies! Look thou upon these pages with favor and compassion. Pardon their many errors and imperfections. Attend them with thy blessing, and shed thou upon the mind and heart of all who shall read them, the light and precious guidance of thy Holy Spirit. May they strengthen the faith, brighten the prospects, and increase the joys of thy people. May they establish the wavering, console the bereft and sorrowing, and be instrumental in thy hands in dispelling the fear of death and the gloom of the grave, and drawing all who read them toward that brighter realm, where decay and death are unknown. And finally, O Christ, when thou shalt come in the clouds of heaven, in power and great glory, to change the living, raise the dead, burn up the world, and judge all men and angels; may both reader and author arise to the resurrection of life, ascend with thee to the mansions thou art preparing for us, and ever dwell with thee, world without end, Amen.

And now unto the ever-blessed and adorable TRINITY—The FATHER, SON, and HOLY GHOST—one God, world without end—be honor and power, dominion and glory, forever and ever, Amen.

NOTE.—It is still the author's purpose to write a similar volume upon *the heavenly world,* and another upon the subject of *future punishment,* its certainty, nature, and duration,—but it is not probable that more than *one* of these volumes can be issued before 1868; as the author has allowed himself to be turned aside by what he deemed a pressing necessity, to prepare a work upon the *Millennium,* or the Second Advent and Reign of Christ in the Earth. This he hopes to issue early in 1867, should Providence grant him life and sufficient health.

INDEX OF AUTHORS CITED.

PAGE
Adrian, Pope........ 310
Athenagoras........ 35
Barnes, Dr. Albert........121, 122, 251, 332
Barrow, Isaac........ 51
Benson, Rev. Joseph........ 55
Beveridge, Prof. William........ 219
Blair, Robert........65, 212
Boethius........ 43
Bogue, Dr. David........ 61
Buck, Rev. Charles........ 61
Bush, Prof. George...131, 132, 135, 136, 140, 141, 142, 146, 149, 174, 175
176, 182, 186, 276, 277, 282, 367
Butler, Dr. John J........ 58
Calvin, Rev. John........ 59
Cary, (lexicographer)........ 148
Clarke, Dr. Adam........55, 104, 385
Clement........ 33
Coxe, A. C........ 63
Dante........ 65
D'Aubigne........ 310
Dick, Dr John........61, 148
Dick, Dr. Thomas........267, 270
Doddridge, Philip........51, 62
Donegan, Dr. James........ 147
Drew, Samuel........189, 193
Dwight, Dr. Timothy........60, 64, 148, 293
Edwards, Dr. Jonathan........ 60
Eusebius, Pamphilus........ 36
Felton, Dr. Henry........ 51
Flatt & Storr, German Professors........ 46
Gaussen, Prof. S. R. L........359, 361
Gill, Dr. John........57, 148
Gray, Prof. Alonzo........ 230
Griffin, Dr. Edmund D........ 60
Groves, (lexicographer)........ 147
Hagenbach, (Hist. of Doctrines)........ 32
Harbaugh, Rev. H........ 289
Herman (the poet)........ 63
Herbert (the poet)........ 64
Herodotus........ 148
Helffenstein, Dr. Samuel........ 52
Hippolytus........40, 41
Hiscock, Rev. Edmund T........ 57
Hitchcock, Dr. Edw......164,194,197,200,201,234,252,293,346,359,380,381
Hobart, Bishop John Henry........ 157
Hodge, Rev. A. A........61, 148
Hody, Dr. Humphrey........21, 34, 35, 36, 38, 40, 42
Hopkins, Bishop (of England)........ 52
Horne, Rev. Geo. (Dean of Canterbury)........ 345
Horne, Dr. Thos. Hartwell........ 105
Irenæus........ 35
Josephus, Flavius........22, 112, 277

PAGE
Justin Martyr........ 34
Kingsley, Bishop Calvin........55, 220, 236, 240, 389
Kip, Bishop Wm. Ingraham........28, 30, 31, 32
Klopstock (the poet)........ 63
Knapp, Rev. Geo. Christian........ 48
Landis, Rev. Robert W........ 26
Latham, Rev. A........ 334
Lexicographers, various........147, 148
Lightfoot, Dr. John........ 26
Lucian........ 40
Macknight, Dr. James........167, 181, 306
Millman (the poet)........ 64
Minucius........ 40
Montgomery, James........65, 212
Morrison (the traveler)........ 21
Mosheim, Dr. John Lawrence Van........39, 41, 167
Nelson, Rev. David........220, 229, 243
Origen........ 41
Osterwald, Rev. John Frederic........37, 53
Parkhurst, John (lexicographer)........ 147
Pearson, Bishop John........39, 48
Polycarp........ 33
Pollock, Rev. Robert........ 242
Pope, Alexander........ 331
Priestly, Dr. Joseph........ 92
Ralston, Rev. Thomas N........ 50
Robinson (the lexicographer)........ 147
Ruffinus (an early writer)........ 43
Sanderson, John (a noted traveler)........ 20
Sandy, John........ 20
Scott, Dr. Thomas........ 51
Schmucker, Dr. S. S........ 47
Sears, Edward H........ 175
Secker, Archbishop........26, 50
Sherlock, Dr. William........143, 144
Sigourney, Mrs. Lydia H........ 295
South, Bishop Robert........50, 148
Stockton, Rev. Dr........ 56
Storr & Flatt, German Professors........ 46
Swedenborg, Emanuel........132, 173
Taylor, Isaac (Physical Theory, &c.)........248, 250, 291, 292
Tertullus (an early Christian writer)........ 38
Thevenot, Melchisedeck........ 21
Titianus, Syrus........ 35
Tupper, Martin Farquhar........66, 230
Ursinus........ 47
Ware (the poet)........ 380
Watson, Rev. Richard........46, 55, 197, 217, 242, 300
Watts, Dr. Isaac........65, 212
Wesley, Rev. John........53, 148
Wesley, Rev. Charles........54, 64, 110, 118
Wesley, Samuel, Jr........ 64
Whateley, Archbishop........199, 227, 259, 261, 290, 310
White, Rev. Henry Kirk........64, 361, 362
Young, Dr. Edward........ 374

INDEX OF POETIC QUOTATIONS.

PAGE

All crimes shall cease, and ancient frauds shall fail........................ 331
An angel's arm can't snatch me from the grave............................ 375
And darkness and doubt are now fleeing away........................ 362
And now the trump of wondrous melody.................................... 337

Before the ploughman fell his steers.. 242
Bury the dead and weep.. 65
But when shall spring visit the mouldering urn............................ 361
By death and hell pursued in vain.. 320

Companion dear! the hour draws nigh....................... 295
Corruption, closely noted, is but a dissolution of the parts............ 230
Corruption, earth, and worms... 65

Fierce meteors, with the lightning's blaze conspire........................ 343
For though past all his essence is diffused.................................. 288
Forgotten generations live again... 64

Glory to God in full anthems of joy.. 380
God my Redeemer lives...65, 212
Grave, the guardian of our dust......................................65, 212
Green turfy grave-yards, and tombs of marble............................ 337

Hasten, Lord the glorious time.. 326
Horror all hearts appalls... 340

If any one shall violate this sepulchre..................................... 31
If I have ever caused thee pain.. 369
I know the time shall come... 63
In his blessed life I see the path.. 374
In this identic body I... 54
It seems as all were over now... 63

Jesus shall reign where'er the sun.. 318

Let sickness blast, let death devour....................................... 382
Lift your glad voices in triumph on high.................................. 375
Lives again our glorious King... 118

PAGE

Man; starting from his couch, shall sleep no more........................ 342

No sigh, no murmur the wide world shall hear............................ 331

Restore thy trust, a glorious form... 65

Set the false witnesses aside.. 13
Soon shall ocean's hoary deep... 335
Sound the trumpet, roll the drum... 341

Take, then, my body as the soul departs*................................. 243
'Tis done; again the conquering chief appears............................ 338
The blessed in the new covenant.. 65
These ashes, too, this little dust... 64
The seas shall waste, the skies in smoke decay........................... 343
The time draws on, when not a single spot................................ 65
The trumpet! the trumpet! the dead have all heard....................... 64
The trump shall sound, the dead shall wake............................... 64
Then let the worms demand their prey...................................... 64
Then the last judgment day shall come..................................... 54
Thou shalt rise, my dust, thou shalt rise................................63, 381
Thus we the pledge receive.. 55

Vain the stone, the watch, the seal... 110

What though my body run to dust... 64
Whence but from heaven, could men unskilled in arts..................... 129
When he first the work began.. 130
When shriv'ling like a parchment scroll................................... 336
Who breathed into our earth.. 54
Who counting on long years of pleasure here.............................. 333
Why do they wish for the hollowed out rocks............................... 373

Yet, these, new rising from the tomb.....................................64, 268
Yet we shall meet to soothe thy pain....................................... 295

* This is the only poetic passage that is original with the author; and it may not be amiss to confess its paternity in this obscure part of the volume.

INDEX OF SCRIPTURE QUOTATIONS.

GENESIS.

CHAP.	VERSE.	PAGE.
V	24	74
XVIII	14	241
XXII	18	72

NUMBERS.

CHAP.	VERSE.	PAGE.
X	2, 3	336
XXIII	10	278
XXIII	19	241

DEUTERONOMY.

CHAP.	VERSE.	PAGE.
XVIII	15	363
XXXII	39	22
XXXIII	39,40	78
XXXIV	5, 6	376

I. SAMUEL.

CHAP.	VERSE.	PAGE.
II	6	79

II. SAMUEL.

CHAP.	VERSE.	PAGE.
XX	9	384

II. KINGS.

CHAP.	VERSE.	PAGE.
II	1–18	75

JOB.

CHAP.	VERSE.	PAGE.
XIV	10–15	79
XIX	23–27	81

PSALMS.

CHAP.	VERSE.	PAGE.
II	6–8	101, 312
II	7, 8	320, 329
XVI	8–11	83, 100
XVII	15	85
XXII	27, 29	329
XLIX	14, 15	85
LXXII	7–15	321

PROVERBS.

CHAP.	VERSE.	PAGE.
XIV	32	278

ECCLESIASTES.

CHAP.	VERSE.	PAGE.
III	14	229
XI	3	278
XII	7	71

ISAIAH.

CHAP.	VERSE.	PAGE.
II	2, 3	329
III	11	278
IX	6, 7	312
XI	4, 6–9	322
XXV	7	329
XXV	8	86, 368, 374

34

ISAIAH

CHAP.	VERSE.	PAGE.
XXVI	19	21, 86
XXXV	10	320
XLIV	4	22
LIV	11–13	322
LV	3	101
LX	16–20	323
LXIII	1	374
LXVI	23	329

JEREMIAH.

CHAP.	VERSE.	PAGE.
VI	16	383
XXIII	5–6	312

EZEKIEL.

CHAP.	VERSE.	PAGE.
XXXVIII	1–10	88, 89, 332
XXXIX	6–11	332

DANIEL.

CHAP.	VERSE.	PAGE.
II	44	313
II	35	320
VII	9, 10	338
VII	14	320
XI	13–15	314
XII	2, 13	90, 296

HOSEA.

CHAP.	VERSE.	PAGE.
XIII	14	91

AMOS.

CHAP.	VERSE.	PAGE.
IX	11	314

ZECHARIAH.

CHAP.	VERSE.	PAGE.
IX	9, 10	313, 320
XII	10	331
XIII	1	331
XIV	5	335
XIV	9	329

MATTHEW.

CHAP.	VERSE.	PAGE.
VI	15	385
XII	39, 40	101

MATTHEW.

CHAP.	VERSE.	PAGE.
XIII	31, 32	321, 329
XVI	27	334
XVII	1–3	75, 376
XIX	26	243
XIX	30	334
XX	18, 19	102
XXI	31	315
XXII	20	316
XXII	23, 28	24
XXV	23	344
XXV	31, 32	302, 335, 339
XXV	34	343
XXV	41, 46	343
XXVI	29	344
XXVI	31, 32	103
XXVI	42	384
XXVII	10, 12	308
XXVII	11, 42	316
XXVII	52, 53	145, 206, 375
XXVII	62, 64	103, 108
XXVII	65, 66	109
XXVIII	1–8	115
XXVIII	6	134
XXVIII	8–10	118
XXVIII	11	110
XXVIII	12–15	111
XXVIII	16, 17	120

MARK.

CHAP.	VERSE.	PAGE.
I	15	315
VIII	31, 32	102
IX	1	315
IX	7	363
XV	43–45	105, 315
XVI	1	109
XVI	1–8	115
XVI	9	118

LUKE.

CHAP.	VERSE.	PAGE.
I	16, 17	308
I	31–33	313
VII	39–44	98
VIII	1	315
IX	27	315
IX	43–47	271

LUKE.

CHAP.	VERSE.	PAGE.
X	9, 11	315
XI	20	315
XII	13, 14	318
XIV	13, 14	94
XVII	20, 21	315
XIX	11	315
XX	27–33	96
XX	34–36	97
XX	37, 38	77, 97, 178
XXIV	1–9	116
XXIV	21	317
XXIV	36–43	119
XXIV	38	134

JOHN.

CHAP.	VERSE.	PAGE.
I	49	316
II	19–22	102
V	25	169
V	28, 29	95, 275, 278
V	28, 29	297, 300, 337
VI	15	316
XI	23, 26	95, 177
XVIII	36, 37	317
XIX	2, 3	316
XIX	19–22	316
XIX	31–34	104
XIX	39–40	105
XX	25	119, 134
XX	26–29	120
XX	27	135

ACTS.

CHAP.	VERSE.	PAGE.
I	3	152
I	6	317
II	22–36	136, 149
II	24	373
II	25–32	83
III	14, 15, 26	151
III	22	363
IV	10	151
V	30–32	124, 151
IX	3–5	262
X	39–41	124, 151
XII	19	111
XII	22, 23	184

ACTS.

CHAP.	VERSE.	PAGE.
XIII	26–33	153
XIII	29–31	125
XIII	29–37	138
XIII	32–37	84, 100
XV	15, 16	314
XVII	2, 3	153
XVII	18–32	224
XVII	31, 32	153
XXII	6	154
XXIII	6	72
XXIII	8	78
XXIV	14, 15	24
XXIV	15	185, 297
XXIV	21	154
XXVI	6–8	25, 72, 154
XXVI	22, 23	84, 376
XXVI	32, 33	154

ROMANS.

CHAP.	VERSE.	PAGE.
I	3, 4	156
II	28, 29	319
V	12	71, 367
V	17	367
VI	3–10	156
VI	5	143
VI	9	364
VIII	11, 23	157, 377
XI	26–29	331
XIV	17	318

I. CORINTHIANS.

CHAP.	VERSE.	PAGE.
IV	20	318
XV	3–8	155, 158
XV	6	121
XV	12–23	159
XV	13–17	366
XV	20–22	298, 368, 376
XV	21	185
XV	35–38	160, 161
XV	39–42	249
XV	42–44	33
XV	53	133
XV	50, 53	251
XV	51, 53	162, 185, 3[illegible]7
XV	54	86
XV	55	91

II. CORINTHIANS.

CHAP.	VERSE.	PAGE.
V	10	339
V	1-4	180

GALATIANS.

CHAP.	VERSE.	PAGE.
I	6-12	388
I	7	383
I	11, 12	159
III	7-9, 29.	319

EPHESIANS.

CHAP.	VERSE.	PAGE.
IV	9	140
V	29	369

PHILIPPIANS.

CHAP.	VERSE.	PAGE.
III	21	268, 275

COLOSSIANS.

CHAP.	VERSE.	PAGE.
II	8	243, 383

I. THESSALONIANS.

CHAP.	VERSE.	PAGE.
I	7-10	301
I	8-10	344
III	13	335
IV	13-17	162, 305
IV	16	336

II. THESSALONIANS.

CHAP.	VERSE.	PAGE.
I	7, 8	334

II. TIMOTHY.

CHAP.	VERSE.	PAGE.
I	10	374
II	18	383

TITUS.

CHAP.	VERSE.	PAGE.
I	11	388

HEBREWS.

CHAP.	VERSE.	PAGE.
I	11, 12	343
IX	27	339
XII	5	74

I. PETER.

CHAP.	VERSE.	PAGE.
I	3, 4	375

II. PETER.

CHAP.	VERSE.	PAGE.
II	4	342
III	4	335
III	7-12	342
III	10	246

II. JOHN.

CHAP.	VERSE.	PAGE.
I	10, 11	389

JUDE.

CHAP.	VERSE.	PAGE.
I	14	335

REVELATION.

CHAP.	VERSE.	PAGE.
I	7	339
I	12-18	262, 374
VI	16, 17	339
X	1-6	333
XI	15	329
XX	1-3	328
XX	4-6	306
XX	7, 8	332
XX	9, 10	332
XX	11	336
XX	12, 13	339
XX	12-15	299, 301
XX	13	335
XXII	11	278

GENERAL INDEX.

ABSURDITY of Jewish account of the resurrection of Christ, 112.
Adam, the primeval body of, may be a model of the resurrection body, 220, 274.
Adam Clark, views of, 55.
Advent, the second, of Christ, order and time of, 334.
Affinity, chemical, may be the power employed in the resurrection, 233.
African, see Negro.
Akiba, Rabbi, extract from, 18.
Anastasius, the Pope, letter to, 43.
Anastasis — αναστασις — resurrection — definitions of the term, 39, 147–149. Accommodated sense of, 179.
Anastasis, by Prof. Bush, quotations from, 131, 132, 136, 141, 146, 149, 150, 174, 175, 176.
Apollonius, alleged miracles of, 144.
Apostles, death of the, note, 127. Credibility of as witnesses of Christ's resurrection, 125–127, 141. Belief of as to his resurrection, 155.
Apostles' Creed, antiquity of the, 38. Import of, 39.
Apostolic Constitution, origin of and extract from, 40.
Apocrypha, quotations from the, 19.
Archbishop Whately, views of, 12. See Whately.
Archbishop Secker, extract from touching the belief of the ancient Jews, 26. See Secker.
Argument of the book, &c., 13.
Arnold, Prof. E., note from, 258.
Assay office, illustration from the, 232.
Athenagoras, opinion of, respecting the nature of the resurrection, 35.
BARNES, Dr. Albert, note respecting, 121. Extracts from, 329–331.
BARROW, Dr. Isaac, extract from, 51.
Baptism an emblem of the resurrection, extract from Bishop Hobart, 157.
Benson, Joseph, quotation from, 49.
Beveridge, Bishop, extract from, 49.
Bodies, love for our, a proof of the resurrection, 368, 370.
Body, the resurrection, nature of, 133. To be material, 247. Spiritual, 251. Incorruptible, 253. Immortal, 253. Powerful, 254. Glorious, 261. Need not include limbs lost during life, 210. Nor all matter ever connected with the body, 212. Various in appearance, 272. In nationality, color, &c., 273. Of the righteous and the wicked to differ, 274–277. Of children, 272. Uses of in another life, 282–295. Of great utility now, 283, 284. Our love for, 285. Medium of knowledge hereafter, 290. Means of recognition, 292. Monument of Christ's victory, 294.
Body of Christ, actually dead, 105. Embalmed, 105–107. Its resurrection anticipated by the Jews, 108. Guarded against, 108, 109. Sepulchre sealed, 109. Gone from the sepulchre, 110. Actually arose, 131. Never found or even looked for, 113. Great difficulty of disposing of a dead body, as shown in the case of Prof. Webster and Dr. Parkman, 114. Labored to prove his own corporeal identity, 135. Seen alive by Mary Magdalene and Peter, 118. By two other disciples, and then the ten, 119. To the eleven, at Jerusalem, to seven in Galilee, 120. To five hundred, 121. To James alone, 122. By all the disciples, 123. Seen to ascend to heaven, 123. Seen by Saul of Tarsus, 123. By St. John A. D. 96, 123. If Christ never arose what became of his body, 141. A specimen of proper resurrection, 143.
Bodies of the saints, which arose, near Jerusalem, 145. What became of them, 146.
Boethius, confession of, 43.
Bogue, David, extract from, 61.
Bones, barks full of Jews brought to Jerusalem, 20.
Buck, Rev. Charles, quotation from, 61.
Bush, Rev. Geo., views of, 11. Respecting

Christ's resurrection, 131. Argument against a corporeal resurrection, 139. Strange assumption of respecting Elijah, 75, 131. Respecting the body of Christ, 131, 140, 142, 149. Concessions of, 63, 132, 136, 145, 146, 147.
Burial service of the Jews, extract from, 22.
Burning of the world, 342.
Butler, Dr. John J., cited, 58.
CALVIN, John, Extracts from, 59.
Cannibalism, objection to a corporeal resurrection drawn from the practice of, 233. Answer to by Bishop Kingsley, 236-244.
Carnis resurrectionem, import of, 39, 45.
Catacombs of Rome, their testimony, 29. Inscriptions in the, 29, 30.
Catechism, the Heidelberg, cited 47. Scotch Presbyterian, 60.
Change of the living at Christ's second coming, 162, 337.
Chemistry, wonders of, in collecting scattered particles, 231-233.
Christians, the early, belief of as to the nature of the resurrection, 28-32, 70.
Chief-priests, no doubt satisfied of Christ's resurrection, 111.
Children, bodies of, in the resurrection, 272.
Christ, teachings of upon the subject of the resurrection, 93-99. Must be interpreted in the light of existing facts, 94. Never combated the views of the Pharisees as to the resurrection, 93. Did contend with the Sadducees, 94. Endorsed their notion of a physical resurrection, 97. At the grave of Lazarus, 94. When opposed by the Sadducees, 96. At Capernaum, understood by the Jews to teach a physical resurrection, 98. Predicted his own resurrection, 98, 100. Fully endorsed the prevailing theory, 98, 99.
Christ, the resurrection of, predicted by the prophets, 100, 136-138. Foretold by Christ, 101. His body really dead, 103. Delivered to Joseph, embalmed, and buried as a dead body, 104-106. Is guarded, 109. Is gone, 110. Never found, 113. Often seen heard, and handled, 118-122. Labored to prove his own corporeal identity, 135. Ascended in a material body, 139. Seen to ascend to heaven, 123. Professor Bush's idea of, 131, 132. (See body.)
Churches, views of the various, respecting the nature of the resurrection, Romish, 45. Greek and Lutheran, 46. Church of England, 48, 52. German Reformed, 47, 48. Reformed Dutch, 52, 53. Protestant Episcopal, 53. Methodist Episcopal, 53, 56. Baptist, 57. Free Will Baptist, 58. Presbyterian and Scotch Presbyterian, 59. Reformed Presbyterian, 66. Independents, 61. Moravians, 62.
Clark, Dr. Adam, extracts from, 55, 85. Respecting the spear in the Saviour's side, 104. "We will persuade him," note, 112. In regard to the alleged stealing of Christ's body, 113.
Clement, opinion of, 32. Argument of founded upon the Phœnix, 29. Extract from his epistle, 33.
Confessions of faith cited, Romish, 45. Greek, 46. Lutheran, 46, 47. Church of England, 48. Reformed Dutch, 52. Protestant Episcopal, 53. Methodist Episcopal, 53. Scotch Presbyterian, 60.
Conflagration of the world, 342.
Constitutions, apostolic, origin of and quotation from, 40.
Conversion, not the resurrection, 167-172.
Corporeal identity, what essential to it. See identity.
Council of Toledo, extract from, 43.
Creed, the apostles', antiquity of, 38. Meaning of the, 39.
Cyprian, opinion of, 32.
DANIEL, quotation from in proof of a physical resurrection, 90.
Darius, sealing a stone, 109.
David, prophecy of, respecting Christ's resurrection, 83. Expounded by Peter and Paul, 83, 84.
Day of Judgment, 338-342.
Death of the Apostles, note, 127.
Defects, physical, in the resurrection, 270.
Denominations, views of the various, as to the nature of the resurrection, 45-67.
Dick, Dr. John, of Glasgow, on the word αναστασις, 61, 148.
Distinctions, moral, to reappear in the resurrection, 277. All others to pass away, 279.
Doddridge, Philip, on the nature of the resurrection, 62.
Doroemus, Dr. of New York, chemical feat of, note, 232.
Drew, Samuel, theory of stated, 12. Considered at length, 189-198. Quotations from, 189-193. Objections to theory, 195-198.
Dry bones, Ezekiel's vision of, based upon the idea of a corporeal resurrection, 88, 89.
Dwight, Dr. Timothy, cited, as to the nature of the resurrection, 60. As to the meaning of αναστασις, 148.
EAR, power of the, in the resurrection, 256.
Eagle, a golden, reproduction of after it is dissolved, 232.
Early Christians, belief of in a corporeal resurrection, 28-32, 70.
Edwards, Dr. Jonathan, on the nature of the resurrection, 60.

Elijah, search for the body of, 114. Not dissolved to dust, 75, 131, 141, 142.
Embalming of Christ's body, 105–107.
Emblems, natural, of the resurrection, 345–362.
Enoch and Elijah, the translation of, a proof of a corporeal resurrection, 74. Assumption of Prof. Bush respecting, 75, 131.
Epiphanius, remarks of, respecting Origen, 42.
Esdras, quotations from, 19.
Evangelists, accounts of the, of Christ's resurrection consistent and natural, 114–116.
Evidences of Christ's resurrection, 100–127. Summary of the, 128, 129.
Eye, the human, power of in the resurrection, 255.
Ezekiel, vision of the dry bones, based upon the idea of a corporeal resurrection, 88, 89.
FELIX, Minucius, extract from, 40.
Felton, Dr. Henry, sermon of, mentioned, 51.
First resurrection, 304. Nature of the, 308, 319. Order of the, 328.
Flesh, the resurrection of the, 39.
GERM theory of Mr. Drew, mentioned, 12. Defined, 189, 193. Partially endorsed by Dr. Hitchcock, 194. A mere hypothesis, 195. Obviates no difficulties, 195. Virtually denies the resurrection of the body, 197. Contrary to all examples, 198.
Gill, Dr. John, views of, cited, 57, 148.
Gnostics, views of, 11, 167.
Greek Church, extent of it, 46.
Greeks, the learned, objections of, to the doctrine of the resurrection of the body, 167.
Griffin, Dr., quotations from, 60.
Guard, a Roman set over the tomb of Jesus, 109. Left the sepulchre, 110. Report of the, 112. Penalty for falling asleep, 112.
HADES, import of the term, 100.
Hagenbach's History of Doctrines, extract from, 32.
Heaven, a place as well as a state, 287. Has a material basis, 289.
Helffenstein, Dr. Samuel, statement of his belief, 52.
Herod, idea of, respecting John, 24. Imprisons Peter, 111.
Herodotus, quotations from, 147.
Hippolytus, Mosheim's description of, and an extract from, 40, 41.
Hitchcock, Dr. views of, 12. Quotations from, 38, 40, 164, 194, 252.
Hobart, Bishop, extract from respecting baptism, note, 157.
Hodge, Rev. A. Alexander, on the import of αναστασις, 61.
Hody, Dr. Humphrey, on the resurrection, quotations from, 21, 34, 35, 36, 42, 43.
Hopkins, Bishop, of England, his views of the resurrection, 52.
Horne, Thos. Hartwell, cited in regard to the Jewish custom of embalming, 105.
Hosea, quotation from, in proof of a physical resurrection, 91.
IDENTITY, corporeal, what essential to it, 197, 198, 202–214, 210–222.
Illustrations—Whately's of house, 200. Reply to, 204. Authors of watch and soldiers' body, 202–204. From state of body at death, 214. From excessively fat persons, 216. From magnet collecting steel fillings, 231. Chemist detecting poison in a dead body, 231, 232. From work in an assay office, 232. Golden eagle dissolved, 232. From golden vases, 225. From chemical affinity, 232, 233. From burial and resurrection of a slave, 279, 280. Caterpillar flying, 283.
Incredulity of Thomas, as to Christ's resurrection, 134, 135.
Irenæus, opinion of, 32. Quotation from as to the nature of the resurrection, 35.
Isaiah, cheering vision of a future resurrection, 86. Prophecies of explained, 86, 88.
JEHOSHAPHAT, the dead to arise from the valley of, 20.
Jews, the ancient belief of, touching the resurrection, 17, 93. Their understanding of the Old Testament, 69. Of Deuteronomy xxxiii. 39, 78. Of 1 Samuel ii. 6, 79. Modern, extract from liturgy of, 26.
Job, hope of, for a resurrection of the body, 79–82.
Josephus, Flavius, extracts from on the possibility of the resurrection, 228. The bodies of the wicked to be sources of misery, 277.
Judgment, the day of, 338–342. Final act of the, 343.
Justin Martyr, testimony of, 34.
KINGSLEY, Bishop, quotations from, on the nature of the resurrection, 55. In answer to objections, 236–241.
King, Hon. Preston, allusion to death of, note, 254.
Kip, Bishop, extract from, 28, 30, 32.
Knapp, George Christian, his idea of the resurrection, 48.
LAZARUS, resurrection of, 177. Body of bandaged like that of Christ afterwards, 106.
Lee, Dr. Luther, note respecting, 234.
Lexicographers' definitions of the term *αναστασις—anastasis*, 147.
Lightfoot, Dr., extract from, 26.
Lucian, testimony of respecting the primitive faith, 40.
Luke, testimony of, as to Christ's resurrection, 152.

Lyons, letter from the churches of, 36, 37.
MACCABEES, quotations from the, 19.
Macknight, statement of, respecting the learned Greeks, 167. Exposition of 2 Corinthians v. 1–4, 181.
Magnet, wonders performed by the, 231.
Mahzar, or Prayer-book of the Jews, quoted, 21.
Martyr, Justin, testimony of, 34.
Matter, to continue for ever, 291.
Miller, Hugh, reference to death of, note, 254.
Millennium, the import of the term, 311. Christ's kingdom not temporal, 318. True notion of the millennium, 320, 329–331. Objections to millenarian theory, 323–326. Order of the, 329.
Minucius Felix, testimony of, respecting the resurrection, 40.
Miracles, the pretended, of Pythagoras and Apollonius, 144, 167.
Mosheim, statement of, respecting the Apostles' Creed, 39.
Mount of Olives, to be cleft asunder, 19. The dead to rise from the, 20.
NEGRO, with double voice, note, 258. Death and resurrection of, 279, 280.
Nelson on infidelity quoted, 242.
"New Church" theory of the resurrection, 11. Of Christ's resurrection, 131–144. General theory stated and refuted, 173–188.
OBJECTIONS to a corporeal resurrection stated, 224. Those of Origen and the Platonists, 224–226. That our bodies are gross and corruptible, 226. Dissolved and substance widely scattered, 227. Devoured by cannibals, &c., 233. That the risen dead could not all stand on the earth, 244. That it would remove much of the globe, 244. That such a body would be of no utility in another life, 246, 282.
Old Testament, teaching of respecting the nature of the resurrection, 68–92.
Olives, Mount of, to be cleft asunder, 19. The dead to rise from the, 20.
Oracles, Sybilline, extract from the, 34.
Order of the resurrection, 162.
Origen, views of, 12. Mosheim's description of, 41. Citations from, and remarks of Epiphanius respecting, 43.
Osterwald, John Frederick, extract from in regard to the faith of the early Christians, 38.
PARKMAN, Dr., reference to the disposition of his body by Prof. Webster, note, 114.
Pearson, statement of, respecting the Apostolic Creed, 39. Citation from, 48, 49.
Peter, argument of as to Christ's resurrection, 137. Sermon of, on the day of Pentecost, 149. Other teachings of in respect to the resurrection of Christ, 149–152.
Physical defects in the resurrection, 270.
Pharisees, belief of, 22.
Phœnix, the, an ancient symbol of the resurrection, 29.
Poetry, see Index of Poetic Quotations, 395.
Poison, detection of, in a human body, 231.
Polycarp, character of, as drawn by Eusebius, 34.
Prayer-book of the Jews, cited, 21.
Priests, the Chief, no doubt satisfied that Christ had risen from the dead, 111.
Priestly, Dr. concessions of, note, 92.
Pythagoras, alleged miracles of, 144.
RALSTON, Rev. Thomas N., quotation from, 57.
Redemption by Christ, implies the resurrection of the body, 71–73.
Regeneration, not the resurrection, 167–172.
Resurrection, a generally admitted, 11. Various theories of, 111. A corporeal implied in redemption, 71–73. Of various persons by the Prophets and Christ, 76. Character of ibid.—"New Church" or Swedenborgian theory of, stated and refuted, 173–188. Germ, theory of, stated, 189, 193. Dr. Hitchcock's endorsement of, 194. Not taught in 1 Corinthians xv. 36–38, 195. Natural emblems of the, 345.
Resurrection, the doctrine of the, should be understood, 382. Preached more, 385. Defended by the ministry, 387.
Resurrection Body, nature, powers, and uses of—See "Body."
Resurrection of Christ, nature of, 132–144. Belief of the Apostles as to its character, 135. Preaching of respecting, 136, 138, 140. Evidence of the, 100–130. Viewed in the light of the "New Church" theory, 131–144.
Resurrection, the general, time of, 302. Extent of, 296.
Resurrection, the first. See First Resurrection.
Resurrection of the saints near Jerusalem, 145. What became of their bodies, 145, 146.
Resurrection, the spiritual or moral, 168.
Resurrection, a corporeal, objections to. See "Objections."
Resurrection, of the wicked, 396. To have different bodies from the righteous, 274–277. To arise at the same time, 300. To be a medium of suffering, 277.
Resurrection, ἀναστασις — *anastasis* — meaning of the term, 39, 61, 63, 147–149.
Ruffinus, letter from to Pope Anastasius, 43.
SADDUCEES, belief of the, 23, 24, 77. Opposed by Christ, 94, 178.

Saints, bodies of the, which rose after Christ arose, 145. Promised translation of a proof of a corporeal resurrection, 162.
Sameness, bodily. See "Identity."
Sanderson, John, extract from, 20.
Sandys' travels, cited, 20.
Sarchos anastasis—σαρχος αναστασις—use and import of, 39.
Satan, the binding of, 327. Loosing of, 332.
Siamese Twins, conversation with the, 370.
Scars on Christ's risen body, 271.
Schmucker, Dr. cited, 47.
Scotch Preacher, eloquent extract from the, 117.
Scott, Thomas, quoted, 51.
Sears, Edmund H., quoted, 175.
Secker, Archbishop, cited, 26.
Sects, the various modern, belief of as to a physical resurrection, 45–67.
Seeds found in Celtic tombs, 360.
Sepulchre of Christ, new, in solid rock and near Jerusalem, 107. Guarded, stone at the door and sealed, 108.
Sherlock, quotation from, in respect to Christ's resurrection, 143, 144.
Soldier, the body of a, illustration drawn from, 203.
Soldiers, guard of. See Guard.
South, Robert, extracts from as to the nature of the resurrection, 50. As to the meaning of αναστασις, 148.
Speculative questions considered, 269.
Spring, and its emblems of the resurrection, 346–363.
St. Paul, teachings of, as to Christ's resurrection, 153–155.
St. Stephen's dying testimony to Christ's resurrection, 152.
Stockton, Dr. Thos. H., cited, 56.
Stone at mouth of lion's den sealed,note, 109. At door of sepulchre, 109.
Swedenborg, Emanuel, cited, 132, 173. Theory of the resurrection, 11, 112. Absurdity of, 141. Formally stated and refuted, 173–188. Contradicts the Scriptures, 184. A novelty, 182. Confounds death and the resurrection, 183. Objections of his followers, 246.
Sybilline, Oracles, cited, 34.
TABERNACLE, use of the term in reference to heaven, 180.
Talmud, cited, 26.
Taste and smell in the resurrection, 258.
Term, definition of, 15, 16.
Tertullus, opinion of, 32, 38.
Testimony of the Apostles to Christ's resurrection, strength of, 125–129.
Theories, various, of the resurrection state, 11, 12. The popular defined, 14. Of the Gnostics and Friends, 11, 167. New Church, 173. Mr. Drew's, 189, 190. Partially endorsed by Dr. Hitchcock, 194. Objections to, 195–198. New body of common elements, 199. Objections to it, 200–208. True theory, 210–223. See also "resurrection."
The dead, our love for, a proof of a future resurrection, 371.
Thomas, incredulity of, 134. Our Lord's course towards, 135.
Time, the end of, 333.
Titianus Syrus, cited, 35.
Toledo, extract from the council of, 43.
Tomb in which Christ lay, new, in solid rock, &c., 107.
Tombs, Celtic, seeds found in, 360.
Translations of Enoch and Elijah, a proof of a corporeal resurrection, 74. Assumption of Prof. Bush respecting the, 75. Of the bodies of the saints who live at Christ's second coming, 162, 163.
Trumpet of the resurrection, 336.
Twins, the Siamese, conversation with, 270.
URSINUS, quotation from, 47.
Uses of the resurrection body in another life, 282–295. Useful now, 284. Love for, 285. A means of communion with the material universe, 286. Medium of knowledge, 290. Of personal recognition, 292. Monuments of Christ's victories, 294.
VARIETY in the resurrection in size and appearance, 272. In nationality, color, &c., 273.
Vienna and Lyons, letter from the churches of, 36.
Vision of the dry bones, Ezekiel's, based upon the doctrine of a literal resurrection, 88, 89.
WATCH thrown overboard, illustration drawn from, 202–204.
Watson, Rev. Richard, extracts from, 55, 195.
Webster, Prof., efforts of, to dispose of the body of Dr. Parkman, note, 114.
Wesley, John, cited, 56, 148.
Whately, Archbishop, cited, 12, 14. Illustration of, 200. Reply to views of, 202–209.
Wicked, the, to arise, 296. With the righteous, 300. To have different bodies from the righteous, 274–277. To be a medium of suffering, 277.
Witnesses, the Apostles the especial of Christ's resurrection, 123, 125, 153. Character, knowledge, and number of, 125. Did not expect it, 126. No motive for deceiving, 126. Endorsed by God, 127.
World, burning of the, 342.

DR. MATTISON'S THEOLOGICAL WORKS.

I.

THE DOCTRINE OF THE TRINITY; *or, a check to Modern Arianism, as taught by Unitarians, Hicksites, New Lights, Universalists, and Mormons; and especially by a sect calling themselves Christians, by* HIRAM MATTISON, D.D., ninth edition, 18mo., 162 pages. Price, in cloth, 75 cents.

REV. GEORGE PECK, D.D.

After quoting the title of the book, Dr. Peck says: The above title-page is fully sustained by the arguments of the book. Any one who wishes to see, within a small compass, the arguments and false expositions of Scripture, by which the errorists named endeavor to sustain their views of the person and work of Christ, completely refuted, should procure this little book. It is a capital thing to circulate among the people where any type of Unitarianism is rife.—*Christian Advocate and Journal.*

REV. CHARLES PITMAN, D.D.

This is a most able defence of the doctrine of the Holy Trinity. The argument is comprehensive, vigorous, and Scriptural. We have read the work with much interest, and most cheerfully recommend it as a powerful vindication of a doctrine which lies at the foundation of the evangelical system.—*Missionary Advocate.*

REV. ABEL STEVENS, L.L. D.

An able little volume in defence of the doctrine of the Trinity. * * The line of argument is vigorously and closely traced, and in a style adapted to popular readers.—*Zion's Herald.*

REV. NELSON ROUNDS, D.D.

An able defence of the doctrine of the Trinity. The author has done good service to the cause of truth in the volume before us, and we trust it may be productive of much good.—*Northern Christian Advocate.*

REV. LUTHER LEE, D.D.

We take rank with Trinitarians, and regard Mr. Mattison as having done good justice to the subject. He is a close reasoner, and possesses a mind well adapted to polemic investigation.—*True Wesleyan.*

REV. SAMUEL I. PRIME.

So brief, concise, and clear a defence of the doctrine of the Trinity cannot fail to be timely and beneficial.—*New York Evangelist.*

THE PRESBYTERIAN. (Philadelphia.)

The author has done a good service in attacking that grand feature of almost all modern heresies—the denial of the Godhead of the Son and Holy Spirit. His treatise seems to be peculiarly adapted to plain, honest readers, and in general circulation.

THE NEW YORK RECORDER.

This small volume is wisely intended to meet a practical want, by defending the doctrine of the Trinity—not so much against scholastic speculation as against the more popular forms of error.

ALBANY SPECTATOR.

We do not hesitate to commend this little work to every member of the Evangelical Church; and to all who would exalt Jesus Christ, as very God, Lord over all, and blessed for ever. It handles every form of Arian error ungloved, and having exposed the false doctrines of the Campbellites, Hicksites, Western New Lights, Universalists, Mormons, and especially a sect calling themselves "Christians," glories in the mission and Godhead of the Redeemer. * * *

ALABAMA BAPTIST.

This is an exceedingly well-written and valuable work—clear, concise, logical, and Scriptural. The author shows himself a complete master of his subject, explaining what is explicable, and proving what is provable. His plan is original, but happy; and his style is easy and attractive.

THE OLIVE BRANCH. (Boston.)

This is a timely production—serving to quicken attention to what must ever be a central truth of Christianity.

II.

THE IMMORTALITY OF THE SOUL, *considered in the Light of the Holy Scriptures; the Testimony of Reason and Nature; and the Phenomena of Life and Death.* By REV. HIRAM MATTISON, D D.

This is a 12mo. of four hundred pages, in clear and beautiful type, good paper, and well bound, with a steel-plate likeness of the author. Price, in muslin, $1 50.

REV. D. D. WHEDON, D.D.

Mr. Mattison has in the present volume ably exhibited the argument for immortality, both from Scripture and reason. * * The work is interspersed with poetical quotations, and animated throughout with a high glow of Christian sentiment. Altogether it is well calculated, not so much for the thorough-bred metaphysician, as for popular use.—*Methodist Quarterly Review.*

REV. D. CURRY, D.D.

In this work Mr. Mattison has directed his polemical skill against a specific modification of modern heterodoxy, with his characteristic acuteness and comprehensiveness of argumentation. * * * We commend it as a valuable presentation, in popular form, of the most obvious and convincing proofs of this great and fundamental doctrine of religion.—*Christian Advocate and Journal.*

REV. JOHN M. REED, D.D.

The volume which now appears has been constructed from long accumulating materials, and may be considered the author's ripest thoughts on the glorious, though mysterious, theme of immortality, and he is no mean thinker or writer. We do not often notice a more thoughtful book than this.—*Western Christian Advocate.*

REV. ISAAC W. WILEY, M. D., D.D.

We need do nothing more than join in the general commendation which it has received from the press. It indicates much study and research, and is fully entitled to its claim to a good degree of originality, not only in the arrangement of its matter, but also in its arguments and illustrations. It is a valuable contribution to the great subject of immortality and a Future Life.—*Ladies' Repository.*

REV. ABEL STEVENS, L.L. D.

An able and original work, in arrangement, argument, and illustration. In the front is a life-like portrait of the author.—*The Methodist.*

REV. D. D. LORE, D.D.

A book of great pains-taking, and one that will repay perusal.—*Northern Christian Advocate.*

REV. G. W. BRIDGE. (N. E. Conference.)

It is altogether the best thing I have seen, and I have read extensively upon the subject.

REV. J. C. VANDERCOOK, A. M.

Writing to the *Northern Christian Advocate*, Mr. Vandercook thus speaks of this work: (1) The discussion is *popular;* peculiarly free from metaphysical and psychological intricacies. All classes of readers will appreciate the clear and forcible style of the work, and be borne on with increasing interest to the close. (2) It is very *rich in illustration.* So much appropriate, interesting and ever thrilling illustrative incident is seldom found in such a volume. (3) The book is enriched with the *choicest gems of poetry.* A very large number of most appropriate poetic quotations, of rare excellence, are woven into the text with such judgment, taste, and skill, as greatly to increase the interest and edification of the reader. The thousands who have listened with rapt attention to the author's eloquent and masterly delineation, of this and kindred topics from the pulpit, have here an opportunity of reviving those scenes of intense interest and edification. No one, I think, will purchase and read this book without feeling richly compensated.

An eminent Congregational minister writing to the author, says:—"I like your 'Immortality' much. It is clear, full, methodical, and just what I wanted, and you have done justice to the subject."

"A work of great research, and yet of a highly popular cast. It will be found an edifying manual, etc."—*Congregationalist.*

"We can heartily commend this volume to all Christians. The proofs that man is immortal are here stated with a force and clearness which we have never found in any other work. The volume is exhaustive of the subject, and we believe it is destined to become a standard work upon this very important Bible doctrine."—*American Baptist.*

III.

THE RESURRECTION OF THE DEAD; *considered in the light of History, Philosophy, and Divine Revelation.* By H. MATTISON, D.D., with an Introduction by Rev. Matthew Simpson, D.D., one of the Bishops of the Methodist Episcopal Church. 400 pp., 12mo., cloth. Price $1 50.

This work is of the size and style of the one on the *Immortality of the Soul,* and is properly a companion to it. Taken together, they are designed to cover the whole question of a future Life for man, both for Soul and Body; and to include everything, pro and con, that is really essential to a complete understanding of the subject.

IV.

THE MINISTER'S POCKET RITUAL, *a Hand-book of* SCRIPTURE LESSONS AND FORMS OF SERVICE, *for Marriages, Baptisms, the Reception of Candidates into the Church, the Lord's Supper, the Visitation of the Sick, the Burial of the Dead, the Laying of the Corner-Stones of Churches, Dedications, Ordinations, Installations, etc., together with* PRACTICAL SUGGESTIONS TO YOUNG MINISTERS, *upon the best mode of conducting these various services. Adapted to use by all denominations.* By H. MATTISON, D.D.

This is a long and narrow paged 12mo., in large type, and elegantly bound, with a view to its being carried in the side pocket. Muslin, 60 cents.; flexible muslin, 80 cents; flexible morocco, $1.

"A pattern of taste and neatness."—*Christian Advocate and Journal.*

"Every young minister, and most advanced ones, want such a book as this. It is elegantly gotten up, and arranged most admirably. Professor Mattison will receive many thanks for this little work, and we hope some profit."—*American Baptist.*

"This is the most complete work of the kind we have ever seen, in the character and adaptation of the matter, and also in its mechanical execution. It cannot fail to be an excellent auxiliary to every pastor, and especially to junior ministers. The fine collection of lessons and services for funerals alone will repay the expense of the volume every quarter."—Rev. J. C. VANDERCOOK, A. M., Black River Conference.

www.ingramcontent.com/pod-product-compliance
Lightning Source LLC
LaVergne TN
LVHW020100110826
845151LV00001B/39

* 9 7 8 1 4 2 5 5 4 5 0 6 2 *